Marie-Louise Bech Nosch
Time of Textiles in Ancient Greece

CHRONOI
Zeit, Zeitempfinden, Zeitordnungen
Time, Time Awareness, Time Management

Edited by
Eva Cancik-Kirschbaum, Christoph Markschies and
Hermann Parzinger

on behalf of the Einstein Center Chronoi

Volume 15

Marie-Louise Bech Nosch

Time of Textiles in Ancient Greece

—

DE GRUYTER

ISBN 978-3-11-914201-4
e-ISBN (PDF) 978-3-11-222307-9
e-ISBN (EPUB) 978-3-11-222375-8
ISSN 2701-1453
DOI https://doi.org/10.1515/9783112223079

This work is licensed under the Creative Commons Attribution-NonCommercial-NoDerivatives 4.0 International License. For details go to https://creativecommons.org/licenses/by-nc-nd/4.0.

Creative Commons license terms for re-use do not apply to any content that is not part of the Open Access publication (such as graphs, figures, photos, excerpts, etc.). These may require obtaining further permission from the rights holder. The obligation to research and clear permission lies solely with the party re-using the material.

Library of Congress Control Number: 2025944099

Bibliographic information published by the Deutsche Nationalbibliothek
The Deutsche Nationalbibliothek lists this publication in the Deutsche Nationalbibliografie; detailed bibliographic data are available on the internet at http://dnb.dnb.de.

© 2025 with the author(s), published by Walter de Gruyter GmbH, Berlin/Boston, Genthiner Straße 13, 10785 Berlin. This book is published with open access at www.degruyterbrill.com.

www.degruyterbrill.com
Questions about General Product Safety Regulation:
productsafety@degruyterbrill.com

Preface

> And why are you anxious about clothing? Consider the lilies of the field, how they grow; they neither toil nor spin; yet I tell you, even Solomon in all his glory was not arrayed like one of these (*Matthew* 6:28–29).

I am grateful to the *Chronoi* leadership, Eva Cancik-Kirschbaum, Christoph Markschies and Hermann Parzinger, for challenging me intellectually by inviting me to give the annual *Chronoi Lecture 2022* on the topic *Time of Textiles*, and for later inviting me to write this book for the *Chronoi* book series.[1]

The time of textiles challenges me personally as a specialist in Aegean Bronze Age history because Linear B tablets are notoriously undated, apart from taciturn references to 'this year' and 'the past year' and an occasional name of a month. The administrative aim of the Linear B tablets was to be relative and preliminary and hence they do not offer information that can be grounded in a specific year. Most archaeologists argue that these clay tablets all stem from the same burnt layer, the same destruction episode, and hence the same year. This synchronicity has only been questioned by the most recent generation of scholars, and a diachronic perspective on the Linear B records can give new opportunities for the understanding of Mycenaean administration and economy,[2] and also of Bronze Age textiles.[3]

I have written extensively on textiles. Yet, I must admit that *Time of Textiles* perplexed me because it was an approach that I had not considered and that I at first found difficult to put in perspective. I sought the advice of my textile research colleagues, and they were immediately full of ideas, inspiration and intriguing thoughts and perspectives. I am grateful for the input from my knowledgeable colleagues Chiara Spinazzi-Lucchesi, Rachele Pierini, Magali-An Berthon, Silviya Svejenova Velikova, Mary Harlow, Niall McKeown, Else Skjold, Sophus Helle, Christian Ammitzbøll Thomsen, Cecilie Brøns, Peder Flemestad, Beate Wagner-Hasel, Ellen Harlizius-Klück, and Doerte Eriskat. They have all helped me relate textiles to time – and time to textiles.

I was also able to rely on the scholarship of Beate Wagner-Hasel and her investigation of weaving, women and time in Homeric epics,[4] and on Ellen Harlizius-Klück's lexical monograph, *Saum und Zeit. Ein Wörter-und-Sachen-Buch in 496 lexikalischen Abschnitten angezettelt von Ellen Harlizius-Klück* from 2005.

---

1 I found inspiration in Reinecke and Ansari 2016 and their discussion of time.
2 Driessen 1990; 1999; 2000; Driessen and Mouthuy 2022.
3 Nosch 2024.
4 Wagner-Hasel 2000; 2020; Möller and Wagner-Hasel forthcoming.

Ellen Harlizius-Klück's work follows the thread of time and cloth borders from antiquity to the present by exploring textile words and expressions and it is deeply rooted in philosophy and the science of technology.[5]

This book reviews textiles and garments in ancient Greece from a time perspective. I have *used textiles to think with time* and *used time to think with textiles*, to paraphrase Claude Lévi-Strauss. Some chapters are new, some are older texts rewritten from a time perspective. In the footnotes, credits are given to my earlier works.

In order to understand the time of textiles, we need to proceed diachronically and by what Florence Gherchanoc[6] calls a "bricolage de sources" – it is more of a quilt of fabric pieces than a well-designed tapestry of sources. I will not pretend to work like the systematic weavers Arachne or Athena, I will rather take the role of an unskilled weaver, a mender, or work like the *ragpicker, Lumpensammler* or *chiffonier* collecting rags and piecing them together to form a useful cloth.[7]

A note on the Greek sources and words cited: I have in several places homogenised the English translations across sources to render the narrative more coherent, meaning that if the topic is the cloak or *khlamys*, for example, I will use these terms and avoid using other garment terms chosen by the translators such as robe or mantle. I have in many places altered or aligned the translations of the problematic textile term *poikilos:* I rarely translate it as embroidered, and more often choose terms such as decorated, variegated or inwoven, based on research in textile archaeology.[8] Only Greek and Latin texts are given in the original, not e.g., Hebrew or Akkadian. I transcribe Greek terms without accent but indicate (only) long ō (ω) and ē (η).

Textiles are mostly worn on the body and are therefore intimately linked to our identity and history: I will illustrate and discuss how textiles reflect life, memory and time in ancient history, classical archaeology and ancient literature, and

---

5 Harlizius-Klück 2005, 5: "Ich wollte zeigen, dass Saum und Zeit, als Wörter und Sachen, an einem zusammenhängenden Gebiet teilhaben – aber die historische Veränderung von Struktur und Bedeutung dieses Gebietes ließ sich nicht also kontinuierliche Geschichte erzählen. Die These ist, dass die Bedeutungslage des Saumes als Schnittkante, Rand, Marginalie und Diskontinuität und die der Zeit also konstante, kontinuierliche und ordnende Kategorie ehemals umgekehrt war: der Saum stand für den ordnungsgegebenen → Anfang und die Kontinuität der Tradition; die Zeit wurde wahrgenommen in der Form eines Einschnitts, der Wunden im Leben erzeugte, die es durch bindende Gewebe zu heilen galt."
6 Gherchanoc 2006, 240.
7 Sørensen 2024 and Thomsen 2025 with reference to Walter Benjamin.
8 This has been argued for a long time by Alan Wace (1934; 1948, 110–111), who was renowned for his excavations at Mycenae and had been the keeper of textiles in the British Museum. See also Droß-Krüpe and Schieck 2014.

how mores and meanings attached to textiles endure the test of time. I will focus on ancient Greece but I will keep in mind the cross-cultural and diachronic qualities of textiles in the past.[9]

This book also seeks to be relevant to the emerging discussions of sustainability because the relation between fashion, clothes and time is crucial in the efforts for more sustainable production and clothing. Moreover, thinking of garments in terms of cycles and rhythms will have implications for the circular economy and for ecology.[10]

Marie-Louise Bech NoschCopenhagen, June 2025

---

[9] For textiles and clothing in a diachronic and cross-cultural perspective in (European) antiquity, see Barber 1991 and Riis 1993.
[10] Fletcher and Tham 2004, 254.

Contents

1 Time and textiles in ancient Greece —— 1

2 Textiles as a marker of the beginning of time and of an era —— 8
2.1 Narratives of clothing as the beginning of culture and history —— 8
2.2 Creation myths that include dressing and weaving in ancient Greece —— 10
2.3 The time of the first weavers, spinners and dyers in Greek myth —— 13
2.4 The human inventor, discoverer and first finder (prōtos heuretēs) of weaving and dyeing —— 16

3 First textiles —— 19
3.1 The earliest evidence of textile technology from archaeology —— 19
3.2 Periodization of time, dress and weaves —— 22
3.3 Weaves and clothes types as proxies for chronologies and periodizations – and how they challenge them —— 23
3.4 Carbon 14 dating of archaeological textile finds —— 25

4 Textiles and time cycles: chronology, seasons, rhythm, and sequences of tasks —— 28
4.1 Seasonality and timeliness of fibre procurement and textile production —— 28
4.2 The chaîne opératoire and linear time in textile research —— 31
4.3 Gendered time of textiles —— 33
4.4 Rhythm and weaving —— 34
4.5 Rhythm and pulse beats expressed in textile terms by Galen —— 36

5 The long hours to make textiles – Penelope's time —— 38
5.1 How long did it take? Time measurements from experimental textile archaeology —— 39
5.2 How long did it take to spin? —— 40
5.3 How long did it take to make a garment? —— 42
5.4 How long did it take to make a sail? —— 43
5.5 Time and leisure measured through spinning in ancient Greek texts —— 44
5.6 Time and waiting measured through weaving in ancient Greek texts —— 47

6 Textile terms in a time perspective: "Words survive longer than cloth" —— 50
6.1   Textile terms of 2nd millennium BCE Greece —— 50
6.2   Textile and garment terms of the 1st millennium BCE —— 52
6.3   The Greek term kairos with meaning related to textiles and time —— 53
6.4   The Greek terms kairós and krisis and Latin ordior and their meanings related to textile and time —— 57

7 The lifespan and timespan of garments —— 60
7.1   Archaeological textiles as witnesses of a lifetime —— 60
7.2   Married life in a garment: Andromache's wedding veil —— 60
7.3   Garments used and stored over long periods of time in sanctuaries —— 62
7.3.1 Old, useless and frayed clothing, veils and girdles in the Inventory of the Temple of Artemis Kithōnē at Miletus —— 63
7.3.2 Ragged clothing in the Brauron clothing catalogue —— 65
7.3.3 A ragged Tarantine dress at Tanagra —— 66
7.3.4 Ragged linen clothes and textiles at the Hera sanctuary in Samos —— 66
7.4   Clothing passed on from one generation to another —— 67
7.5   Second-hand garments and markets —— 68
7.6   The lifespan of textile tools: heirlooms – loom-weights —— 69

8 Clothing for life chapters, life stages and lifetime —— 71
8.1   Clothing for life stages and ages —— 71
8.2   A girl is born in wool —— 73
8.3   Clothing for the end of a lifetime —— 73

9 Dressing for special transition points in time and status —— 77
9.1   Transition clothing for young Greek male citizens: the ephebic khlamys cloak —— 77
9.2   Transition time for a king: investiture clothing —— 79
9.3   New clothes – new times – for Alexander the Great —— 79
9.4   Passing the cloak and passing the office and responsibility —— 81
9.5   Veiling and unveiling the bride and the Anakalypteria ritual in Athens —— 81
9.6   Belting and unbelting —— 83

10 Annual and cyclic times in festivals for textile work —— 85
10.1 Festivals for weaving Athena's peplos in Athens —— 85
10.2 Festivals for washing Athena's peplos in Athens —— 88

10.3	Clothes and Athena in the Panathenaia, Plynteria and Kallynteria —— **90**	
10.4	The festival of veils and wool? —— **92**	
10.5	Time of textiles in religious festivals outside Athens —— **92**	
10.6	The cyclic time of textile production in religious festivals —— **94**	

11 Woven lifetime – textiles as time capsules of memories in Greek tragedy —— 98

11.1	The reunion of brother and sister through a tapestry —— **98**
11.2	The refusal to recognise a brother from his clothing —— **99**
11.3	A second reunion of a brother and a sister by means of pieces of tapestry —— **102**
11.4	A reunion of a mother and her son through a tapestry —— **104**

12 Dress changes —— 107

12.1	The change from peplos to khitōn in women's clothing in Archaic Greece —— **107**
12.2	From khitōn and back to peplos in the 5th century BCE: dress of the 'good old days' —— **109**
12.3	A new look: the change to more modest male dress in the 5th century BCE —— **110**
12.4	Dress changes or fashion changes? —— **112**

13 Conclusion – following the threads up to today —— 115

Epilogue. The long time of textiles, the short time of a T-shirt —— 119

Ancient sources —— 122

Bibliography —— 126

Index —— 146

1 Time and textiles in ancient Greece

Textiles accompany us throughout our lives, *au fil du temps*, from the cradle to the grave, from diapers to shrouds. They are flexible and tangible materials through which we express gender, age and status. Textile craft precedes metallurgy and pottery.

Aspects of time, seasons and chronology play an important role when working with textiles and clothes. Textiles themselves are ephemeral and rarely survive in archaeological contexts. But when they do, they can show evidence of a long life, in changes and patterns of wear.

In many academic works on time in antiquity, time seems to exist without gender and without much material expression, except for the often-mentioned sundials (which to me look like semi-circular cloaks).[1] Time is mostly treated via texts, with detailed theoretical discussions in ancient political history, medicine and philosophy.[2] In contrast, the time of textiles appears highly gendered, embodied, tangible, and concrete. Textiles seem to follow other timeframes and paces, and they connect us to the past in an intimate and diachronic way because we still wear woven fabrics, as people did in antiquity.

In ancient Greek verbs, time is flexed into past tenses and future forms but also marked according to the action's imperfective durability or its aoristic, punctual nature. Greek prepositions also expressed time as well as place.[3]

Time was in antiquity expressed in diverse Greek terms: *chronos/χρόνος* as the *longue durée* of unbroken processes, *kairos/καιρός* as the brief, decisive moment, *hōra/ὥρα* as season and later as hour, *aiōn/αἰών* as eternity.[4]

But there is also time beyond these Greek terms, meaning how people in antiquity observed, sensed, experienced and understood time. To express this, Mar-

---

[1] Hannah 2009; 2016. Singer 2022.
[2] Despite its title, *Intentional History. Spinning Time in Ancient Greece* (Foxhall, Gehrke and Luraghi 2010), has nothing to do with thread but is about notions of the past in antiquity. Witmore 2023 explores the archaeology of time exemplified in roads, bridges and monuments between Mycenae and Epidaurus and uses textile-related terms and concepts to articulate time: *line, folds, pleats*, but does not include textiles in his discussion of time.
[3] Guilleux 2016, 8, highlights the association of *time* and *place* in the prepositional organisation of several Indo-European languages, such as *before/after* in English, *vor/nach* in German, *avant/après* in French, *pro/meta* in ancient Greek, *ante/post* in Latin.
[4] In antiquity and later they were personified by the young and agile Kairos who seizes the moment (and with his forelock of hair by which he himself could be seized), or *chronos* personified in the old and divine figure of Kronos, a "senior member of the Greek and Roman Pantheon." Panofsky 1967, 73. For a recent overview of studies and concepts of time in antiquity, see Wolkenhauer 2011.

tin Persson Nilsson introduced in 1920 a distinction between the concept of "time-indication" based on various physical phenomena in the world, and "time-reckoning" in which time is regulated and standardised.[5] Natural phenomena, such as the daily sunrise and sunset or the seasons, may be timely points of reference but derive their time meaning from the social and religious activities associated with them.[6]

The planetary and biological change of time we as humans experience every start of the day at sunrise is expressed in saffron-dyed clothing in the *Iliad* 8.1:

Ἠὼς μὲν κροκόπεπλος ἐκίδνατο πᾶσαν ἐπ' αἶαν

Now Dawn the saffron-robed was spreading over the face of the earth

When we today approach time in ancient Greece, we use the modern absolute chronology of calendar years Before the Christian/Common/Current Era (BCE) and within the Christian/Common/Current Era (CE). This was, of course, not a chronological framework in ancient Greece. The year would start at different times in each city-state, in some places at the beginning of the sailing season, in other places after the summer harvest.[7] Time was most of all a physical and biological experience, seen in the sun, the moon, daylight and night, experienced through biological processes including sleep, menstruation and pregnancy and through seasons, climate and ageing. Time could be observed in nature in the ripening of fruits and crops, the coloration of leaves, and the abundance or dearth of water in rivers and lakes. Cultural events such as festivals were held annually and followed the climatic and agricultural cycles. These biological, physical, and climatic time perceptions are highly relevant when approaching the time of textiles because they determine fibre resources and how much clothing was needed.

Anthropology, in particular, has inspired the idea of cyclical time in the past, i.e., that people considered time not as linear but as turning and repeating itself.[8]

---

5 Nilsson 1920, 9: "The *time-reckoning* in the proper sense of the term is preceded by *time-indications* which are related to concrete phenomena of the heavens and of Nature" (...) "time-indications do not stand in direct relation to other time-indications but are related only to a concrete phenomenon, and through that to other time-indications, so that they are of indeterminate length and cannot be numerically grouped together." Nilsson combined ethnographic data from his native Sweden with world cultures and with ancient Greece and Rome, as was customary in early 20th century research, especially in the history of religions.
6 Remijsen 2023, 158.
7 Möller and Wagner-Hasel forthcoming.
8 Knapp 1992 on time concepts used in anthropology, history and archaeology. For a critical assessment of different time concepts, see Bloch 1977 who insists that only linear and cyclical time

A purely cyclical conception of time cannot, however, be found in Classical and Hellenistic textual sources.[9] Years were compared and put in sequence by early historians. "Herodotus, Thucydides, and of course, Polybius have in turn been described as historians with a cyclical view of time. I shall attempt to show that they were not", wrote Arnaldo Momigliano,[10] and this position has been echoed by most historians.

To the ancient Greeks, prehistory or the more remote past was called τὰ παλαιά, and how τὰ παλαιά was linked to the present resulted in diverse configurations.

Hesiod (*Work and Days* 109–170) defined history in terms of five generations (*genoi*). They are not the 25–30 year generations of human families, but longer timespans: the Golden generation lived together peacefully and without the toils of hard work;[11] the Silver generation was less noble and did not honor the gods appropriately; the Bronze generation was terrible and violent, a generation of warriors; the Heroic generation was nobler and more righteous, a god-like generation of heroes and demi-gods who fought at Troy; and finally, Hesiod's own time, the Iron generation of hard-working men with sorrows and pain.

Historical and mythical genealogies were means to grasp time.[12] They are generation-based and family-based chronologies of human life (γενέαι) into which every human being can be placed. Genealogies are biological- and experience-based since many people would know two or three generations before and after them. Successful champions in the Olympic Games would list their ancestors; kings would trace their family tree back to prehistory and mythology;[13] sanctuaries likewise could list a long heritage of celebrity donors going back in history, as for example with the Lindos temple chronicle.[14]

---

exist. Elias 1988 discusses and contextualises various perceptions of time historically and culturally.
9 For a critical assessment of work and ideas about cyclical time thinking in ancient Greece, see Momigliano 1966, 7–8.
10 Momigliano 1966, 11.
11 Baldry 1952.
12 As Mitchel 1956, 48, dryly comments: "Genealogical chronology is the oldest method of reckoning historical time and the most inexact." See also Ball 1979.
13 Möller and Wagner-Hasel forthcoming.
14 Higbie 2003. Shaya 2005. Mitchel 1956 notes how generation-based chronologies are used when Herodotus wants to outline mythological time or time as indicated by oracles such as the Pythia in Delphi.

On the more personal level, the female poet Nossis of the 3rd century BCE wrote an epigram mentioning three generations of women in her family including her mother Theophilis and grandmother Kleocha (*Greek Anthology* 6.265):[15]

Ἥρα τιμήσεσα, Λακίνιον ἃ τὸ θυῶδες πολλάκις οὐρανόθεν νεισομένα καθορῇς, δέξαι βύσσινον εἶμα, τό τοι μετὰ παιδὸς ἀγαυᾶς Νοσσίδος ὕφανεν Θευφιλὶς ἁ Κλεόχας.

Sacred Hera – since you often come down from heaven to see Lacinion with its fragrant incense – take this linen cloth. Theophilis, daughter of Kleocha, and her noble daughter Nossis, wove it for you.

A piece of fine linen cloth, *byssos*, forms the bond between the three women and the goddess, and it is a homemade cloth woven by a mother and a daughter.

The historian Herodotus likewise used generations to scaffold his narrative and to express chronological distances between events.[16] He equates three generations to one hundred years (2.142). But the ancient authors' use of multiple generations was neither very precise nor effective to indicate time and correlate chronologies.

These genealogical and generation-based time perceptions are relevant when approaching the time of textiles because they are reflected in the symbolic and emotional meanings of clothing. Indeed, in the narratives of *longue durée* concerning the beginning of history, mythology and prehistory, the genealogical and generation-based time perceptions often include textile making and the creation of clothing as formative events (see ch. 2).

When ancient Greek historians aimed to describe a sequence of political events, biological, climatic, and physical chronologies were less useful, and complex systems of fixing and describing dates and intervals were used instead. The chronologies of tenures of political or religious offices served as a reliable sequence allowing the labelling of intervals through eponyms using the name of the office holder.[17] Athens had a sequence of archons, Sparta had a sequence of kings and of ephors, and the Hera sanctuary at Argos had a sequence of priestesses: in the year/time of archon X, of ephor Y, of priestess Z became a recognised way to indicate years and intervals of years. Nevertheless, for historians in antiquity it was not a simple process to triangulate a precise time from the names of priestesses, ephors and archons holding offices of different durations and starting

---

15 Lefkowitz and Fant 2016, 10, no. 19. Möller and Wagner-Hasel forthcoming.
16 Mitchel 1956. Ball 1979.
17 Möller and Wagner-Hasel forthcoming.

at different times of the year.[18] From the 4th century BCE the Olympic Games became a pan-Hellenic reference point for time, and in the 3rd century Eratosthenes of Kyrene conceptualised Hellenic chronology as intervals between pan-Hellenic political events, such as the end of the war in Troy, the years of Lykurgus' leadership, the first Olympic Games, the Persian invasion and the Peloponnesian War.[19]

These tenure-based and eponymic perceptions of time are, however, less relevant when approaching the time of textiles; they can, nevertheless, be useful when dating a source or a political event related to clothing.

Thus, not one, but various concepts of time coexisted in antiquity.[20] Greek city-states would define their own elaborate calendars for civil and religious dates.[21] Ancient Greek authors could have very different views of time.[22] As an example: in Homer's epics, time is tensioned between past, present and anticipation of future. Some scholars have coined it the Homeric *hysteron-prōton* model: according to narratological theories, Homeric time is expressed in two 'anachronies', *analepsis* (retrospection) and *prolepsis* (anticipation).[23]

Hence no unified notion of time can be said to exist in Archaic, Classical and Hellenistic Greece. Rather, several concepts of time co-existed, were used and were useful, depending on an author's needs and genre: Hesiod, for example, operated with a number of temporal frames, including cosmic time, the cycles of agriculture, seasons and generations.

But this book is not about time. It is about the time of textiles: how time is articulated and conceived via clothing and textile production and how clothes

---

18 See the ancient Greek historian Thucydides' (Thuc. 2.1) efforts to set the date of the start of the Peloponnesian war in 431 BCE: "For fourteen years the thirty years' truce which had been concluded after the capture of Euboea remained unbroken; but in the fifteenth year, when Chrysis was in the forty-eighth year of her priesthood at Argos, and Aenesias was ephor at Sparta, and Pythodorus had still four months to serve as archon at Athens, in the sixteenth month after the battle of Potidaea, at the opening of spring, some Thebans, a little more than three hundred in number, under the command of the Boeotarchs Pythangelus son of Phyleidas and Diemporus son of Onetoridas, about the first watch of the night entered under arms into Plataea". I thank Möller and Wagner-Hasel forthcoming for this observation.
19 Möller and Wagner-Hasel forthcoming.
20 Momigliano 1966, 4, about time and "very naïve ideas about the uniformity of Greek thought."
21 Rasmussen 2023 presents Attic calendars for offerings and the stipulated value of the sacrificed animals as well as fees paid to priests and priestesses.
22 Fränkel 1931, 103: "Im Ganzen finden wir bei Homer einen unentwickelten Zeitsinn." Momigliano 1966, 9: "Fränkel seems to me to be on perfectly safe ground when he says that the emphasis on Chronos as creator, judge, discoverer of truth is to be found first in Solon, Pindar, and Aischylos. Homer has nothing of all that. He is indifferent to exact chronology and in general to temporal sequences." See Momigliano 1966, 9–10 for a critical assessment of Fränkel's work.
23 Genette 1980, 35–48. Bergren 1983, 39–42.

can convey time, seasons, ages, and periods. Clothes are a functional response to a series of human needs and challenges: climate, temperature, shelter, and comfort. Clothes are also linked to social aspects of human life such as status, pride, privacy and sense of belonging. Anthropologists argue that humans have an innate desire for adornment, and this theory has been further expanded to focus on how clothes are used by humans to establish rank, hierarchies, differences, to form social groups, and to stand out.[24] Moreover, ancient cultures had notions of modesty, which implied shame, and which also connected with clothing.[25]

"Unfortunately the tissues of history today have only one dimension that is readily measured: it is calendrical time, which permits us to arrange events one after another. But that is all", wrote George Kubler in his book *The Shape of Time. Remarks on the History of Things*.[26] In this book, I challenge this view and will attempt to go beyond calendrical and linear time.

I will work with the time of textiles as a weaver, with warp and weft, interlacing and weaving them together into a new fabric of understanding the past. My focus is on Archaic, Classical and Hellenistic Greece and how textiles and dress studies can contribute to a nuanced understanding of time in antiquity. It is timely, because as Hans van Wees puts it, "The old and far-from-lively field of scholarship on Greek dress has in recent years been given a new lease of life by the study of clothes as a means of non-verbal communication".[27]

Textiles can, and at times do, symbolize eternity. In ancient times, the spinning goddesses of fate were called *Moirai* by the Greeks, *Parcae* by the Romans, and the *Norns* (named Urdr, Verdandi, Skuld) in Nordic mythology. These goddesses spin, measure and cut the thread of a person's life (Fig. 1). In Graeco-Roman antiquity, one's lifespan was often metaphorically thought of as a thread spun at birth.[28] The weaving of this thread could be seen as representing an individual's life choices. The thread itself became a symbol of time. The linen thread from Latin *linum*, flax, botanically *Linum usitatissimum* of the *Linaceae* family, lies at

---

24 Schneider and Weiner 1986.
25 To dress and undress has crucial implications. A woman's shame and modesty, *aidōs*, is protected by her clothing, and undressing means shedding her decency. When the Persian King Candaules suggested that his bodyguard Gyges should look at his naked queen, Gyges was horrified (Herodotus 1.8,3–4): see Cairns 1996.
26 Kubler 1962, 83.
27 van Wees 2005a, 1. For textiles and non-verbal communication, see Schneider and Weiner 1989.
28 For metaphorical uses of textiles and thread in antiquity, see Wagner-Hasel 2006. Fanfani, Harlow and Nosch 2016.

the root of our word 'line' (Latin *linus*),²⁹ which we use to depict time as a *timeline*. Hence, the thread is closely linked to a linear perception of time.

Figure 1: Modern representation of one of the Moirai, Atropos, cutting the thread of life. From the funerary stele of George P. M. Maurogenes in the church of Panagia Hecatontapyliana on the island of Paros. Atropos is presented with the tools of all three Moirai: the spindle, the cutting device (a modern pair of scissors), and the ball of yarn.
Photo: Wikimedia Commons / Tom Oates, CC BY-SA 3.0, https://commons.wikimedia.org/wiki/File:Atropos.jpg (last access 04.07.2025).

---

29 Threads are constituent parts of a weave but thread, yarn and rope were commodities in themselves and also useful tools, for example in construction: see Mertens 1991.

2 Textiles as a marker of the beginning of time and of an era

Some say that history begins with writing. We textile historians see the weaving of fabrics as the beginning of history. In prehistoric times, clothing was initially made from animal skins and furs carefully processed and adapted to be worn on a human body, a technology we still use for skin clothing, footwear, skin gloves and fur coats.

Much later, textiles were woven into tiny bands or human-sized clothing. The first weavers wove textiles in the shape of animal skins or treated the woven fabrics in such a manner as to appear as animal furs.[1]

The production of textiles and clothing are among the most long-lasting technologies since they are attested so early and are still in use today; we still dress in textiles woven of spun thread. The technology to make thread has changed over time and more and new fibre types have appeared, but the basic technology of spinning and weaving is still the same.

Foundational myths involving textiles and clothing are found in the oldest works of literature of Mesopotamia, Archaic Greece, Judaism, Christianity and Islam.[2] These myths are articulated through dressing scenes. They reflect a belief in a fundamental shift from nature to culture, from prehistoric times with naked humans to historic times with humans dressed in clothes.[3] This chronological divide between naked and clothed is set much earlier than the traditional divide between prehistory and history via the invention of writing.

2.1 Narratives of clothing as the beginning of culture and history

The Sumerian epic of creation known as the *Debate between Grain and Sheep* tells the story of how the first humans lived with and as animals and without clothing. The Sumerian text uses the term *tug$_2$-ga* to designate clothes (lines 12–25).

---

[1] Barber 1991. Riis 1993. Nosch 2023.
[2] Wolkenhauer 2011, 271–328. Nosch 2023. Drewsen, Harlow, Mannering and Nosch 2024. On time aspects and the beginning of time in myths of origin and eschatological myths, see Hubert and Mauss 1905, 7.
[3] The concept of the naked and wild (in contrast to clothed and civilised), continues to have influence, particularly from a western colonial perspective: see Höpflinger 2019.

The people of those days did not know about eating bread.
They did not know about wearing clothes;
they went about with naked limbs in the Land.

Like sheep, they ate grass with their mouths
and drank water from the ditches.

In the Babylonian *Epic of Gilgamesh*, a young man lives with animals on the Mesopotamian steppes. His name is Enkidu, and he is a hunter. When Enkidu is transformed into a civilized human, he starts wearing clothes. It happens through the intervention of a woman, Shamhat, who serves the goddess Ishtar. The transformation from wild hunter to socially embedded man happens via sexual intercourse, food and clothing. He is naked, she is dressed:

Lines 175–179

With the gazelles he grazed on grass,
with the herd he rushed to drink,
with the beasts he quenched his thirst.

Shamhat saw him, the man of the wild,
this brute born in the wasteland's womb.

Lines 188–202

Shamhat untied her skirt,
spread her legs and worked her charm.
She was brave and smelled his scent,
threw off her clothes and brought him down.

She showed the wild man what women can do
and his lust wrapped him around her body.
For six days and seven nights Enkidu was aroused
and made love to Shamhat.

When he had had his fill of her delights,
he turned back to the herd.
But the gazelles saw him and ran,
the herd of the wild fled from him.

Enkidu had sullied his spotless body.
The herd was running, his knees were stuck;
Enkidu was weakened and could not keep up,
but now he could reason and think.

Naked Adam and Eve lived peacefully and naked in the Garden of Eden and they felt no shame, as narrated in *The Book of Genesis* in the *Old Testament* (*Gen.* 2.25). But when they defied God and ate the forbidden fruit, they experienced shame for the first time because of their nakedness, and therefore they made clothes (*Gen.* 3.7–11, 23):

> Then the eyes of both were opened, and they knew that they were naked; and they sewed fig leaves together and made themselves aprons. And they heard the sound of the Lord God walking in the garden in the cool of the day, and the man and his wife hid themselves from the presence of the Lord God among the trees of the garden. But the Lord God called to the man, and said to him, "Where are you?" And he said, "I heard the sound of thee in the garden, and I was afraid, because I was naked; and I hid myself. "He said, "Who told you that you were naked?"

Sewing is therefore the first technology ever to be practiced by humans, according to *Genesis*. Adam and Eve sewed their first clothes of leaves, but God later provided clothes made of animal skin (*Gen.* 3:21), which we may assume were likewise sewn:

> And the Lord God made for Adam and for his wife garments of skins, and clothed them

Hence, Adam and Eve engaged in sewing and dressing as their first activities after Paradise and before starting farming and animal husbandry.

2.2 Creation myths that include dressing and weaving in ancient Greece

In Greek mythology Pandora, the first woman, is dressed by Athena in silvery or shining clothing (*argypheē esthētes*), and she is girded (*zōse*), the girdle being a typical female clothing accessory. Her dress included an elaborate veil (*kalyptrē*). These many female dressing details are narrated in early 7th century BCE Boeotia by Hesiod[4] (*Theogony* 573–575):

> ζῶσε δὲ καὶ κόσμησε θεὰ γλαυκῶπις Ἀθήνη
> ἀργυφέῃ ἐσθῆτι· κατὰ κρῆθεν δὲ καλύπτρην
> δαιδαλέην χείρεσσι κατέσχεθε, θαῦμα ἰδέσθαι·
>
> The goddess, bright-eyed Athena, girdled and adorned her
> with silvery clothing, and with her hands she hung a
> finely-made veil from her head, a wonder to see.[5]

---

[4] On Hesiod's description of Pandora and the myth's possible root in Egyptian and Mesopotamian ideas, see Blundell 1986, 14–18. See Zeitlin 1995 for a comparison to *Genesis*. On Eva and Pandora, yet without discussing their shared textile identities, see Schmitt 2002.
[5] I have modified the translation of some dress details from Powell 2017.

Pandora is dressed, not as a neutral human being nor as a wife, but as a *nymphē* or *parthenos*, an unmarried girl.⁶ She is dressed by Athena (*Works and Days* 68–69):

ζῶσε δὲ καὶ κόσμησε θεὰ γλαυκῶπις Ἀθήνη

And the goddess glancing-eyed Athena gave her a girdle and ornaments,

But even before being dressed, Pandora is taught to weave by the goddess Athena herself (*Works and Days* 60–64):

Ἥφαιστον δ' ἐκέλευσε περικλυτὸν ὅττι τάχιστα
γαῖαν ὕδει φύρειν, ἐν δ' ἀνθρώπου θέμεν αὐδὴν
καὶ σθένος, ἀθανάτης δὲ θεῆς εἰς ὦπα ἐΐσκειν
παρθενικῆς καλὸν εἶδος ἐπήρατον: αὐτὰρ Ἀθήνην
ἔργα διδασκῆσαι, πολυδαίδαλον ἱστὸν ὑφαίνειν:

He [Zeus] ordered the famed Hephaistos immediately
to mix earth with water and to place inside the voice and strength
of a human being, and to make the lovely desirable shape of a young
girl with a face like the immortal goddesses. And he commanded Athena
to teach her crafts, how to weave elaborately decorated cloth,

In the passages from Hesiod quoted above, Pandora is designated by the terms *zōse* and *erga* and these terms recall classical Athena with her epithets *Zōstēria* and *Ergane*.

Weaving is a temporal marker of the beginning of 'civilized' society in Greek literature and philosophy.⁷ Ruby Blondell interprets the image of wool working in Plato's *Statesman* as a paradigm of achieving unity.⁸ Seeking a definition of the ideal statesman, the dialogue explores two figures: the shepherd and the weaver. The dialogue progresses chronologically from the time of Cronus, a primitive world of pasture with only one gender,⁹ to the time of Zeus, the world of civilization and culture where the king weaves the fabric of society populated by men and women. The shepherd procures raw fibres while the king-weaver transforms the wool into a new and more complex product.

The idea of the primitive older times of pastoralist life occurs in many parts of Greek literature.¹⁰ In the 9th book of the *Odyssey*, the savage Cyclops Polyphemos

---

6 Gherchanoc 2006, 245.
7 Blondell 2005.
8 Blondell 2005, 23. See also Lane 2009.
9 Blondell 2005, 35.
10 Blondell 2005. Wagner-Hasel 2000, 82–91.

personified the lonely shepherd, in skin clothing or naked, living outside human community.

With the time of Zeus came weaving and women, society and complexity.[11] The Age of Zeus was initiated with the divine gifts of fire, metallurgy and weaving from Prometheus, Hephaistos and Athena, as well as agriculture (Plato, *The Statesman* 274 c). Plato omits Pandora as the first weaver and focuses on Athena.[12] In another passage by Plato (*Laws* 679 a–b), an Athenian explains to a stranger how people lived peacefully before the invention of metals by means of pastoralism, weaving and cooking.

> ΑΘ.
> Πρῶτον μὲν ἠγάπων καὶ ἐφιλοφρονοῦντο ἀλλήλους δι' ἐρημίαν, ἔπειτα οὐ περιμάχητος ἦν αὐτοῖς ἡ τροφή. νομῆς γὰρ οὐκ ἦν σπάνις, εἰ μή τισι κατ' ἀρχὰς ἴσως, ᾗ δὴ τὸ πλεῖστον διέζων ἐν τῷ τότε χρόνῳ· γάλακτος γὰρ καὶ κρεῶν οὐδαμῶς ἐνδεεῖς ἦσαν, ἔτι δὲ θηρεύοντες οὐ φαύλην οὐδ' ὀλίγην τροφὴν παρείχοντο. καὶ μὴν ἀμπεχόνης γε καὶ στρωμνῆς καὶ οἰκήσεων καὶ σκευῶν ἐμπύρων τε καὶ ἀπύρων εὐπόρουν· αἱ πλαστικαὶ γὰρ καὶ ὅσαι πλεκτικαὶ τῶν τεχνῶν οὐδὲ ἓν προσδέονται σιδήρου· ταῦτα δὲ πάντα τούτω τὼ τέχνα θεὸς ἔδωκε πορίζειν τοῖς ἀνθρώποις, ἵν' ὁπότε εἰς τὴν τοιαύτην ἀπορίαν ἔλθοιεν, ἔχοι βλάστην καὶ ἐπίδοσιν τὸ τῶν ἀνθρώπων γένος.

> Athenian:
> In the first place, owing to their desolate state, they were kindly disposed and friendly towards one another; and secondly, they had no need to quarrel about food. For they had no lack of flocks and herds (except perhaps some of them at the outset), and in that age these were what men mostly lived on: thus they were well supplied with milk and meat, and they procured further supplies of food, both excellent and plentiful, by hunting. They were also well furnished with clothing and coverlets and houses, and with vessels for cooking and other kinds; for no iron is required for the arts of moulding and weaving, which two arts God gave to men to furnish them with all these necessaries, in order that the human race might have means of sprouting and increase whenever it should fall into such a state of distress.

The entire world could even be conceived as being created as a textile. In the 6th century BCE cosmogony by Pherekydes of Syros, Zeus offers a mantle (*pharos*) – richly decorated and woven by himself – to his bride Chthonie. The decoration depicts the earth/Ge and the ocean and thereby it contains a weave of the world as it was about to be created.[13]

Philo of Alexandria, *On Dreams* 1.203–204, uses the adjective *poikilos*, colourful or variegated, to describe the world, and it is a term often used for textiles.

---

11 Blondell 2005, 48, 52
12 Blondell 2005, 45, 48.
13 Schibli 1990, 50–69, F68. Scheid and Svenbro 2003, 56–58. Gherchanoc 2006, 263.

And indeed, he describes the entire word as a variegated piece of weaving (*hyphasma*):

τὴν γὰρ ποικιλτικὴν τέχνην ἐνόμισαν μέν τινες οὕτως ἠμελημένον καὶ ἀφανὲς εἶναι πρᾶγμα, ὥστε ὑφάνταις αὐτὴν ἀνέθεσαν. ἐγὼ δ᾽ οὐ μόνον αὐτήν, ἀλλὰ καὶ τοὔνομα τέθηπα, καὶ μάλισθ᾽ ὅταν εἰς τὰ γῆς τμήματα καὶ τὰς ἐν οὐρανῷ σφαίρας καὶ ζώων καὶ φυτῶν διαφορὰς καὶ τὸ παμποίκιλον ὕφασμα, τουτονὶ τὸν κόσμον, ἀπίδω.

For the art of variegation has been looked upon by some as so obscure and paltry a matter that they have relegated it to weavers. I on the contrary regard with awe not only the art itself but its very name, and most of all when I fix my eyes upon the sections of the earth, upon the spheres of heaven, the many different kinds of animals and plants, and that vast variegated piece of fabric, this world of ours.[14]

2.3 The time of the first weavers, spinners and dyers in Greek myth

In ancient Greek mythology the gods were experts in technology. They are not the inventors of crafts but patrons and donors who offer their knowledge to humans.

Goddesses knew the art of spinning and weaving. Aphrodite had her golden spindle or distaff. Athena was the expert weaver[15] who taught women to work, here meaning to weave:[16]

κούρην τ᾽ αἰγιόχοιο Διὸς γλαυκῶπιν Ἀθήνην,
οὐ γάρ οἱ εὔαδεν ἔργα πολυχρύσου Ἀφροδίτης,
ἀλλ᾽ ἄρα οἱ πόλεμοί τε ἅδον καὶ ἔργον Ἄρηος,
ὑσμῖναί τε μάχαι τε, καὶ ἀγλαὰ ἔργ᾽ ἀλεγύνειν –
πρώτη τέκτονας ἄνδρας ἐπιχθονίους ἐδίδαξεν
ποιῆσαι σατίνα<ς τε> καὶ ἅρματα ποικίλα χαλκῶι·
ἣ δέ τε παρθενικὰς ἁπαλόχροας ἐν μεγάροισιν
ἀγλαὰ ἔργ᾽ ἐδίδαξεν ἐπὶ φρεσὶ θεῖσα ἑκάστηι.

There is the daughter of goat-rider Zeus, steely-eyed Athena, for she does not like the doings of Aphrodite rich in gold: she likes wars and the doings of Ares, battles and fights, and fine workmanship – she first taught joiners on earth to make carriages and chariots ornamented with bronze, and she taught fine workmanship to tender-skinned girls in their houses, putting it into each one's mind.

---

14 With a few alterations in the translation.
15 Athena is the inventor and patroness of weaving according to Plato, *The Statesman* 279 c–d. See also Plato *Symp.* 197 A and Pausanias 1.24.1. For the Graces representing divine versions of the *ergastinai*, see Wagner-Hasel 2000, 142–144; 2002; 2020, 155–169.
16 *Homeric Hymn to Aphrodite* V.8–15.

Pandrosos and her sisters Aglauros and Herse, the *Kekropidai*, the daughters of Kekrops, were celebrated in myth as the inventors of weaving.[17] Pandrosos and Aglauros had their individual cults with priestesses assigned to them.[18] Aglauros' sanctuary was the place where ephebes received their weapons,[19] and perhaps also their cloak, the *khlamys*. She was also involved in the *Plynteria* festival of washing Athena's clothing.[20] Pandrosos and Aglauros have further important associations: one of the mythical kings of Athens, Erichthonios, was hidden as a baby in a basket but was discovered by them.[21] Thus there appears an entanglement of the genealogies of Athens and its dynasties with weaving and with Athena. This myth of the Kekropidai sisters is mirrored in the ritual of the *arrhēphoroi* girls[22] (see ch. 10).

Baby Erichthonios was a son of gods but born out of wool: Hephaestus had raped his sister Athena and she wiped off his semen with a tuft of wool and threw it on the ground, and from the wool and the earth grew Erichthonios. His name is of uncertain etymology but some scholars associate it with *erion* = wool and *chthōn* = earth, ground.[23] If this is correct, Athens' ruling dynasty started and originated in wool, and a connection between wool, reproduction and the generation of life is expressed through myth. In a similar vein, in the myth of the Argonauts the golden fleece endows Jason with legitimate royal power.[24]

Thread and the act of spinning were metaphorically connected to one's lifespan and destiny through the *Moirai* and their spinning, measuring and cutting the threads of life, from birth to death.[25] They connected the moment of birth and the moment of death. Hecabe, the queen of Troy, recalls her dead son at

---

17 Brulé 1987, 35, 99, 150 note 191. Kearns 1998, 100. Shapiro 1995.
18 Pausanias 1.18.2. In the Attic *Decree of the genos Salaminioi concerning the resolution of a dispute*, lines 41–47, dated 363/2 BCE, provisions of bread are made for the priestess of Pandrosos at the occasion of the Skira festival: Lambert 1997. A priestess of Pandrosos named Philistion is attested ca. 150 BCE: see Raubitschek 1945.
19 Shapiro 1995, 40 and note 19 with sources.
20 Hesychius, *s.v. Plynteria*. The Athenian ephebes accompanied the statue of Athena to the sea where it was washed.
21 Pausanias 1.18.2. Calame 1977, 236–237.
22 Burkert 1966.
23 Pausanias 3.14.6. Brulé 1987, 13–14 and 140 note 6.
24 Jenkins 1985, 127.
25 Hesiod, *Theogony* 901–906. Moira means share or portion. *Il.* 15.185–204 use the word to designate how the sons of Kronos divided the world between them into three parts for which they cast lots. Hesiod, *Theogony* 411–428 tells that Hecate received a *moira* of land. See discussions in Thomson 1972, 38–39 and Pirenne-Delforge and Pironti 2011, 98.

the end of the *Iliad* (24.209–210) by remembering how the *Moirai* had spun his thread of life:

τῷ δ' ὥς ποθι Μοῖρα κραταιὴ γιγνομένῳ ἐπένησε λίνῳ, ὅτε μιν τέκον αὐτή.

In this way for him did resistless Fate spin with her thread at his birth, when I myself bore him.

The *Moirai* were three sisters: Klotho 'Spinner', Lachesis 'Allotter', and Atropos 'Inevitable'.[26] They were spinners of lifetime. Moreover, through their father Zeus' union with the goddess Themis, they had the *Hōrai* 'Hours' as half-sisters.

The *Moiria* also offered protection to women at the crucial and dangerous moment of giving birth, as did Artemis and Eileithyia,[27] and all of these divinities were associated with textile attributes or offerings: the Moirai with spinning, Artemis with her golden spindle, and Eileithyia, who was called *eulinon*[28] in the classical era and who received wool offerings in the Mycenaean period.[29] There is also a female divinity named Rhapso 'Seamstress' in Attica.[30]

Arachne is another mythological founding mother of weaving and spinning. Her name is clearly derived from the Greek word for spider.[31] The story of Arachne is mainly known from Ovid,[32] and we cannot be sure what stories were told about her in Greece centuries earlier. She is said to be a motherless

---

26 Lachesis appears to be named from *lachos*, a portion given or received by the process of casting a lot. Atropos' name may be connected with *trephō*, turn, Thomson 1972, 47 suggests that Atropos has an initial a- to render the meaning more intensive, and thus is a parallel to *atraktos*, so her name means "Turner", and personification of the spindle.
27 In Pindar, (*Ol.* 6.40), Eileithyia and the *Moirai* appear side by side as birth helpers. Artemis states that the *Moirai* gave her the assignment to help women give birth in Callimachos, *Hymn to Artemis* 22–25: ᾗσί με Μοῖραι γεινομένην τὸ πρῶτον ἐπεκλήρωσαν ἀρήγειν, ὅττι με καὶ τίκτουσα καὶ οὐκ ἤλγησε φέρουσα μήτηρ, ἀλλ' ἀμογητὶ φίλων ἀπεθήκατο γυίων (*For these the Fates assigned me from my very birth to bring aid, since my mother when she gave birth to me and carried me did not suffer, but took me from her own womb without pain.*).
28 Pausanias 8.21.3 cites an old hymn dedicated to Eileithyia *eulinon*: Λύκιος δὲ Ὠλὴν ἀρχαιότερος τὴν ἡλικίαν, Δηλίοις ὕμνους καὶ ἄλλους ποιήσας καὶ ἐς Εἰλείθυιαν, εὔλινόν τε αὐτὴν ἀνακαλεῖ. (*The Lycian Olen, an earlier poet, who composed for the Delians, among other hymns, one to Eileithyia, styles her 'the clever spinner'.*).
29 Nosch and Perna 2001.
30 *IG* II² 4547 lists the following divinities together: Hestia, the Pythian Apollo, Leto, Artemis Lochia, Eileithyia, Genethliai nymphes and Rhapso.
31 On weaving and spiders in Bronze Age iconography, see Nosch and Ulanowska 2021.
32 *Metamorphoses* book 6. This book starts with the story of Arachne and ends with Philomena, two weaving protagonists with catastrophic fates.

child of a wool dyer in Lydia. She challenged Athena and audaciously claimed to be the better weaver, and for this she was punished.[33]

Finally, even the rather unlikely figure of Herakles is associated with the working of textiles. The discovery of purple dye from murex was attributed to him in Pollux's 2nd-century CE *Onomastikon* (1.46). Herakles's dog accidentally bit on a murex sea snail, and its mouth became tainted purple. A nymph called Tyro, her name probably a reference to the Phoenician city of Tyre, saw the bright purple colour and asked Herakles for a dress dyed in this hue. The mythical discovery thus unites serendipity, the desire for textile luxury, and love.

2.4 The human inventor, discoverer and first finder (prōtos heuretēs) of weaving and dyeing

The inventor, discoverer, or 'first finder' (*prōtos heuretēs*) is a prominent figure in ancient Greek history writing.[34] They were a source of fascination to classical audiences, and some ancient authors published lists of inventors in so-called *heuremata* catalogues, or catalogues of discoveries.[35] The *heuremata* lists historicize inventions and inventors and the origins of crafts and techniques, τέχναι, and create a sense of time, continuity and tradition.[36] As Krystina Bartol notes:

> The motif of the *protos heuretes* was deeply rooted in Greek horography too, where the annalistic method of organising the past dominated. In local histories, the category of first finder or discoverer becomes part of their eulogising technique, in which *spatium mythicum* is well integrated with history. (Bartol 2006, 86)

The genre is often ethnocentric, celebrating inventions by Greeks. It connects with the double meaning of the Greek word *archē* as both 'beginning' and 'leading', with the Greeks usually therefore both first and best.[37] The inventor, discoverer,

---

33 See Miller 1986 for a feminist and literary reading of Arachne. Frontisi-Ducroux 2003, 221–272 explores the metamorphosis of women and spiders.
34 Kleingünther 1933 (without discussion of textile crafts). Bartol 2006. Wersinger-Taylor 2018. Zhmud 2006.
35 Thraede 1962, 183: "[…], dass die Form der Kataloge, so fragwürdig sie uns scheint, einer eigenen Gattung antiker Bildungstradition entspricht."
36 Bartol 2006, 86. Zhmud 2001; 2006.
37 Bardol 2006. Wersinger-Taylor 2018.

'first finder' is usually a man, historical or mythical, and his inspiration is induced by divine input.[38]

The sources on inventors are mainly authors from Roman times or later, but it is assumed that they rely on older literature and traditions.[39] Impressing one's audience by showing off one's knowledge of the number and range of inventors and inventions seems more important than accuracy or documentation.[40] Interestingly, inventors of textile-related crafts are rarely mentioned.

First finders, discoverers, inventors and heurematography tie theoretically into 'the invention of the past' and intentional history as a:

> projection in time of elements of subjective, self-conscious self-categorization which construct the identity of a group as a group.[41]

There seems to be a care to link inventions with specific places for which a particular technology had a long craft tradition.[42] For example, creators and inventors of textile crafts were often associated with Lydia or places in Asia Minor that were historically renowned for their textile production and trade. In general, however, inventions in the sphere of clothing and textiles are not a focus in the inventor catalogues but appear in-between many other technical and intellectual innovations.

Pliny the Elder (*Natural History* 7.191–221) gives a long account of inventions and inventors. Most inventors were divinities or mythical figures such as King

---

38 In modern times, this effort was repeated in the celebration of ancient Greece as the unique source of European culture as coined by Ernest Renan's expression "le miracle grec" in the late 19th century, see Wersinger-Taylor 2018, 2. Bruno Snell's *Die Entdeckung des Geistes* from 1946 and Richard Onians' *The Origins of European Thought* from 1951 are highlighted by Wersinger-Taylor 2018 as representatives of this trend.
39 Thraede 1962, 158–159.
40 Kleingünther 1933, 1: "Teils von einem durchaus wissenschaftlichen Sammlerinteresse getragen – besonders im frühen Peripatos – wurde die Heurematagraphie vielfalt zum Tummelplatz elender Skribenten, die das Publikum mit θαυμάσια unterhalten wollten und sich nach Auffassung des Altertums vor albernsten Kombinationen nicht scheuten." Thraede 1962, 172: "Gerade auch für die Analyse der Erfinderkataloge kann man sich gar nicht deutlich genug machen, dass die Tendenz nahezu aller Erfinder-Traditionen außerhalb des Peripatos nicht auf Sachen, sondern auf Namen ging und es sich im Denkmodell εὕρεσις – μίμησις in erster Linie um das Interesse an der Geschichte und den sie stiftende Namen handelte, nicht aber um historische Verifizierbarkeit."
41 Foxhall and Luraghi 2010, 9.
42 Thraede 1962, 172: "Als Namen, deren Geltung wichtiger ist als historische Richtigkeit in der Sache, kommen hier für die älteste Tradition vor allem die lokalpatriotischen Zuschreibungen an Heroen und Städte in Betracht."

Cadmus of Thebes, though inventions could also be assigned to whole peoples (e.g. the art of writing to the Assyrians). After the inventions of cities, bricks and walls, Pliny passes on to the production of textiles before other crafts (7.195–196):

> Aegyptii textilia, inficere lanas Sardibus Lydi, fusos in lanificio Closter filius Arachnae, linum et retia Arachne, fulloniam artem Nicias Megarensis, sutrinam Tychius Boeotius
>
> woven fabrics by the Egyptians, dyeing woollen stuffs by the Lydians at Sardis, the use of the spindle in the manufacture of woollen by Kloster son of Arachne, linen and nets by Arachne, the fuller's craft by Nicias of Megara, the shoemaker's by Tychius of Boeotia

As we can see, according to Pliny the inventors of textile technologies range from ethnic groups (Egyptians and Lydians[43]), semi-mythical figures such as Arachne and her son Kloster (from κλωστήρ, thread, spindle), to named men from Megara and Boeotia.

In *Fables* no. 274, a 2nd-century CE text attributed to Hyginus, we find a catalogue of creators and discoverers, among which are two connected with textiles:

> Be\<l\>one prima acum repperit, quae Graece βελόνη appelatur.
>
> Belona first invented the needle, which in Greek is called belonē
>
> Lydi surculis lanam \<in\>fecerunt, postea idem s\<t\>amen
>
> The Lydians first dyed raw wool with a substance from twigs, and afterward learned to dye the thread.

What was the driver of such textile innovations? In Athenaeus (12.64), a man called Polyarchus, surnamed the Luxurious, claims that pleasure and comfort generate innovations and inventions. In contrast, the philosopher Democritus (68 B 154) is credited for a saying about nature as a source of technical innovation and that people had learned weaving from spiders.[44] Whatever the truth of such suggestions, people in antiquity clearly had an interest in the development of textiles, represented in both myth and other forms of literature. We have seen that such literary evidence, while culturally illuminating, is, however, also questionable. Let us next examine what the archaeological evidence can reveal.

---

[43] On the textile industry in Lydia, see Roebuck 1959, 57: "a Greek tradition ascribed the invention of dyeing cloth to the Lydians (Pliny NH 7.56 [196]; Hyginus Fables 274). The textile industry centered at Sardis is known only from the fifth century (Scholia to Aristophanes *Ach.* 112; *Peace* 1174) but was probably much older and developed from small beginnings as a household craft under the patronage of the Lydian and Ionian nobility."
[44] Reported in Plutarch, *De sollertia animalium* 20.

3 First textiles

The need for clothing as protection probably arose when our ancestors lost their body hair approximately three million years ago. Clothing not only protects us against cold, but also against insects, discomfort, thorns, UV-radiation and heat.

3.1 The earliest evidence of textile technology from archaeology

Once humans migrated from the warmer regions of the African continent, they reached colder climates where cover and clothing became necessary for survival. Genetic analyses demonstrated that eventually, about 100,000 years ago, human body lice (*Pediculus humanus*) had developed into two distinct types with two distinct biotopes: head lice in the scalp and body lice on the skin and in clothes and fur.[1]

Recent excavations at Neanderthal sites confirm that they had knowledge of plant fibre processing, twisting and cord making: at the Middle Palaeolithic site of Abri du Maras, Ardèche, 41,000 to 52,000 years ago, a tiny piece of bast fibre cord was created from three fibre bundles that had been s-twisted into 2 yarns and then z-plied into a cord.[2] Another site in Swabian Jura contained ivory tools that the archaeologists interpreted as Neanderthal fibre tools for spinning or plying.[3] A 17,000-year-old 6-plied cord was uncovered in Lascaux.[4] Regarding early fibre technology and time, the archaeologists state that:

> Fibre acquisition, processing and production may have also played an important role in scheduling daily and seasonal activities. String and rope manufacture are time intensive activities and large amounts of string are required for the production of carrying objects such as bags.[5]

---

[1] Toups et al. 2011.
[2] Hardy et al. 2020.
[3] Conard and Malina 2016.
[4] Soffer and Adovasio 2010. Conard and Malina 2016.
[5] Hardy et al. 2020.

The mention of 'carrying objects' recalls the *carrier bag theory* by Elizabeth Fischer, who presented the bag as carrying device for infants or food used by hunter-gatherer as an early and formative feminine technology.[6]

Early humans survived partly because of an ability and willingness over many thousands of years to cover naked skin with that of an animal.[7] They used hides and furs from animals which were processed into soft and pliable materials and adapted to the human body. Since the Palaeolithic, humans have made clothing by cutting animal skin and fur into human shapes and sewing them together. The first sewing threads were probably made from animal sinew or tendons or from plant fibres such as flax, hemp, nettle, or tree bast. We can be certain that creating thread from fibres, by twisting, twining and spinning, had developed by the Palaeolithic period as needles made out of bone and furnished with eyes and dating back 30,000 years have been found in excavations.[8] The archaeologist Bo Gräslund has even claimed that humanity's greatest invention was not fire, but the needle.[9]

That sewing, spinning, twisting, plying, fibre processing and, eventually, weaving are among the earliest technologies developed by humans is confirmed by archaeological findings: bone needles and the earliest woven impressions in clay are much older than evidence for agriculture, animal husbandry, pottery, or metallurgy.[10]

Weaving probably developed later in human history than sewing in skins, although scholars suggest that weaving, plaiting and braiding have been used since the Upper Palaeolithic, based on finds of tools and figurines (Fig. 2).[11] The material finds support this early date: the earliest textile imprints in clay are ca. 30,000 years old;[12] the oldest preserved archaeological woven textiles are between

---

6 Fisher 1979 in the chapter "The Carrier Bag Theory of Evolution". The carrier bag as a crucial invention is convincing but not necessarily as a woven or plaited textile, since a hunter-gatherer bag could be made of skin, leather, tendons, sinew, or plaited fibres and twigs. The theory gained prominence in another field, namely feminist and literary studies, in the 1986 essay "The Carrier Bag Theory of Fiction" by Ursula Le Guin that presents 'story' as a vital carrier bag of culture maintained by women's voices.
7 Gilligan 2010. Nosch 2023.
8 Gilligan 2010, 48–53.
9 Gräslund 2017, 86. I thank Maria Sjöberg for this reference.
10 Adovasio et al. 1996.
11 Soffer et al. 2000.
12 Adovasio et al. 1996.

10,000 and 6,000 years old, and are all made of plant fibres and originated in the Levant, the Middle East, and Egypt.¹³

Figure 2: Mizin, Ukraine, ca. 20,000 years old mammoth ivory incised with patterns that resemble techniques using threads, such as tablet-weaving, braiding, or weaving. With kind permission from The National Museum of the History of Ukraine.

Anthropologist Tim Ingold has argued that weaving is a 'foundational' craft, suggesting that weaving is not a kind of making but *vice versa* – weaving constitutes all kinds of making and making is a modality of weaving: "Weaving epitomizes human technical activity".¹⁴

Wool from animal fibres appeared in the 3rd millennium, and the earliest preserved wool textiles come from Mesopotamia. In the Bronze Age, wool use expanded into Europe and radically transformed technology, agriculture, animal husbandry, landscapes, soil erosion and human visual expression to such an extent that we might well speak of the *Wool Age* instead of the *Bronze Age*.¹⁵

However, archaeological textiles from antiquity are rare and belong to what prehistoric archaeologist and plant fibre expert Linda Hurcombe has termed the problem of the "missing majority" as almost all the evidence has disap-

---

13 Skals et al. 2015. Bender Jørgensen et al. 2023. Kvavadze et al. 2009 assumed that plant fibre finds from 30,000 BP could be flax but we have argued against this in Bergfjord et al. 2010.
14 Ingold 2000, 64.
15 Nosch 2015.

peared.[16] As archaeological artefacts, they clearly had a limited lifetime, though we will discuss some isolated survivals later.

3.2 Periodization of time, dress and weaves

Periodization is the main analytical tool for associating phenomena in a chronological sequence and thereby in a mutual relationship of *before* and *after*. It can be defined as a period of time to which a certain unity is to be attributed and which is to be distinguished to a certain degree from the preceding and subsequent periods. Our study of the past operates generally operates via such sequences of periods, either conceptually or, in the case of archaeology, concretely (with superposed soil layers where the thickness of a soil layer mirrors a duration of time).[17]

Importantly, in Greek, *periodos* as a term and concept contains a sense of rhythm and returns (see ch. 4.4).[18]

Christian Jürgensen Thomsen (1788–1865) was a pioneer of periodization as one of the most important principles in modern archaeology. He was an assistant at the National Museum of Denmark and had access to a wide range of archaeological artefacts, of which he was able to make comparative analyses. From the mid-1820s, Thomsen developed a three-period system which shaped the modern division of antiquity into three main periods: the Stone Age, Bronze Age and Iron Age, named after the materials that weapons and tools were made of.[19] This represented a revival of the concept of technological succession from stone to bronze to iron of ancient authors like Hesiod.[20] Thomsen's fundamental taxonomic system still characterizes our approach to prehistoric cultures globally.

As an alternative periodization, textile fibres could form the chronological framework for Europe and one could divide history into the Plant Fibre Age, the Wool Age and the Man-made Fibre Age of the modern era. Long before the fibre-based ages was the Skin Clothing Age that lasted perhaps until 30,000 years ago when plant fibre textiles were first developed. Around 5,000 years

---

16 Hurcombe 2014.
17 Sometimes these sequences of periods are underpinned by typology, sometimes cross-cut. Witmore 2023, 30, 50.
18 Meyer 1901, 3: "Insbesondere ist es nicht zufällig, aus dem rhythmischen Begriff der ‚Periode' als einer metrischen oder stilististichen Einheit irgend welche Folgerungen auf den der historischen Periode zu machen."
19 Thomsen 1836; 1837; 1848. For the historical roots and a critical assessment, see Heizer 1962. Wagner-Hasel 2000, 306–307; 2017, 42; 2020, 329–330.
20 See above, ch. 1, and Heizer 1962, 262.

ago wool became a fibre resource and the Wool Age began.²¹ Approximately 2000 year ago silk and cotton fibres became known broadly in Europe and initiated an age when fibres were traded across continents, and this age continued till the 20th century with the introduction of synthetic and oil-based fabrics. In contrast to the metal-based ages, the fibre-based ages never fully supplanted each other but supplemented each other. After all, we still wear skin and fur clothing in many places on the planet today.

3.3 Weaves and clothes types as proxies for chronologies and periodizations – and how they challenge them

The simplest weave types are tabbies, with weft threads running over and under every second warp thread. This weave is found in all ancient cultures. Another weave is known as twill: in this weave, weft threads run in different sequences with one, two or three wefts crossing the warp. Twill as a weave type has been associated the specific period of the European Iron Age²² and has been seen as a chronological marker of Iron Age textiles. Margarita Gleba, however, reviewed ca. 300 Iron Age textile fragments from Italy and Greece and compared them in terms of weave and other structural parameters. She observed more of a geographical than a chronological difference in Iron Age textiles: the textile fragments from Italy demonstrated a greater variety of weaves and techniques, several of which were closely associated with the European Iron Age. Tabby textiles woven in single, primarily z-twisted yarns were the most common, and most tabbies were balanced (with the same number of warp and weft threads). There were also many weft-faced wool tabbies (with more wefts than warp threads), often with so many wefts beaten in that the warp had become invisible.²³ Significantly, over a quarter of the textiles were woven in balanced 2/2 twill weave and with tablet-woven borders, so this weave seems a salient feature of Iron Age Italy.²⁴

---

21 Nosch 2015.
22 Barber 1991. Mannering 2017, 118: Scandinavian Bronze Age textiles (1700–500 BCE) are tabby woven while most pre-Roman fabrics (500–1 BCE) are woven in 2/2 twill. Twill can be used as a dating criterion in Scandinavia, but not tabby, since this weave continues from the Bronze into the Iron Age. See Nosch 2019.
23 Gleba 2017, 1208; 2025, 425–429.
24 Gleba 2017, 1210; 2025, 427.

The Iron Age textiles from Greece are different: they are all balanced tabbies or weft-faced tabbies. The balanced tabbies were mostly of linen, while the weft-faced tabbies were mostly of wool.[25]

Overall, Greece and the Near East weave balanced or weft-faced tabbies in the 2nd and 1st millennia while in Italy and Central Europe twills and tablet-weaving appear in the 1st millennium. Hence, when focusing on textiles, new regional chronologies emerge which challenge older periodizations.[26]

Dress is also used for periodization in art history and archaeology, with Greek dress being used to define periods and assign artefacts to certain eras and chronologies, such as Dorian dress that preceded Ionian dress.[27] In the transition between the Late Bronze Age and the Early Iron Age in the Aegean, a new dress trend appeared in both male and female dress with the extensive use of dress-pins and fibulae. Fixing garments with metal devices is very common in the Iron Age, especially in the 8th to 6th centuries, but not very common in the Bronze Age and does not appear in clothing depicted in Minoan or Mycenaean frescoes. Yet, a closer look reveals that this Iron Age dress trend actually started before the Bronze Age finished – numerous fibulae and dress-pins occur in Late Bronze Age layers.[28] This suggests that 'Early Iron Age clothing' was adopted before the transition into the Iron Age had started. As we shall soon see (cf. ch. 12), Herodotus and Thucydides reported further significant changes in dress in the 6th and 5th centuries BCE.

Another textile-technical development that does not align with the division between the Bronze Age and Iron Age is the appearance of a new weaving device, the spool, which forms a technological bridge between the Late Bronze Age and the Early Iron Age.[29] Typical Bronze Age loom-weight types are spherical, pyramidal or discoid; the new type of loom-weight – the spool – appears across the eastern Mediterranean area at the end of the Late Bronze Age. Spools can be used on warp-weighted looms for fine, open weaves, weft-faced weaves, and twills.[30] They appear in the last two centuries of the 2nd millennium, especially in Late Helladic

---

25 Gleba 2017, 1215; 2025, 420–425.
26 With reference to the periodization of Roman times via textiles, Gleba 2017, 1229 and 2025, 434 observed that weft-faced tabby became the preferred weave of the Romans; this shift suggests that the Greek plain tabby textile culture eventually supplanted the indigenous Italic twill tradition.
27 The same ethnic or regional terms are used to designate Greek dialects and Classical and Hellenistic architecture in art history.
28 On pins and fibulae in archaeology, see Kilian 1974. Kilian-Dirlmeier 1984. Ložnjak Dizdar 2018. On pins and fibulae in iconography, see Brøns 2014, and in sanctuaries, Brøns 2016, 421–430.
29 Rahmstorf 2011, 320. Nosch 2019, 593–594.
30 Andersson Strand and Nosch 2015.

3.4 Carbon 14 dating of archaeological textile finds

IIIC settlements, and they may suggest the arrival of migrants with their own weaving toolkits for the warp-weighted loom.[31]

3.4 Carbon 14 dating of archaeological textile finds

Time is incorporated into a textile's organic fibres, and therefore textiles can be used to establish a precise moment of time.[32]

When organisms are alive, they replenish their Carbon 14 supply continually through respiration, the food chain, or photosynthesis, providing them with a constant amount of the 14C isotope. But once plants are harvested, animal hair is shorn, and silk threads are produced, they no longer absorb carbon from their environment and the unstable 14C isotope begins to decay. Since it decays at a constant rate, textiles can be dated based on the residual amount of 14C in the organic matter. It is a "natural chronometer to reconstruct the ages of organic materials."[33] Retrieving 14C thus helps to answer the basic question of "when".

One should note that the 14C dating of textiles only indicates the time of the plant fibre harvest or the collection of the animal fibres or silk filaments. These raw materials are then spun and woven into a fabric that can be used for decades or generations before the textile is placed in a grave or discarded.[34] The 14C timeframe of textiles therefore reflects the time of production and not necessarily the time of consumption or last use.

---

[31] Rahmstorf 2003, 400–401.
[32] Hajdas et al. 2014.
[33] Fedi et al. 2024.
[34] Fedi et al. 2024 are less concerned about such time gaps: they argue that textiles are vulnerable and short-lived, and therefore not likely to be used for a very long time. While they note a possible time delay between the harvest of fibres, the time of spinning and weaving and the time of use, they consider this time delay limited and hence unproblematic. Fedi et al. 2024, 127. "Therefore, we can expect a time delay between the collection of the raw material and the preparation of the fibre and the thread, and, finally, the manufacturing of the work. Fortunately, when speaking about textiles, raw materials come from short-living organisms and, also considering that they can be fragile and highly degradable, we can expect just a minor delay between the cut or the collection and the manufacturing, well within the typical uncertainties we can obtain in radiocarbon dating. In addition, a textile can be teared up, or it can lose its mechanical properties, or it can be also easily subjected to strong wear: due to this, the possibility of re-using the same material for a different product after lot of time since the first use is not so likely."

While the validity of 14C analyses of textiles has been debated in the past,[35] 14C analyses have provided new insights into the age of textiles and rectified previously assumed dates.[36]

The 14C dating of garments uncovered in bogs in Jutland in Denmark did not align with their assumed dates based on the interpretation of the styles of the clothes: some garment types clearly belonged stylistically to the Late Bronze Age, yet the 14C suggested an Early Iron Age date.[37] We must conclude from this that either typical 'Late Bronze Age clothing' continued to be worn in Early Iron Age communities, or, perhaps, that Late Bronze Age styled clothes were deposited in the Early Iron Age bog burials.

The new 14C dating of some textile finds in Greece has also revealed apparent inconsistencies, assigning them to the Late Bronze Age instead of the Iron Age, i. e. hundreds of years earlier than the original contextual estimate of their date.[38] The extraordinary 10th century BCE burials at Stamna in Aetolia stem from the Early Iron Age, i. e. after the fall of the Mycenaean palaces. Many different types of textiles were deposited in large bronze tripod cauldrons, ranging from very fine to very coarse, and made from plant fibres or wool. They were woven in the tabby technique, which confirms that Stamna belonged to the weave traditions of Greece and the Eastern Mediterranean of balanced or weft-faced tabbies.[39] Human bones wrapped in fabric were also found in the tripod cauldrons and some of the Stamna textiles were dyed with purple from the murex sea snail, a dye that was highly valued for its colour fastness and durability.[40] What do

---

35 Turnbull et al. 2000. Hajdas et al. 2014, 637–638.
36 For a 14C rectification of the dating of textiles from a more recent context, see Fedi et al. 2024: A silk-knitted textile was stored among carbonized finds from Pompeii. It is knitted of thin unspun silk threads with tiny loop sizes of ca. 1 mm, which shows that it was knitted on very thin needles. The technique is the so-called *stockinette* with alternating rows of knit stitch and purl stitch. While some types of knitting are known in antiquity from Egypt, and *nålebinding* has been known for millennia, knitting in this kind of technique and quality is not attested in Roman times; moreover, the knitted pieces are not carbonised as were other textile fragments from Pompeii; and silk was a very rare fibre in Roman times. It was therefore attractive to assume that these pieces of knitting were from the 18th century excavations of Pompeii. Recently, however, 14C tests dated them to the 15th to 16th centuries CE, before the excavations started, and the fragments possibly came from dumps and had mistakenly been mixed up with the Pompeian textile fragments during storage.
37 Mannering et al. 2010, 263: "An important result is however, that finds previously dated to the Late Bronze Age have now been down dated in time and cluster with the majority of the other finds."
38 Kolonas et al. 2017.
39 Gleba 2017.
40 Kolonas et al. 2017.

these textiles tell us about time and memory? Based on the pottery finds, the grave was sealed off in the 10th century BCE. But 14C dating of the textiles surprisingly indicated that some of the grave good textiles were several generations older than the grave. This expands our historical and archaeological understanding of the lifespan of burial textiles.

The potential age of the Stamna textiles invites us to consider whether there was a tradition of offering clothing and textiles from parents, grandparents and even great-grandparents to the deceased in the grave. These textiles must have had a special meaning for the family of the deceased. They could have been kept for a hundred years before they were placed in the tripod cauldron at Stamna.

Perhaps textiles should be considered among the most important and precious grave goods precisely because they connected generations and stood the test of time.[41]

---

[41] Wagner-Hasel 2000, 217 concluded that the weaving of funerary textiles demanded much longer cooperation between women and much more time than the construction of the grave monument: "Für ihre Fertigung bedarf es der dauerhaften Kooperation, des Aufwandes von Zeit und Energie über Jahre hinaus, während die Herstellung eines Grabmals und die Verwandlung der Güter des Toten in *aethla* und damit in dauerhafte Gedächtniszeichen nur punktuelle Kooperation erforderlich macht. Jedoch haftet den metallenen *aethla* und dem steinernen *sema* in ihre Materialität ein Moment der Dauerhaftigkeit an, während die textilen Gedächtniszeichen, die verbrannt werden, nach periodischer Erneuerung verlangen."

4 Textiles and time cycles: chronology, seasons, rhythm, and sequences of tasks

The complexity of textile production generates by itself processes and sequences that last a certain time and that are fixed to certain times of the year.

4.1 Seasonality and timeliness of fibre procurement and textile production

There were four seasons in the ancient Greek agricultural year – spring, summer, autumn and winter. In Archaic Greece, seasons were expressed by the term ὥρα, *hōra*, plural *hōrai*, which only later gained the meaning of hours. The four seasons of antiquity were not equally long. They were:[1]

- Summer, *theros*, lasted from mid-May to mid-September. This was the time of shearing sheep and harvesting flax and other textile crops and of bleaching linen cloth.
- Fall, *phthinopōron*, lasted from mid-September to late October.
- Winter, *cheimōn*, lasted from late October to the spring equinox. During this season fibre processing, spinning and weaving would take place.
- Spring, *ear*, lasted from spring equinox to mid-May.

One could argue, however, that two seasons dominated in ancient Greek perceptions of the year: the long summer and the shorter winter. Thucydides (2.1) outlined how his account of the Peloponnesian War would be narrated according to these two main seasons:

> καὶ γέγραπται ἑξῆς ὡς ἕκαστα ἐγίγνετο κατὰ θέρος καὶ χειμῶνα.

---

[1] Nilsson, 1920, 72: "The Greeks complete the circle of the year with the three seasons winter, spring, and summer (χειμών, ἔαρ, θέρος), but in Homer the fruit-harvest, ὀπώρη, already appears with the pretensions of an independent season. Alkman has these four (Fragm. 76 Bergk). The principle of nomenclature is however different: the first three names are derived from climatic phenomena, ὀπώρα from the fruit-harvest. Now since four climatic periods are naturally to be distinguished – cold, warmth, and two transitional periods – the logical consequence is that the fourth season should also be referred to the climate, and indeed to the still unnamed period of transition between summer and winter. This period however does not coincide with ὀπώρα, but follows it. The latter term is therefore corrected to φθιν- or μετόπωρον; the ὀπώρα naturally persists as the fruit harvest."

> The events of the war have been recorded in the order of their occurrence, summer by summer and winter by winter.

In ancient Greece, there was a seasonal time for each textile task.

Procuring textile fibres has its own temporality and timeliness and depends on seasons, climates and altitudes. Flax and hemp were sown in March/April in the Aegean and Southern Europe and harvested in June/July, with a maturation time of ca. three months.[2] Harvesting one hectare of flax takes one person 25–30 working days.[3] Plant fibre yields are ca 10% of the harvested stalks, depending on how fine a fibre is needed and how the fibre treatments are done.[4] The timing of plant fibre preparation is flexible and extendable, depending on many other factors such as labour, climate and weather. Harvesting flax or hemp stems needs days of warm and dry weather for rippling. After retting, the stems again need warm and dry weather for drying before breaking and heckling. The climate will define how long a time is needed. It is therefore difficult to give precise estimates for plant fibre processing in antiquity. Waiting time, wind, and free time from other tasks count as time factors. Likewise, for the later stages of plant fibre processing, the bleaching of linen requires periods of warm and dry weather.

Procuring wool fibre also has its own temporality and timeliness. Sheep moult their wool every summer. One sheep would yield 750 grams of usable wool in the Bronze Age, as attested both in the Linear B tablets and in Near Eastern documents, and this amount can be assumed for Classical and Hellenistic Greece as well.[5] Wool was plucked in the Bronze Age and in the Iron Age wool shearing was made possible with iron scissors. Both plucking and shearing should be done at the natural moulting time to free the sheep of the old wool and let a new coat of wool grow. Plucking one sheep takes ca. 50 minutes, as has been tested experimentally. Eva Andersson Strand writes:

> It is important to pluck the wool at exactly the right time: if started too early the fibres are not weakened enough, if waiting too long, the old fibres will be mixed with the new, both with the result that it will be hard (for the sheep and the plucker) to pluck the wool.[6]

---

2 Nosch 2014b.
3 Andersson Strand 2012, 25 with bibliography. In the Nile Valley, sowing takes place in November.
4 Nosch 2014b. In Ribe, Denmark, historians and archaeologists grew flax and concluded that 1 ton of flax stalks could yield enough fibres to make 100 kilos of cloth: see Ejstrud et al. 2011.
5 Nosch 2014c.
6 Andersson Strand 2012, 30 with references.

Weaving took place in winter and spring. The chorus of Aristophanes' *Birds* summarises the relationship between seasons and wool working, and also gives some interesting insights into the difference between summer and winter garments and the comercialization of clothes, when they sing (*Birds* 713–715, J. H. Frere's rhyming translation):

Χορός
ἰκτῖνος δ' αὖ μετὰ ταῦτα φανεὶς ἑτέραν ὥραν ἀποφαίνει,
ἡνίκα πεκτεῖν ὥρα προβάτων πόκον ἠρινόν: εἶτα χελιδών,
ὅτε χρὴ χλαῖναν πωλεῖν ἤδη καὶ ληδάριόν τι πρίασθαι.

Chorus
The shepherd is warned, by the Kite reappearing,
To muster his flock, and be ready for shearing.
You quit your old cloak at the Swallow's behest,
In assurance of summer, and purchase a vest.

This text also shows how clothes were commercialised and sold when not needed, and also that there was a difference between summer and winter clothes.

Some days of the month are best suited for certain textile-related tasks, according to Hesiod. Shearing sheep is best on the 11th or 12th day; the 12th day is also the best suited to start warping and heddling the loom. Hesiod's explanations of the proper time to undertake tasks derived from his beliefs about the animal world: these are also apparently the days that spiders spin and ants gather their pile (Hesiod, *Works and Days*, verses 774–779):

ἑνδεκάτη δὲ δυωδεκάτη τ', ἄμφω γε μὲν ἐσθλαί,
ἠμὲν ὄις πείκειν ἠδ' εὔφρονα καρπὸν ἀμᾶσθαι:
ἡ δὲ δυωδεκάτη τῆς ἑνδεκάτης μέγ' ἀμείνων:
τῇ γάρ τοι νῇ νήματ' ἀερσιπότητος ἀράχνης
ἤματος ἐκ πλείου, ὅτε ἴδρις σωρὸν ἀμᾶται:
τῇ δ' ἱστὸν στήσαιτο γυνὴ προβάλοιτό τε ἔργον.

the eleventh and the twelfth, both excellent days
for shearing sheep and for gathering in the gladdening wheat;
but the twelfth is much better than the eleventh.
On this day the high-soaring spider weaves its web
in the full of the day, when the Wise One heaps her pile.
On that day the woman should set up her loom and get on with her work.

Hesiod and Aristophanes' texts suggest that people in antiquity connected seasons and textile production-related tasks and they also saw a parallel between birds' migrations, ants' and spiders' constructions and humans' organisation of textile tasks, alongside other tasks of the agricultural year. Hence, textile production was conceptually part of agrarian and nature-based rhythms and cycles (Fig. 3).

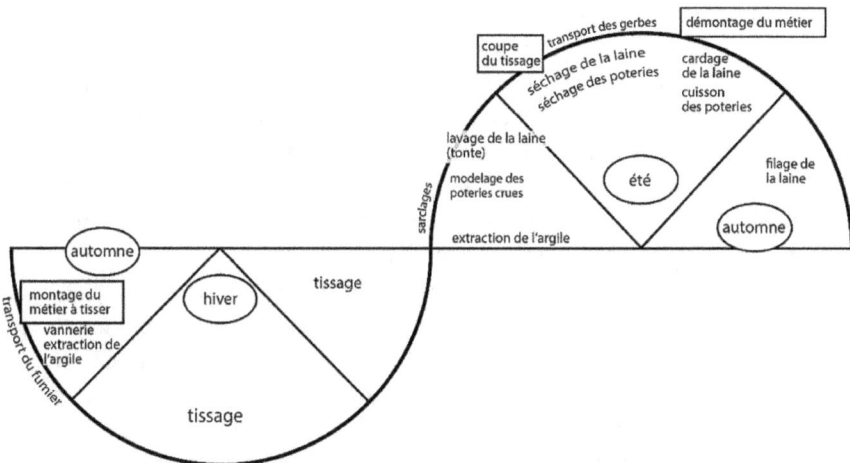

Figure 3: In Kabylian villages of mid-20th century Algeria there were two main seasons, with weaving taking place in winter. Pierre Bourdieu (1963, 56) observed how weaving belongs to one of the two annual seasons among the Kabyle Berber people: "The mythico-ritual system appears to be built about a cluster of contrast between complementary principles. In opposition to plowing and sowing there is the harvest; to weaving, the seasonal counterparts of plowing, the firing of pottery is opposed. Spring is opposed to autumn, summer to winter, all aspects of a larger and clearer contrast between dry season (spring and summer) and the wet season (autumn and winter)." Figure edited and reworked by MLBN, from Bourdieu 1980, 361.

4.2 The chaîne opératoire and linear time in textile research

Textile production is presented in many scholarly works according to the anthropological theory and framework of *chaîne opératoire*, as a chain of actions following a fixed sequence, in a linear form, as a chain. It organises the processes of textile production in a time sequence. Catherine Perlès calls it a succession of mental operations and technical gestures.[7] The *chaîne opératoire* has enabled a fine-grained and nuanced reading of textile technology and craft. The concept stems from early 20th-century social anthropology[8] and has become very influential in

---

7 Perlès 1987, 23, quoted in Sellet 1993, 103.
8 On cultural technology: Mauss 1936. Leroi-Gourhan 1964 and Lemonnier 1983.

archaeological textile research.⁹ It was initially mainly used for lithic technologies.¹⁰

The framework of *chaîne opératoire* is indeed useful for understanding theoretically how textiles are made, but it operates in a void, largely emptied of people, society and culture. It appears as a sequence of processes or "stages"¹¹ rather than a sequence of human choices. Moreover, it appears teleological or deterministic in scope, with a fixation on a productive goal, and, in that, it recalls the industrial processes of the 20th century. Finally, the *chaîne opératoire* tends to only cover the pathway from production to product; yet we know that the finished cloth continues its own trajectory and the processes continue with mending, repair, washing and changing the clothing into new items.

Agata Ulanowska, in a critical assessment of the *chaîne opératoire*, calls it an 'operational syntax' to highlight its intrinsic nature as a logic of production. She uses it as a cognitive framework that can illustrate the gaps in the archaeological evidence.¹² Other scholars, likewise, have emphasized the entangled nature of textile production that is only partially sequential, and not necessarily best perceived as a chain or sequential line of actions.¹³ The *chaîne opératoire* in its simplistic form fails to articulate other aspects of textile production, such as skill, time, labour, scales, diversification of products, social organisation and place of production. Moreover, the *chaîne opératoire* contains a notion of time progression yet fails to illustrate how much time is needed for each sequence.

Another difficulty is that the framework of *chaîne opératoire* is aligned with a temporality that moves in one direction only, with the notion of time as "a series of instants succeeding one another along an abstract line oriented in a single direction."¹⁴ Hence, the directionality of the *chaîne opératoire* can be compared to narratives with a strong focus on conclusions as the peak of the story or "the pole of attraction".¹⁵ The *chaîne opératoire* contains a certain narrativity, and, as Paul Ricoeur hypothesised, narrativity and temporality are closely related.¹⁶

---

9 Andersson Strand 2012. Harlizius-Klück 2016, 751–753 and fig. 45.1.
10 Sellet 1993, 106: "a chronological segmentation of the actions and mental processes required in the manufacture of an artefact and in its maintenance".
11 Andersson Strand 2012, 22.
12 Ulanowska 2020.
13 Harlow and Nosch 2014.
14 Ricoeur 1980, 174.
15 Ricoeur 1980, 174.
16 Ricoeur 1980, 169–170.

4.3 Gendered time of textiles

Textile production was gendered both in its tasks and where it took place. Pasture and shepherding were men's work and took place outside the house; fibre work was women's work and took place at home.[17] The gendered textile production moreover unfolded at different times.

Sofie Remijsen has explored gendered time in rabbinic texts and investigated the existence of different temporalities for men and women:[18]

> a female temporality in which the duration and order of household tasks and of biological cycles loomed large, and a male temporality determined by the more rigid schedules of public life.[19]

In rabbinic texts, female temporal shifts were set primarily by the menstrual cycle because the monthly alternation of periods of purity and impurity regulated both women's and men's behaviour.[20] A concrete piece of cloth plays an important role in keeping track of women's time. In the *Mishna* of the first centuries CE are collected and edited older rules, traditions and laws for Jewish communities. In the stipulations about women's bodies, purity must be controlled daily by pieces of cloth inserted in the vagina to test if there were signs of blood which would signal the time of the monthly impurity.[21] The cloth name is translated as 'test rag' or 'examination cloth'.[22]

Gendered time is also expressed and materialised in the clothing donated to Greek sanctuaries because such donations mostly coincided with important moments in women's lives: wedding, pregnancy, and birth. In a relief from Echinos of the late 5th century, a mother presents her new-born baby to the goddess Artemis; above them on a cloth line hang textiles and garments (Fig. 4). "The scene

---

[17] Jenkins 1985.
[18] Remijsen 2023, 163: "The gendered aspect is stronger for biological rhythms. With the menstrual cycle, women physically experience a biological rhythm that is close to the civil month, which could theoretically have been experienced as a marker of time."
[19] Remijsen 2023, 159.
[20] Remijsen 2023, 158. On women's bodies as metaphors for time in Jewish literature, see Gribetz 2017, 176: "In ancient Jewish literature, one of the dominant metaphors used for time is that of a women's body and its cycles (menstruation, pregnancy and birth as well as fertility)." Gribetz 2020, 165: "Rabbinic sources about menstrual purity required women to count their days and keep track of their bodies' time on a daily basis".
[21] Gribetz 2020, 166.
[22] Gribetz 2020, 302, note 137. Etymologically, it connects to 'witness', not to a root of 'cloth', but means 'cloths that serve as witness'. I thank Arjan Bakker for his help with these references.

marks the culmination of an important cycle for the mother, and as the baby reaches out to the goddess, a new cycle has begun."[23]

I believe we could consider the many clothing dedications as tokens of women's time: their biological phases and their social life chapters.

Figure 4: An important moment in a family's life. A mother presenting her baby to Artemis in her sanctuary, with garments hanging above them. Relief from Echinos near Lamia, late 5th century BCE. Published by Dakoronia and Gounaropoulou 1992.
Photo: Wikimedia Commons / Grb16, CC BY-SA 3.0, https://commons.wikimedia.org/wiki/File:Lamia_ofiara_dziekczynna_476kB.jpg (last access 04.07.2025).

4.4 Rhythm and weaving

Production time is the duration of time it takes to make an object. But craft also has another internal temporality composed of rhythm. Rhythm and repetition of movements are constituent elements of making, according to anthropologist Tim Ingold. Through rhythms and repetitions, the craftsperson creates the object. This

---

[23] Cole 1998, 35. Cole 1998, 34, stresses the bond between garment donation and time occasion when she states that "These were valuable items, representing the best clothing their donors possessed, given to the divinity to mark very special occasions. Their value for the city was reckoned not only by the value of the garment but by the meaning of those occasions."

perspective resonates well with textile production and its many rhythmic and repetitive movements and sequences.[24]

Making cloth created a background rhythm of female life in ancient Greece that is both visible and audible if one knows where to see and hear it.[25]

One of the most iconic and permanent acoustic rhythms of life in antiquity was the sound of weaving, which would have been a constant backdrop to daily domestic life. A warp-weighted loom's rhythm and sounds are diverse: the sound of opening the shed by pulling or pushing the heddle bar with the attendant clanking sounds of pending clay loom-weights or stones; the quiet sound of inserting weft yarn and pushing it into place with a *kerkis*, an implement used as shuttle, pin beater or weft-beater;[26] and two to three blunt, loud sounds of the weaving sword beating the weft upwards into place. On a two-beam loom or a ground loom, the sound of the beating of the weft would be similar to that on the warp-weighted loom, but there would be no sounds from clanking loom-weights.

These rhythmic sounds would have filled most households.

A coarse weave of ten weft threads per cm means 1000 beating sounds and changes of shed for every meter of woven fabric. One meter of denser fabric of thinner threads of 30 wefts per cm would generate 3000 noisy beats per meter of woven fabric.

An average weaving pace of about 50 cm during an 8-hour day, while weaving a coarse fabric with 10 threads per cm^2, means beating the weft 500 times each day. This generates a loud sound approximately every minute (75 beats per hour). In a test of weaving sailcloth on a warp-weighted loom, a very experienced weaver achieved the maximum weaving speed of inserting 86–88 wefts per hour, hence 86–88 beating sounds per hour.[27] Weaving thus creates a constant acoustic rhythm throughout the day.

The rhythm would depend on the weave quality, on the skill of the weaver and the width of the fabric. It is plausible that people in antiquity would have recognised what cloth was being woven and by whom from the rhythm and beat sounds alone.

---

24 Ingold 2000, 61–62.
25 Nosch 2014a.
26 Manessy-Guitton 1977, 242–243. Flemestad et al. 2017.
27 Dimova et al. 2021, 769.

4.5 Rhythm and pulse beats expressed in textile terms by Galen

Rhythms appear everywhere in nature: in seasons, gestation, and the manner in which our bodies follow rhythms defined by hormones, pulse beats, melatonin, and heartbeats. These rhythms work at different paces; yet they do not run in parallel, they are entangled and mutually dependent and together form ecosystems of slow and fast rhythms.[28]

It is perhaps no coincidence that the medical writer Galen (129–217 CE) chose to use terms from weaving when describing the human pulse and its beats.[29] Galen had a detailed understanding of the pulse and used it as a diagnostic tool and his analyses and conclusions are contained in various works. In some passages the noun *pyknotēs* designates the density or frequency of pulse beats.[30] Peter Singer translates Galen's terms for pulse beats as 'close', *pyknoi*, in contrast to pulse beats that are *araioi* 'spaced out'.[31] These adjectives are also used in relation to the craft of weaving and are terms for thread density in a fabric where *pyknos* designates a dense weave, i.e. with many weft beats.[32] It is attractive to imagine that weave density was associated with the sound of frequent weave beats and frequent pulse beats, both semantically and as experience.

There are also bonds between the pulse beat and the clothing term *khitōn* in Galen's works, perhaps because of its properties as flexible and permeable: the *khitōn* is the 'outer wall' of the artery,[33] and two layers of fibres in the walls of

---

28 Fletcher and Tham 2004.
29 I am grateful to Peter Singer and Orly Lewis for sharing their extensive knowledge on Galen with me. For the pulse theories by the Pneumatists and Galen, see Coughlin and Lewis 2020.
30 Singer 2022, 137–139. Singer 2022, 138: "Galen defines *pyknotès* in terms of length, or shortness, of the interval between the end of one pulse and the beginning of the next. It is, indeed, the 'closeness' of one pulse beat to the next".
31 Singer 2022, 139. Galen defines *araios* and *pyknos* in *Health* (II.5, 53–54 Koch, 120–121 Kühn): "What is properly speaking porous is that which is run through with large channels, just as what is dense is what is run through with small ones;" Translation from Singer 2023, 222.
32 A cloak, *khlaina*, can be dense (*pyknos*) as the cloak that Eumaios offered as cover for the night to Odysseus in *Od.* 14.520–521, 529. Moreover, in Mycenaean Greek, *pu-ka-ta-ri-ja* designates wool textiles, see Nosch 2012.
33 In *Diff. Puls.* 1.3 (VIII.500–1 Kühn), Galen states: "It is also necessary that it be in [3] some state of tension, so that is it acting either with difficulty and feebly, or readily and vigorously; and that [4] the actual tunic of the artery be soft or hard, but also [5] the internal breadth be as it were empty or full." Translation from Singer 2022, 136, note 27. See also Galen, *De usu pulsuum* (V.158 Kühn): "You will understand clearly what is being said, if you expose the heart of an animal and take off its covering, which people call the pericardial tunic, without penetrating the rest of the

the stomach are called *khitōnes*.³⁴ Clothing and textile terms are thus integrated in the language in many ways, as metaphors and as useful descriptors in technical texts.

---

thorax." Translation from Johnston and Papavramidou 2024, 95. Galen, *Diff. Puls.* 2.3 (VIII.575 Kühn) uses *khitōn* for the wall of an artery. See also Miller 2023 on Galen and time.
34 Galen, *Nat. Fac.* 3.8 (II.168–II.172 Kühn), see Lewis 2023, 271–272.

5 The long hours to make textiles – Penelope's time

Textile manufacturing processes are many and long. The process of spinning is more time-consuming than weaving: several hands must be spinning before weaving can even begin.

Time is essential for textile production and cloth's value is directly related to the spinning and weaving time. Large pieces of cloth, and/or cloth woven of very many thin threads represent time investments whose value can be hard to grasp for a modern audience and are often overlooked in the historical assessments of the past.

An iconic example from ancient Greek literature illustrates how time-consuming textile production was: none of Penelope's many suitors, who courted her during her husband Odysseus's long-term absence, found it strange that Penelope was weaving the same piece of cloth every day for three years.

Penelope herself revealed her weaving and unravelling tricks to a visiting beggar (who in reality was Odysseus, her husband) (*Od.* 19.136–147):

> ἀλλ' Ὀδυσῆ ποθέουσα φίλον κατατήκομαι ἦτορ.
> οἱ δὲ γάμον σπεύδουσιν: ἐγὼ δὲ δόλους τολυπεύω.
> φᾶρος μέν μοι πρῶτον ἐνέπνευσε φρεσὶ δαίμων,
> στησαμένη μέγαν ἱστόν, ἐνὶ μεγάροισιν ὑφαίνειν,
> λεπτὸν καὶ περίμετρον: ἄφαρ δ' αὐτοῖς μετέειπον:
> κοῦροι, ἐμοὶ μνηστῆρες, ἐπεὶ θάνε δῖος Ὀδυσσεύς,
> μίμνετ' ἐπειγόμενοι τὸν ἐμὸν γάμον, εἰς ὅ κε φᾶρος
> ἐκτελέσω—μή μοι μεταμώνια νήματ' ὄληται—
> Λαέρτῃ ἥρωϊ ταφήϊον, εἰς ὅτε κέν μιν
> μοῖρ' ὀλοὴ καθέλῃσι τανηλεγέος θανάτοιο:
> μή τίς μοι κατὰ δῆμον Ἀχαιϊάδων νεμεσήσῃ,
> αἴ κεν ἄτερ σπείρου κεῖται πολλὰ κτεατίσσας.

> I miss Odysseus; my heart is melting.
> The suitors want to push me into marriage,
> but I spin schemes. Some god first prompted me
> to set my weaving in the hall and work
> a long fine cloth. I said to all my suitors,
> "Although Odysseus is dead, postpone
> requests for marriage till I finish weaving
> this sheet to shroud Laertes when he dies.
> My work should not be wasted, or the people
> in Argos will reproach me, if a man
> who won such wealth should lie without a shroud."

Her weaving is called *pharos*, a fine mantle. Her trick is induced by a god, she claims, who told her to weave on a large loom in the main hall of the palace. Then at night, she unravels the threads. Only when a disloyal servant betrayed Penelope did the suitors understand the trick – it was not the unusually long weaving and waiting time that raised their suspicion.

One wonders how she could weave in public in the main hall, not hidden away, and unravel at night without being seen by the suitors.

5.1 How long did it take? Time measurements from experimental textile archaeology

A note of caution about time: it is difficult to draw firm conclusions about how much time people in the past spent on textile production.[1] It would depend on what textile they produced, its size and quality, the fibres and the tools they used. It would also depend on their skill, motivation, concentration, the time available, whether they hurried or not, if weaving was a pastime or a necessary living condition.[2] Experimental archaeology cannot give a firm answer about the time spent on textile production but it provides answers to what is possible given ancient textile tools and the final quality of cloth produced. It can also estimate the minimum length of time required for various textile processes.

Fibre procurement and fibre preparation first involve time in shepherding animals or in growing fibres. Next comes the time for harvesting large quantities of fibres from animals or plants, quantities which are substantially reduced in weight by each processing step.[3] This takes time: to harvest 1 ha of flax by hand takes 25–30 days for one person,[4] and to ripple 54.5 kilos of flax takes 37

---

[1] van Wees (2005b, 45 and note 11) gives estimates of sizes and time consumption but does not explain clearly on what basis the estimates were made. He assumes that a short, coarse wool cloak would take 24 hours or 3 working days to make, while a woman's finest large linen *peplos* would take 1200 hours or 150 days: see van Wees 2005a, 16–17 and van Wees 2005b, 46.
[2] See Ejstrud et al. 2011, 14–15 on time estimates in experimental archaeology and Ejstrud et al. 2011, 14: "The reason is that the human factor is all important in such studies. The time taken to perform some task is highly reliant on the skill and motivation of the person doing the work. And we can measure neither skill nor motivation of prehistoric people."
[3] For example, experiments have demonstrated that after harvesting 54.5 kilos of fresh flax, a total of 25.6 kilos of dry stalks remained after drying and rippling the stems, see Ejstrud et al. 2011, 43.
[4] Andersson Strand 2012, 25 with references.

hours for one person.⁵ The most time-consuming processes by far are fibre preparation and spinning. A general estimate often used in experimental textile archaeology gives a weaving pace of 50 cm per day on a warp-weighted loom.⁶

At the Center for Textile Research (CTR), we have tested systematically how long it takes to prepare, comb, spin and weave using ancient techniques experimentally. We have worked exclusively with highly experienced textile craftswomen active in the field of experimental archaeology, we have only used exact copies of archaeologically attested tools, and we have used plant and animal fibre that were similar to ancient fibre qualities.

5.2 How long did it take to spin?

Before spinning could begin came another very time-consuming and crucial task: fibre preparation, e.g., wool cleaning, sorting and combing. CTR textile experts could prepare only ca. 114 grams of wool per working day of 8 hours.⁷

The pace of ancient spinning was measured via numerous spinning trials in experimental archaeology. Experienced spinners in the CTR concluded that it takes longer to spin fine, thin threads than thicker and looser yarns.⁸ It was more time-consuming on a light spindle whorl than on a heavy spindle whorl and it was faster to spin long fibres than short fibres.⁹

CTR spinners achieved the following spinning results: from 100 grams of wool, they were able to spin an average of 623.5 meters of yarn with a spindle whorl weighing 18 grams, and 1031 meters of yarn with a spindle whorl weighing 8 grams.¹⁰

Two experienced spinners conducted drop spinning tests in Italy and confirmed that the size and weight of the spindle whorl had an effect on the spinning and the thread but they also observed how the spinners and the fibre preparation and many other factors impacted the final yarn product.¹¹ They achieved a wool

---

5 Ejstrud et al. 2011, 43. Ejstrud et al. 2011, 44 estimate that 20–25 m² cultivated flax would suffice to produce a linen shirt.
6 Andersson and Nosch 2003, 199 give 70–80 cm per day. Andersson Strand 2012, 35.
7 Olofsson et al. 2015.
8 These measurements can shed light on textile production in terms of time and quality of production. See Firth and Nosch 2012. Nosch and Sauvage 2023.
9 Andersson Strand 2012, 33–34.
10 Andersson and Nosch 2003, 198, 201, stated that 1 kilo wool yields between 3.9 and 14 kilometers of thread depending on the wool quality and we estimate 6.5 kilometer of thread for a fabric woven with 12 threads per cm. Andersson Strand and Nosch 2015.
11 Ciccarelli and Perilli 2017, 162.

spinning pace of 20 m per hour on spindle whorls of 20–30 grams and a flax spinning pace of 16 m per hour on spindle whorls of 20–30 grams.[12]

In other spinning tests with spindle whorls of bone and clay, on high and low whorls, and with wool and flax,[13] a team of spinners in Italy found that it took significantly longer to spin flax than wool. The Italian team could spin 36–45 m of wool yarn in one hour but only 23–33 m of linen yarn.[14] Their average was ca. 42 m wool yarn or 24 m linen yarn spun per hour on a 7 g spindle.[15] The CTR spinners achieved similar results on an 8 g whorl: 40–41 m wool yarn and 24–31 m linen yarn per hour.[16]

Another experiment tested fourteen spinners and two wool types on spindles of 5, 15 and 52 g, resulting in 140 wool yarn samples.[17] The length of wool yarn spun per hour varied greatly from 10 to 60 m wool yarn but with an average of ca. 30–40 m per hour.[18] Another study found that a spinning pace of 50 m wool thread per hour was a plausible average speed.[19]

A flax spinning experiment with one expert spinner in Ribe could produce ca. 52–60 m linen yarn per hour with an average of 55.8 m yarn per hour.[20] This was a fast spinning pace compared to the slower linen yarn production rate of the two CTR spinners, who spun 24.34 m and 33.29 m per hour, respectively.[21]

---

[12] Ciccarelli and Perilli 2017, 160, tab. 1. See also Andersson and Nosch 2003, 199, 201.
[13] The bone spindle and spindle whorl weighed respectively 4.5 and 7 g, and the wooden spindle weighed 5 g and was combined with a spherical clay spindle whorl of 30 g. Hence, the tools were of quite different weight, 11.5 g and 35 g, respectively: Busana et al. 2024, 143–144.
[14] Busana et al. 2024, fig. 8.7.
[15] Busana et al. 2024, 147: "Regarding the *length*, it was observed that, with the same initial fibre quantity, 25 g, and with the same spinning time, 1 h each test, both sets produced much longer wool yarns than linen yarns. The reason could lie in the greater dexterity and speed of the spinner in drafting the wool fibres from the distaff. Moreover, during the spinning of flax fibre, the rotation speed quickly slows down, requiring a greater number of reactivations and therefore a greater use of time."
[16] Mårtensson et al. 2006a, 8, fig. 6. Mårtensson et al. 2006b, 8, fig. 7. Olofsson et al. 2015, 85.
[17] Kania 2015.
[18] Kania 2015, fig. 10.
[19] Andersson Strand and Mannering 2021, 37.
[20] Ejstrud et al. 2011, 62–64.
[21] Mårtensson et al. 2006a.

5.3 How long did it take to make a garment?

Most garments in antiquity were wraps, veils or cloaks, rectangular pieces of textiles of many sizes that were wrapped, pinned, stitched, or tied to fit on the body.[22] The cloth pieces varied in size from small elongated scarfs and sashes to large cloaks. *Khitōnes* and a few other garments were fitted and sewn, and had sleeves.

The production time of 40 m^2 of cloth for tunics for a classical Greek family consisting of three adult women (perhaps wife, wife's mother, and a slave), one husband and two children were estimated at 200,000 m (200 kilometres) of thread.[23] Karen Carr assumed a spinning rate of 100 m of wool yarn per hour but this is probably too high given that yarn for weaving tunics should be thin. Her estimate for flax spinning is 36 m per hour, based on medieval experiential archaeology expertise, and this figure seems appropriate. In total, for the spinning of yarn for 40 m^2 cloth (half wool and half flax) for the household tunics alone, Carr estimated a weekly spinning time of 77 hours for the 3 women, or 26 hours each. These figures highlight the permanent need for female labour. A more modest annual cloth production of 4 tunics and 1 blanket (a total of 18 m^2) made by three women would mean a weekly workload of spinning and weaving for each adult woman ca. 15 hours.

Hans van Wees argues that it took longer to make women's clothes than men's clothes because he estimates women's clothes to be larger than clothes for men,[24] but this gender difference is not clear from the written or iconographic sources.

An experimental project reconstructed a knee-length, sleeved man's shirt woven with 22 warp threads and 12 weft threads per cm^2 based on an archaeological find of the Viking Age. The shirt is not unlike the tunic found in Chehrābād, Iran (Fig. 8), and also not unlike a man's sleeved *khitōn* from Classical Greece. The craftspersons and archaeologists involved measured and calculated about 107 h

---

22 van Wees (2005b, 45 and note 11) assumes a male *pharos* to measure ca. 2 m^2. A simple cloak would have the size of 1 m^2, or 1 x 2 m for a knee-length wrap, 1.25 x 2.5 m for an ankle-length wrap. A *peplos* would vary in size from 2 x 1.5 m to 2 x 3 m (van Wees 2005b, 46). In comparison, in Scandinavian bog body textiles (dated 500–1 BCE), wraps fall in three standard sizes: large scarves of ca. 1.5 x 0.5 m, wraps of ca. 1.5 x 1 m, and large wraps of ca. 2.5 x 1.4 m, according to Mannering 2017, 116–117.
23 Carr 2000, 164–165.
24 van Wees 2005a, 17, argues that women's clothes are larger in size: "A set of woollen cloak and tunic of average quality would take about 10 days to make, while an equivalent set of veil and large *peplos* would take about a month, and a veil and a large *peplos* of average-quality linen would take about four months."

for setting up the warp, weaving and finishing,[25] with spinning taking about 188 h:[26] in total, ca. 300 h or 42 days with 7 work hours per day.

But spinning and weaving are only two sections of the long *chaîne opératoire*. So how long did it take in total to make this linen tunic? In terms of work hours, the total labour input from sowing flax, harvesting, rippling, retting, breaking, scutching, heckling, spinning, weaving, bleaching and sewing amounted to 355 work hours.[27] The spinning and weaving account for more than 80% of this.[28]

The entire timespan needed to make this shirt is actually more than a year: from sowing in spring, harvesting in summer, treating fibres in late summer and fall, spinning and weaving in winter and spring, bleaching in summer (because dry weather and sunlight is necessary), to finally sewing the finished shirt.

5.4 How long did it take to make a sail?

What do these numbers mean, to give another example, for the manufacture of the sails of a warship in a classical Greek fleet, i.e., a *trireme*?[29] The fabric requirement for the sails of a trireme can be reconstructed as ca. 100 kilos of cloth, representing sailcloth of 125 m^2. Flax sailcloth weighs between 500–720 grams per m^2 so a hypothetical mainsail of 100 m^2 would weigh up to 72 kilos.[30] A hypothetical mast sail of 25 m^2 would have a lower average weight of 500 grams per m^2, which corresponds to 12.5 kilos. In total, 84.5 kilos of sailcloth. There is also a need for cloth for repairs, selvages, reinforced edges, holes for ropes, etc., which gives a final total of probably 100 kilos of sailcloth for a *trireme* warship.

It would require 1 ton of flax stems to make 100 kilos of cloth, since only ca. 10% of the stems' weight represent usable fibres.

For 1 m^2 of sail cloth, woven with 10 threads per cm^2,[31] one needed ca. 2 kilometres of thread, plus 10% for weaving in, i.e., 2.2 kilometres of thread per m^2. In conclusion, 125 m^2 of sailcloth needed 275 kilometres of yarn.

---

25 Ejstrud et al. 2011, 67.
26 Ejstrud et al. 2011, 67. They used mechanically spun yarn in the reconstruction of the tunic.
27 Ejstrud et al. 2011, 79.
28 Ejstrud et al 2011, 80.
29 Dimova et al. 2021. Spantidaki et al. 2023.
30 Dimova et al. 2021, 767, take the *Olympias* reconstruction of a trireme's main sail of 95 m^2 and a foresail of a quarter its size, resulting in a total of 119 m^2 sail cloth.
31 Dimova et al. 2021, 764, used a median of sailcloth density of 10–13 threads/cm^2.

If we transfer these numbers to the time estimates made in experimental textile archaeology, the following working times would be required. At a spinning speed of 50 meters/hour,[32] 5,500 working hours would be needed to spin 275 kilometres of thread. With a hypothetical weaving speed of 50 cm/day, it would take one weaver 400 days to weave 125 m² of sailcloth. Working seven hours per day, 300 days per year, a person would spend around 2 ½ years spinning the yarn and 1 ½ years weaving to make the sailcloth of one *trireme*. This means a total of 4 years of full-time textile work of one person to produce the sails of an Athenian warship.[33] Another study came to similar figures: a *trireme* with 119 m² sailcloth would require at least 4299 hours/18 months of spinning and 2966 hours/12 months of weaving, a total of 7256 hours/2.5 years assuming 356 working days a year and 8 hours work per day.[34]

5.5 Time and leisure measured through spinning in ancient Greek texts

We have seen that spinning is one of the most time-consuming processes of textile work. Women of all ages would spin and they donated their decorated spindle whorls to sanctuaries. Vase paintings illustrate spinning women, sometimes wandering about while spinning, and sometimes concentrating on the task at hand (Fig. 5).

The continued, twisted, drafted, spliced or spun thread serves as metaphor for time, in antiquity and today, and Nicole Guilleux argues that:

> This continuity is precisely the reason why thread as a concrete item is well adapted to metaphorize the abstract notion of time.[35]

---

[32] Andersson Strand 2021, 37.
[33] Spantidaki et al. 2023. Andersson Strand 2021, 42 made similar estimates of the time needed to make a 120 m² wool sail for a Viking Age warship woven in 2/1 twill. "With eight-hour working days, it would take one person three and a half years, with no rest days, to make such a sail." Andersson Strand 2021, 42, estimates a workload of 600 days for sorting and combing wool, 385 days for spinning (on a 40 gram spindle whorl) and 240 days for weaving. The wool yarn was coarse and the weave had 6 threads/cm², thus probably a coarser wool fabric compared to the linen sail cloth of the trireme.
[34] Dimova et al. 2021, 770.
[35] Guilleux 2016, 8.

Figure 5: Elegantly dressed woman standing while engaged in spinning. Attic white ground *oinochoe*. Possibly from Locri in Calabria. Brygos painter, ca. 490–470. London, British Museum, inv. 1873,0820.304.
Photo: © The Trustees of the British Museum, https://www.britishmuseum.org/collection/object/G_1873-0820-304?selectedImageId=83177001 (last access 04.07.2025).

Guilleux has examined the metaphorical matrix of *time = thread*[36] and another metaphorical matrix of *the passing of time = winding yarn into a ball/clew*.[37] Both metaphorical matrices are embodied in the *Moirai*, whom we have already met, with their spinning, measuring and cutting the threads of life, from birth to

---

36 Guilleux 2016, 8–9.
37 Guilleux 2016, 10–11.

death[38] (ch. 2 and Fig. 1). In Greek, winding up yarn is the verb *tolypein*, and the noun *tolypē* means either spun yarn, or skein of yarn, or wool ready to be spun.[39]

The craft of spinning was seen as an appropriate pastime or handiwork for the female elite, as when Arete, the Queen of Phaeacia, sits in the main hall of her palace and spins in the 6th book of the *Odyssey*.[40] She sits by the fireplace and spins purple yarn, exemplifying a modest and wise wife. The following two passages describe Arete but are seen from the perspective of her daughter Nausikaa (*Od.* 6.52–53 and 6.305–306).

> ἡ μὲν ἐπ' ἐσχάρῃ ἧστο σὺν ἀμφιπόλοισι γυναιξὶν
> ἠλάκατα στρωφῶσ' ἁλιπόρφυρα
>
> Her mother sat beside the hearth and spun
> sea-purpled yarn, her house girls all around her.
>
> μητέρ' ἐμήν: ἡ δ' ἧσται ἐπ' ἐσχάρῃ ἐν πυρὸς αὐγῇ
> ἠλάκατα στρωφῶσ' ἁλιπόρφυρα, θαῦμα ἰδέσθαι
>
> You will find my mother
> sitting beside the hearth by firelight,
> and spinning her amazing purple wool.

Helen is another wife who is depicted spinning in the *Odyssey* (*Od.* 4.130–135), spinning wool with her golden spindle. It is a telling scene: the Trojan War is over and she has regained her position as queen of Sparta. Spinning means stability for her.[41] Her spinning tools are costly and her purple yarn is kept in containers of gold and silver. By spending time spinning, Helen conveys leisure, wealth and a return to normal life.

> χωρὶς δ' αὖθ' Ἑλένῃ ἄλοχος πόρε κάλλιμα δῶρα:
> χρυσέην τ' ἠλακάτην τάλαρόν θ' ὑπόκυκλον ὄπασσεν
> ἀργύρεον, χρυσῷ δ' ἐπὶ χείλεα κεκράαντο.
> τόν ῥά οἱ ἀμφίπολος Φυλὼ παρέθηκε φέρουσα
> νήματος ἀσκητοῖο βεβυσμένον: αὐτὰρ ἐπ' αὐτῷ
> ἠλακάτη τετάνυστο ἰοδνεφὲς εἶρος ἔχουσα.
>
> And besides these, his wife gave to Helen also beautiful gifts,—a golden distaff and a basket with wheels beneath did he give, a basket of silver, and with gold were the rims thereof gilded. This then the handmaid, Phylo, brought and placed beside her, filled with finely-spun yarn, and across it was laid the distaff laden with violet-dark wool.

---

38 Pirenne-Delforge and Pironti 2011.
39 Guilleux 2016, 10.
40 Pantelia 1993, 499.
41 Pantelia 1993, 496.

Spending time spinning can have the opposite effect if a man spins:[42] moralising Greek and Roman authors find it an extreme waste of time for a king to spin. The Greek author Diodorus (2.23.1) mocked the Assyrian king Sardanapallus for spinning soft purple wool with the ladies at court:

> Σαρδανάπαλλος δέ, τριακοστὸς μὲν ὢν ἀπὸ Νίνου τοῦ συστησαμένου τὴν ἡγεμονίαν, ἔσχατος δὲ γενόμενος Ἀσσυρίων βασιλεύς, ὑπερῆρεν ἅπαντας τοὺς πρὸ αὑτοῦ τρυφῇ καὶ ῥᾳθυμίᾳ. χωρὶς γὰρ τοῦ μηδ᾽ ὑφ᾽ ἑνὸς τῶν ἔξωθεν ὁρᾶσθαι βίον ἔζησε γυναικός, καὶ διαιτώμενος μὲν μετὰ τῶν παλλακίδων, πορφύραν δὲ καὶ τὰ μαλακώτατα τῶν ἐρίων ταλασιουργῶν

> Sardanapallus, the thirtieth in succession from Ninus, who founded the empire, and the last king of the Assyrians, outdid all his predecessors in luxury and sluggishness. For not to mention the fact that he was not seen by any man residing outside the palace, he lived the life of a woman, and spending his days in the company of his concubines and spinning purple garments and working the softest of wool

5.6 Time and waiting measured through weaving in ancient Greek texts

Women in Homeric epics weave, as a necessity and to make time pass (Fig. 6a–b).[43] Time is measured in the weaving; as the fabric expands on the loom, they can see how much time they have spent weaving and waiting. Maria Pantelia argues that married, elite Homeric women weave in dire situations of domestic instability,[44] and the wives "see their weaving as an escape from a state of domestic disorder."[45] In contrast, when domestic conjugal stability is achieved, Homeric wives "cease their weaving and are depicted as spinning".[46]

We have already met the most famous Homeric weaver: Penelope. Her weaving creates structure and a sense of progression – or sometimes stagnation – in the epic narrative. When will her plot be uncovered? What is she waiting and weaving for: her husband's return or the death of her father-in-law Laertes? The long period of weaving prolongs Penelope's time of freedom before a potential second marriage. Beate Wagner-Hasel[47] states that "In Penelope and her unravelling her fabric, the poet of the Odyssey shows us how she halts time." Yet, Penelope's long weaving time also prolongs Laertes' lifetime – as long as she

---

42 Though Pliny the Elder stated that spinning flax is honourable, even for a man. Plin. *Nat.* 19.3.
43 On Penelope's weaving, see Pantelia 1993. Wagner-Hasel 2000, 152–165, 206–219. Nosch 2014a.
44 Pantelia 1993, 498.
45 Pantelia 1993, 499.
46 Pantelia 1993, 499.
47 Wagner-Hasel 2022, 139.

weaves, he lives on. She, Laertes and her suitors know that the weaving will end eventually, not necessarily when Penelope is satisfied with her fabric, or when the piece appears as finished, but when Laertes dies.

Helen wove battle scenes while captive in Troy, visualizing her version of the Trojan War in her tapestry (*Il.* 3.125–128).[48] The Trojan princess Andromache wove colourful flowers – *throna poikil'* – while she waited anxiously for her husband Hector to return from his duel with Achilles (*Il.* 22.441–442).[49]

Deianera is another faithful wife depicted in Greek literature, spending her time weaving and waiting. In Sophocles' play *Women of Trachis* (performed sometime between 450 and 425 BCE), Deianera wove a new set of clothes (*khitōn, peplōma*) for her husband Herakles while waiting for his return.[50] She exclaims (verses 610–613):

> οὕτω γὰρ ηὔγμην, εἴ ποτ' αὐτὸν ἐς δόμους ἴδοιμι σωθέντ' ἢ κλύοιμι, πανδίκως στελεῖν χιτῶνι τῷδε, καὶ φανεῖν θεοῖς θυτῆρα καινῷ καινὸν ἐν πεπλώματι
>
> For this was my vow, that if ever I saw or heard of his safe return home, I would duly clothe him in this tunic, and reveal to the gods a new sacrificer wearing a new robe.

The garment that had been woven during the long hours of waiting in order to honor his homecoming, however, did not lead to a happy reunion. The garment was stained with what Deianera believed was a love potion, but it killed her husband.

Finally, two weavers in Homer are neither married nor waiting: Kalypso and Kirke. Kalypso weaves in her cave and joyfully sings while she weaves (*Od.* 5.61–62). She is not in a hurry, and neither is Kirke, who also sings in front of her loom (*Od.* 10.220–223). [51] Time only seems long to Odysseus who is held captive on Kirke's island. What Kirke weaves is not described. Later in the narrative, however, she releases Odysseus and equips him with a raft and a sail. Perhaps this was the object of her weaving?

---

[48] Pantelia 1993, 495.
[49] *Il.* 22.440–441.
[50] Doyle 2016, 140–141.
[51] Weaving and singing have communalities as discussed by Snyder 1981.

5.6 Time and waiting measured through weaving in ancient Greek texts — 49

Figure 6: Women spinning and weaving together. Black-figure lekythos, attributed to the Amasis Painter, ca. 550–530 BCE. New York, The Metropolitan Museum of Art, Fletcher Fund, 1931, Object Number: 31.11.10.
Photos: The Metropolitan Museum of Art, public domain, https://www.metmuseum.org/art/collection/search/253348 (last access 04.07.2025).

6 Textile terms in a time perspective: "Words survive longer than cloth"

"Words survive longer than cloth", wrote textile scholar Elizabeth Barber in her monograph *Prehistoric Textiles*.[1] There is an extraordinary continuum of textile terms in ancient Greece, from the 3rd millennium BCE to the 1st millennium CE, and in the other languages of the ancient Near East and the Mediterranean area.[2] The richness and varieties of textual documentation constitute a unique source of information on ancient textiles and their production and consumption in these areas, spanning millennia.

Textile terms can indicate origin, material, or techniques. With time, and over longer distances, these meanings can become blurred or fade, or the terms acquire a new meaning appropriate to a new context.

6.1 Textile terms of 2nd millennium BCE Greece

In the Middle to Late Bronze Age Aegean, i.e. over a period of a thousand years, textiles appear as logograms in no less than three writing systems: Cretan hieroglyphs, Minoan Linear A and Mycenaean Linear B. Each of these writing systems had strategies to convey the full complexity of a textile or garment, and a strong continuity is evident in the logogrammatic rendering of textiles and wool.

Textile logograms were used in Greece Bronze Age Greece to describe textile quality and fibres.[3] In the Bronze Age Aegean scripts, the logograms were endowed with syllables and adjuncts to indicate the names of the textiles or the fibre, and sometimes the textile and garment names were spelled out to achieve precision.[4]

---

[1] Barber 1991.
[2] Various scholars have over the years investigated this rich textile terminology data of the 2nd and 1st millennia BCE in comprehensive works on the role of textiles in ancient societies, or in individual studies on single corpus terminologies, see Veenhof 1972. Waetzoldt 1972. Zawadzki 2006. Michel and Nosch 2010. Gaspa et al. 2017. Quillien 2022.
[3] We still use a logogrammatic system today to describe textile fibres in washing and care instructions. These logograms are internationally accepted and some contain maximum washing temperatures or Latin letters designating the solvents used by professional dry cleaners. The country of manufacture is also indicated and the composition of fibres, e.g., 100% cotton.
[4] Del Freo et al. 2010. Nosch 2012.

Open Access. © 2025 the author(s), published by De Gruyter. This work is licensed under the Creative Commons Attribution-NonCommercial-NoDerivatives 4.0 International License.
https://doi.org/10.1515/9783112223079-007

The Bronze Age term for wool in Mycenaean Greek is attested in the adjective *we-we-e-a*, *werweheha* (cf. Greek *eiros*) meaning 'woolen' or 'of wool' (KN L 178 and L 870).[5] Spinners are *a-ra-ka-te-ja*, a term which appears connected with the classical Greek ἠλακάτη, a spinning implement which is either the spindle[6] or the distaff.[7] There are different technical terms for weaving and they bridge the Late Bronze Age and the 1st millennium BCE. The Greek verb *plekein*, 'to plait' is used both in Mycenaean Greek and in Classical Greek texts. The Greek verb *hyphainein*, 'to weave' is well attested from the Homeric epics onwards but may also have a Mycenaean history in the epithet *u-po-jo-po-ti-ni-ja*, the 'Mistress of Weaving'.[8] The Classical Greek word for loom, *histos*, is found in Mycenaean Greek in the occupational designations *i-te-we*, *histēwei* or *histēwes* 'to the weaver(s)' and *i-te-ja-o*, *histeiāhōn* 'of the female weavers'.[9] Sewing is well attested in Mycenaean Greek with the root **rap-* used for sewing in leather and in textiles, and in the occupational designations *ra-pi-ti-ra₂* and *ra-pte-re*, and the adjective *ra-pte-ri-ja*, which describes stitched reins as part of leather equipment for horses and chariots, and the participle *e-ra-pe-me-na* 'sewn', which refers to garments.

Some textile and garment terms in Mycenaean Greek were only used in the Bronze Age, such as *tu-na-no* and *pu-ka-ta-ri-ja*. Other Bronze Age garment terms continue in use in the Iron Age.[10] The Mycenaean Greek word for a tunic, *ki-to* in Linear B in the 2nd millennium BCE, is derived from a 3rd millennium BCE word with the Semitic root *ktn*.[11] The same root is used in Akkadian to express linen, in Old Assyrian to express a garment made of wool, and in Classical and Hellenistic Greek for the unisex tunic *khitōn*,[12] the female tunic *khitōnion*, and the diminutive for a shorter tunic, the unisex *khitōniskos*.[13] Most Classical texts use χιτών with dialectal variants, in Ionic κιθών, and Doric κιτών. Other Bronze Age garment terms that continue in use are *pa-wo*/φᾶρος and *we-a₂-no*/ἑανός. The wool term *lēnos* in the 1st millennium BCE is from the same root as *hulana* in Hittite and so demonstrates a long history. Also the terms for flax (*ri-no/linon*) and wool (*we-we-e-a* 'woolen' and 'wool' *eiros*) continue in use in the 1st

---

5 Chantraine 1968. Nosch 2015, 174.
6 Barber 1991, 263–264. Del Freo et al. 2010, 341.
7 Neri 2016.
8 Nosch and Perna 2001.
9 Del Freo et al. 2010. Nosch 2015, 177.
10 On Mycenaean textile and garment terms, see Nosch 2012.
11 Nosch 2015, 188.
12 Lewy 1895 derives many Greek textile words from Hebrew or other Semitic languages: Lewy 1895, 82–92 is a chapter on "Tracht", and in Lewy 1895, 121–134, terms for weaving and dyes.
13 Cleland 2005.

raised millennium BCE. Mycenaean wool textile *te-pa* appears in the form τάπης in the 1st millennium.[14]

6.2 Textile and garment terms of the 1st millennium BCE

Many garment terms[15] are new in the 1st millennium or at least previously unattested in the sources and may testify to a change in clothing: the *peplos*, which initially meant a piece of fabric and a garment for both men and women; cloaks with names such as the unisex garments *himation* or *khlaina*; the men's cloak *khlamys*; the loincloth, *zōstra*. *Rhēgea* denotes bedlinen, blankets and sheets. Poor and hardworking men in the 1st millennium BCE wore a garment with one shoulder uncovered, the *exōmis* (a literal description of the garment on the body: from *ex-*, off, and *ōmos*, shoulder).

The *peplos* is an iconic dress term for women's dress but it is actually better attested in modern classical archaeology and art history texts than in ancient texts. *Peplos* has an unknown etymology but has been connected to the Latin *palla* and *pallium*, especially by those scholars who assumed a sharp contrast between Semitic dress terms such as *khitōn* and Indo-European dress terms such as *peplos* or *himation*.[16]

Clothing and textiles are a very rich terminological and semantic field in the 1st millennium BCE, and Losfeld identifies no less than 460 dress terms in his 1991 *Essai sur le costume grec*.[17] Many of these terms are similar or have variant spellings, and it is not always easy to determine what this meant in relation to real clothing and wardrobes.

Clothing and textile terms seem to cluster around certain roots: *pel-* (*plekein, peplos, peplōma*), *kal-* (*kalymma, kalyptra*), *khl-* (*khlaina, khlanis, khlamys*),[18] *st-* (*histos, stolē*), *khit-* (*khitōn, khitōnion, khitōniskos*), *krk-* (*krekein, kerkis, krokē*,[19]

---

14 Pierini 2018.
15 There is a rich bibliography on this topic: Cleland et al. 2007 is an excellent starting point. Spantidaki 2016, 97–105 for textile terms with more than one meaning.
16 Lee 2003, 133 (with reference to Studniczka 1886): "Working within the tradition of scholarship that claimed racial unity among the Indo-European speaking peoples, he suggests that the early Greeks originally wore a Doric (that is, a pure Hellenic, Indo-European, Aryan) garment, the *peplos*, but that at some later time they suffered a sort of Semitic infiltration in the form of the Ionic *chiton*. As a result of the Persian Wars, however, the Greeks resumed their national costume as a means of asserting their Hellenic identity".
17 Losfeld 1991.
18 Flemestad 2022, 148 note 1057 and Chantraine 1968, *s.v:* "termes visiblement apparentés."
19 Manessy-Guitton 1977, 236–237. Neri 2016, 197.

perhaps *krokos*, if it is not Minoan) and *zō-* (*zōstra, zōma, zōnē*). The headcoverings *kalyptra* and *kalymma* derive from the verb *kalyptō*, to cover, to conceal.[20] Several female headgear terms include *deō-*, to bind (*krēdemnon, desmata*), or they have very literal and descriptive names, such as 'little roof' *tegidion* (from *tegos*, roof), 'before the face' *prosōpida*, and 'curtains' (of the face) *katapetasma*.[21]

Clothing terms of the 1st millennium BCE often indicate how one would wear them on the body or how one would dress up in them, because they are prefixed with prepositions such as 'around' *peri, amphi*, 'on' or 'over' *epi* in the compounds of outer garments such as *ampekhonon, ampekhonē, enkyklon, epiblēma*, and *periblēma*. For example, the verb *amph-echomai*, to have around, gained the meaning 'to drape'. Dressing and undressing are likewise described by verbs with these prepositions such as to clothe (ἀμφιάζω, ἀμφιέννυμι), and the verbal adjective *apoduteon* meaning 'one must strip'.

The longevity of textile and garment terms appears in the wide use of metaphors related to clothing and weaving, and this semantic field and its metaphors continue to develop throughout antiquity.[22]

6.3 The Greek term kairos with meaning related to textiles and time

Some ancient terms and concepts relating to time have an etymological connection to terms and concepts relating to textiles.

There are two similar Greek words, καιρός and καῖρος. *Kaîros* is a technical term in weaving: it denotes the device that divides the warp threads into two sheds. It can be a plaited band of yarn or a wooden rod[23] that holds each set of warp threads separated, aligned and in place; hence, in a tabby weave the *kaîros* divides the warp threads into even and odd numbers.

Photius writes the following about the word:

---

20 Llewellyn-Jones 2003, 23–39.
21 Llewellyn-Jones 2003, 23–29, 34, 62–64.
22 Fanfani et al. 2016. On textile and clothing metaphors, see Delalande et al. 2024, 25: "on retire l'impression que toutes les métaphores vestimentaires perdurent à travers les siècles et à travers les langues. Elles seraient alors comme une sorte d'invariant anthropologique. Cela tient pour une part à la réalité universelle et journalière du vêtement. (…) Mais ce succès est aussi, semble-t-il, le résultat de ses emplois dans des textes canoniques." Hence, cloth and garment metaphors had become canonised by their presence in important works of reference in antiquity, such as Homer and Plato as well as the *Old Testament*.
23 Harlizius-Klück 2005, 104, 234.

καῖρος · σειρά τις ἐν ἱστῷ δι' ἧς οἱ στήμονες διείργονται

kaîros: a band in the loom with which the warp-threads become separated.²⁴

The *Etymologicum Magnum* states, with more details:

καλεῖται καῖρος καὶ καίρωμα ἡ παραπλοκὴ τοῦ στήμονος ἡ διαπλεκομένη ὑπὲρ τοῦ μὴ συγχεῖσθαι αὐτόν

Is called καῖρος and καίρωμα the woven band that is braided into the warp-threads to ensure that they don't mingle.²⁵

Καιρός, however, means the opportune moment, the right time, the right timing, and also opportunity, limit, boundary, threshold, transition, and passage.²⁶ Erwin Panofsky, in his essay "Father Time", defines *kairós* as "the brief, decisive moment which marks a turning point in the life of human beings or in the development of the universe".²⁷

In contrast to the more permanent and ongoing *chronos* time, *kairós* is momentary, contextualised, diverse, and experience-based.

As we shall see below, some scholars have explored the shared notions of καιρός and καῖρος and suggested linking the two under the same "Zeichenmantel".²⁸ *Kairos* has no obvious Greek etymology but has been interpreted as having a Semitic root, with the linguist Heinrich Lewy arguing that *kairos* is related to Hebrew words for thread.²⁹

It was Robert B. Onians in *The Origins of European Thought. About the Body, the Mind, the Soul, the World, Time and Fate* (1951) who first advanced the idea that the concept of καιρός in Greek philosophy is related to the technical weaving word καῖρος. Onians argued that both terms contain a notion of *opening* or *hole*.³⁰

The ancient lexicographer Hesychius first translated *kairós* as time: καιρός · χρόνος; immediately afterwards, he explained the term *kaîros* as 'thread' or 'weft-thread': καῖρος · μίτος; and he adds the lexeme *kairōmata*:

καιρώματα · τὰ διαχωριστικὰ τῶν στημόνων πλέγματα

---

24 My translation.
25 My translation.
26 Sipiora and Baumlin 2002. Miller 2023, 156–179.
27 Panofsky 1967, 71.
28 Harlizius-Klück 2005.
29 Lewy 1895, 125.
30 Onians 1951, 343–351. Kerkhoff 1973, 258, followed Onians's interpretation of a weaving meaning in *kairos* as opening or hole and translated it as "Einschlag (am Webstuhl)".

the twisted elements that separate the warp threads.³¹

The linguist Pierre Chantraine also noted the double meaning of *kairos* in his *Dictionnaire étymologique de la langue grecque*.³² Chantraine, like Onians, distinguished between καιρός and καῖρος, the former as the polysemantic concept of right time and opportunity, the latter a technical weaving term. Regarding καῖρος, Chantraine concludes:

> l'étymologie est obscure (...), mais le mot rends peut-être compte de καιρός, qui pourrait être un emploi figuré.

This possible figurative or etymological bond between καιρός and καῖρος led other scholars to conclude a semantic link, e.g., that *kairos* means the right moment to insert the weft in the warp. According to Eric Charles White:

> There is the 'critical time' when the weaver must draw the yarn through a gap that momentarily opens in the warp of the cloth being woven.³³

This means, according to White, that:

> *kairos* refers to a passing instant when an opening appears which must be driven through by force if success is to be achieved.

Monique Trédé(-Boulmer)'s monograph *Kairos. L'à-propos et l'occasion. Le mot et la notion d'Homère à la fin du IVe siècle avant J.-C.* surveyed all attestations of *kairos* in Greek literature from Homer to the late 4th century BCE, plus its occurrence in epigraphy and later Greek-writing scholars such as Plutarch.³⁴ She presented seven different etymologies of *kairós*.³⁵ Although she concluded that its etymology remains uncertain,³⁶ she favoured associating *kairós* metaphorically and concretely with the semantic field of 'cut', 'divide', 'separate' and 'decide' (*couper, trancher, séparer, decider*), and hence to the root **ker-*, linked to κρίνω and κείρω.³⁷ She disagreed with Onians' translation of 'opening' or 'hole'.³⁸ Instead,

---

31 My translation.
32 Chantraine 1968.
33 White 1987, 13, mentions that weaving is integral to the understanding of *kairos*; however, weaving is not integrated into his thinking or conclusions about *kairos* and *kaironomia* in his erudite book. Sipiora 2002, 1, only mentions the connection to weaving by referring to White.
34 Trédé 1992; second edition as Trédé-Boulmer 2015.
35 Trédé 1992, 51–52.
36 Trédé 1992, 15–21.
37 Trédé 1992, 16, 53.

she suggested the paired meanings of *"coupure-séparation"* and *"jointure-adjustment"*, which render aspects of both καιρός and καῖρος.[39]

Two works from 2005 explored the shared notions of καιρός and καῖρος: According to the classical philologist Ruby Blondell:

> weaving requires the kind of flexible, practical intelligence which enables one to adapt to circumstances and recognize the right moment – the *Kairos* – for appropriate action of various kinds (cf. *Rep.* 370 b). This is the art of due measure.[40]

Textile scholar and philosopher Ellen Harlizius-Klück likewise emphasised the weaving connotations of *kairos*, and how it is connected conceptually to division and separation and to practical movements in a loom when warp threads are divided into sheds. She noted *kairos*' role as divider of the warp threads into even and odd numbers in a tabby. Further, she linked *kairos* with *kanōn*, a word which has a wide semantic extension in philosophy and mathematics. The *kanōn* was a weaving device, namely the heddle rod (Latin *regula*), which enables the weaver to divide and change shed and is one of the main regulating elements of a loom.[41]

Art historian Barbara Baert has explored *kairós* as a concept in philosophy and studied the personification of Kairos in art.[42] She observed how *kairós* may be related to the Greek term for a lock of hair (κάρ): hair is something that may be seized with the hand, in the same way that one can seize the moment.[43] She links hair to thread and textiles as similar textures.

Interestingly, in the two Homeric epic works, *kairos* is used with both meanings. It appears in the *Iliad* as an opportune moment, and as a weaving term in the *Odyssey*. In the *Iliad* (4.186, 8.84 and 8.326) we find the adjective *kairios* (καίριος) and the noun *kairion* (καίριον) with a quite specific meaning of the right place on a body to deal a lethal blow in battle. But in a passage in the *Odyssey* (7.107), the adjective appears with a textile-related meaning as the hapax *kairousseōn*[44] to describe how well and how tightly Phaeacian women weave linen cloth:

---

38 Trédé 1992, 74: "si nous ne suivons pas Onians dans son interprétation de καιρός/καῖρος comme 'ouverture', nous considérons, comme lui, que καιρός et καῖρος sont un seul et même terme dont deux accentuations différentes opposent deus spécialisations de sens."
39 Trédé 1992, 74.
40 Blondell 2005, 56.
41 Harlizius-Klück 2005, 104, 234.
42 Baert 2016. See also Panofsky 1967.
43 Baert 2016, 201–202.
44 καιρουσσέων is explained by Hesychius as μεμιτομένων (woven) from μίτομαι, to weave. Trédé 1992, 25 note 1, believes that the passage is a later interpolation: "Le lien entre καιρουσσέων et notre *kairos* resta à établir."

καιρουσσέων δ' ὀθονέων ἀπολείβεται ὑγρὸν ἔλαιον.
And from the closely-woven linen the soft olive oil drips down

6.4 The Greek terms kairós and krisis and Latin ordior and their meanings related to textile and time

In ancient texts, *kairós* often appears with *krisis* and the verb *krinein*, meaning to separate, select, cut, and decide.

In medical works in antiquity, the terms *kairós* and *krisis* cover a broad semantic field and both refer to time.[45] *Kairós* refers to 'right time' or 'opportune moment' with the plural form *kairoí* referring to the sequence of crucial moments in the development of a disease.[46] *Krisis* means judgement, assessment, and decision, or a decisive moment or turning point in the development of the illness.[47]

Vivien Longhi, in his monograph *Krisis ou la décision génératrice. Épopée, médecine hippocratique, Platon* (2020) rarely discusses the textile aspects of the term *krisis*. Yet, he chose an image of Penelope contemplating her loom to illustrate the cover of his book (cf. Fig. 7).

Longhi does, however, mention one connection between *krisis* and textiles, namely the link to *kerkis*, the shuttle or the weft-beater, and thus by extension to weaving.[48]

> [...] on constant une proximité phonétique entre le vocabulaire du tissage (κερκίς) et le vocabulaire de la séparation (διακρίνειν).[49]

The Greek verb *krinō* and weaving appear in a passage by Plato (*Cratylus* 388 B) where weaving is used as a metaphor for statemanship.

ΣΩ.
κερκίζοντες δὲ τί δρῶμεν; οὐ τὴν κρόκην καὶ τοὺς στήμονας συγκεχυμένους διακρίνομεν;

Socrates:
And what do we do when we weave?
Do we not separate the mingled threads of warp and woof?

---

45 Singer 2022, 102–105.
46 Singer 2022, 102–106.
47 Singer 2022, 106. *Kairos* can be reduced to the root **kr* from which derives the Greek verb *keirō*, κείρω, and of the same root is also *krinō*, κρίνω and its derived noun *krisis*, κρίσις with the sense of separating and hence deciding: see Harlizius-Klück 2005, 115–116 and Trédé 1992, 51–53.
48 Manessy-Guitton 1977.
49 Longhi 2020, 194.

Figure 7: Penelope contemplating her tapesty, print by Max Klinger (1857–1920). New York, The Metropolitan Museum of Art, Gift of Robert L. Isaacson, 1979, Object Number: 1979.674.3. Photo: The Metropolitan Museum of Art, public domain, https://www.metmuseum.org/art/collection/search/384495 (last access 04.07.2025).

Some Latin terms may form more uncertain links between ideas of time and textiles but should nevertheless be presented briefly here.

Tempus, Latin for 'time', derives from the Greek verb *temnein*, 'to cut', and hence tempus means something cut out, just like *textus* means something woven.[50]

Latin verb *ordior* means 'I begin' and indicates a beginning of time. It also has a textile-related meaning of warping: to set up the loom and to begin to weave. The French verb *ourdir*, to warp, is from the same root.[51] Nicole Guilleux explored *ordior* and the related term *ōrdō* and argued convincingly that the technical and specialised meaning of warping and adjusting threads in the warp came before its

---

50 Trier 1940, 110–111 moreover assumes a shared terminology between Greek *tapes* (τάπες), blanket or carpet, as found in French *tapiserie*, and the root *temp-* for time.
51 Harlizius-Klück 2005, 133, 137–138. Guilleux 2016, 12.

generalised meaning of starting.⁵² The verb marks the beginning of time, and warping marks the beginning of weaving. *Ordior* also includes setting up the heading band and starting to weave on the warp-weighted loom. The heading band is a kind of pre-weave as it is the initial weaving before the actual weaving starts. The heading band sets the warp threads in order and fixes them in the band; later, when the weave is finished, the heading band appears as a band or ribbon on one side of the cloth. This is what is called the *praetexta* in Latin, the pre-woven band in Roman clothing.⁵³

---

52 Guilleux 2020. She suggests a relationship between Latin *ordior* (warping threads, weaving and, by extension, beginning) and the Greek forms ὄρδημα (clew of wool yarn) and ὄρδικον (small *khiton*) of items made of thread/yarn.
53 Harlizius-Klück 2005, 149–150. Guilleux 2020, 471.

7 The lifespan and timespan of garments

7.1 Archaeological textiles as witnesses of a lifetime

Textiles, especially clothes, are witnesses to lifetimes. They testify to the time in which they were made and to the lifespan of the wearer. This has inspired scholars to describe a garment in terms of a biography.[1]

One example is the tunic found in Chehrābād in northern Iran (Fig. 8). It is dated to the Sassanian period. Woven from plain cotton, it belonged to a salt miner who died when the mine collapsed. Due to the salt, the tunic was very well preserved. It is knee-length with long sleeves. The yarn is hand-spun and the tunic hand-woven. Perhaps it had been made by the salt miner's family members. The warp is z-spun and the weft is s-spun, and because the s- and z-spun yarns have slightly different thread diameters, textile archaeologists have concluded that at least two persons spun the 4.5 kilometres of yarn for the tunic. The yarn is spun tight, so tight that it still holds its twist today: a good quality yarn, indeed.[2]

The situation is different when it comes to the tunic's weave quality. Whoever wove this fabric was no expert but was a learner or a beginner, or someone careless or in a hurry: the weave has numerous weaving mistakes. Perhaps the weaver paid less attention because it was work clothing for a miner. The many weaving mistakes appear only to the trained eye: superficially the weave seems of good quality and the mistakes are not clearly visible.

Whoever sewed the tunic may have known the miner's shape and size and the nature of his work in the salt mine as they adapted his clothing to his work activities: gussets were inserted in the armpits and by the hips to allow more freedom of movement.

7.2 Married life in a garment: Andromache's wedding veil

Also in ancient Greek literature, a garment is personal and holds a story. Andromache, at the time of her wedding to Hector, was gifted a special veil (*kredēmon*) by the goddess of love, Aphrodite. Andromache still wore this veil on the day her husband was killed. On that heart-breaking day, Andromache was standing weaving in the palace hall of Troy, and when she learned of Hector's death, she fainted.

---

1 Apparudai 1986. Tarlo 2007. Skjold 2016.
2 Grömer and Aali 2020.

7.2 Married life in a garment: Andromache's wedding veil

Figure 8: Tunic of Chehrābād, Iran. Photo: N. Kanani, Museum Zanjan. With kind permission from the excavators.

The text combines this tragic moment with references to multiple types of head-wear: in addition to the wedding veil (*kredēmon*), she wore bright head-wear (*desmata sigaloenta*) consisting of several items: a headband/frontlet (*ampyx*), a hair-net (*kekryphalos*), a hairband (*anadesmē*) and a wreath or plaited band (*plektē*) (*Il.* 22.466–472):

> τὴν δὲ κατ᾽ ὀφθαλμῶν ἐρεβεννὴ νὺξ ἐκάλυψεν,
> ἤριπε δ᾽ ἐξοπίσω, ἀπὸ δὲ ψυχὴν ἐκάπυσσε.
> τῆλε δ᾽ ἀπὸ κρατὸς βάλε δέσματα σιγαλόεντα,
> ἄμπυκα κεκρύφαλόν τε ἰδὲ πλεκτὴν ἀναδέσμην
> κρήδεμνόν θ᾽, ὅ ῥά οἱ δῶκε χρυσῆ Ἀφροδίτη
> ἤματι τῷ ὅτε μιν κορυθαίολος ἠγάγεθ᾽ Ἕκτωρ
> ἐκ δόμου Ἠετίωνος, ἐπεὶ πόρε μυρία ἕδνα.

> Then black night veiled her eyes. She toppled backward,
> and breathed her spirit out. She tossed away
> the shining knotted headdress from her head –
> the circlet, veil, well-braided band, and scarf

that golden Aphrodite gave to her the day that Hector of the glittering helmet
paid lavish bridal-gifts to lead her off
in marriage from the house of Eetion.

The wedding of Hector and Andromache seems to have taken place before the Trojan War,[3] hence at least a decade earlier, so Andromache wore and kept this precious headdress for many years.

7.3 Garments used and stored over long periods of time in sanctuaries

Greek temple inventory lists from the Late Classical and Hellenistic periods show that sanctuaries received, inventoried and stored both children's and adult clothing, mainly women's.[4] Such inventories of clothing are preserved in many parts of the Greek world: in Attica, in Boeotia, on Samos, Delos and Rhodes and at Miletus.

Significantly, time plays a role here because of the age of the dedicated garments. Several of them are recorded as old or ragged. Once donated they might then be stored and inventoried in the temples for years. This is the case for some garments dedicated to Artemis at Brauron, to Artemis Kithōnē at Miletus, for clothing dedicated to Demeter and Kore in Tanagra, and at Samos for the clothes dedicated to Hera. Thus, the tradition of keeping and inventorying dedicated clothes for a very long time is attested across Greece, across centuries and in sanctuaries of different divinities. Most are for female divinities but in Samos we also find garments inventoried as dedications to Hermes.

Dedicated garments are sometimes recorded as being either rags (*rhakoi*), frayed (*katakekommenoi*), useless (*ēkhreōmenoi* or *akhreioi*), or old (*palaioi*).[5] These old clothes were of all kinds, including cloaks, *khitōns* and fine clothing dyed with purple or saffron. It is possible that the garments were already heavily used before they were donated to the shrines, but, nonetheless, there is ample evidence that the shrines stored, displayed and cared for the textiles for a very long time.

---

3 Sappho (fragment 44, *P.Oxy.*X 1232) wrote a poem about the wedding celebration of Hector and Andromache. The celebration was held on Aphrodite's island Cyprus and does not mention a veil but it mentions Andromache's purple-dyed dresses (κάμματα πορφύρα). "Hector and his companions are bringing the lively-eyed, graceful Andromache from holy Thebe and ever-flowing Placia in their ships over the salt sea; and (there are) many golden bracelets and (perfumed?) purple robes, ornate trinkets and countless silver drinking-cups and ivory."
4 For a full discusssion of votive clothes in Greek sanctuaries, see Brøns 2015; 2016, 120–165; 2019.
5 Günter 1988, 229. Brøns 2016, 120–122.

In the extensive temple inventories from Brauron (kept as copies on the Athenian Acropolis),[6] only one dedicated garment is described explicitly as new. Liza Cleland argues that the garments had been worn, and often made, by those who dedicated them.[7] Silvia Milanizi concludes that "these gifts still conserved the memory of generation after generation of piety."[8] Cecilie Brøns has demonstrated just how common it was for temples to store old and ragged clothing.[9] Such garments are specifically recorded in temple inventories of Brauron, Tanagra, Samos and Miletus.

Let us look at the evidence of some of the inventories in more detail.

7.3.1 Old, useless and frayed clothing, veils and girdles in the Inventory of the Temple of Artemis Kithōnē at Miletus

The city of Miletus was famed for its production of clothing since the Archaic Age. An inventory list of clothing has survived from the late 2nd century BCE.[10] The upper part of the inscription is damaged but Wolfgang Günter (1988) argues convincingly that it is a dedication to Artemis Kithōnē. The inventory systematically lists garments (lines 5–11: *kalaseiris, himatia, khlanides*, a *karpasos* garment, a *sindonitēs* garment, linen *othonai*, and ephebic *khlamydes*), then female headgear (lines 12–17: *prosōpidia* and *epikrēna*) and then girdles and belts (lines 18–22: *lēmniskoi, strophoi*, and *zōma*). It then records a special donation by Anaios (lines 22–24). The garments and accessories are made of wool, flax or silk.

Time is expressed through the garments. Most of them were either old (*palaioi*), useless (*ēkhrēōmenoi*), or frayed (*katakekomenoi*). This is true for a *kalasiris, himatia*, purple garments, light cloaks (*khlanides*), *sindonites, othonai*, ephebic *khlamydes, prosōpidia*, linen pieces, head-dresses, ribbons, girdles/belts, and children's cloaks and clothing.

κα<λά>σειρις μεσογλαύκινος περίχρ[υ]-
[σ]ος παλαιὸς ἠχρηωμένος, ἱμάτιον σελ<ά>γινον (?) περιπόρφυρ[ον]
παλαιὸν ἠχρειωμένον, ἁλουργέα παλαιὰ κατακεκομμένα
ἀχρεῖα ὀκτώ, χλανίδες παλαιαὶ ἀχρεῖαι κατακεκομμέναι τ-

---

6 On the Brauron catalogues (IG II² 1514–1531), see Cleland 2005. Cole 1998, 36–43.
7 Cleland 2005, 6, 9.
8 Milanezi 2005, 80.
9 Brøns 2016, 120–122.
10 Herrmann et al. 2006. Inventory number 1378. Greek text from Günter 1988, translation from Brøns 2016, 399–400 with amendments from Günter 1988 and by MLBN. See also Cole 1998. Brøns 2015, 53–55.

7 The lifespan and timespan of garments

[ρ]εῖς, ἱμάτια πορφυρᾶ βαπτὰ ἀχρεῖα κατακεκομμένα τρία, κά[ρ]-
πασος παλαιός, σινδονίτης παλα[ι]ὸς ἀχρεῖος, ὀθόναι λιναῖ π-
[α]λαιαὶ ἀχρεῖαι τρεῖς, ἄλλαι ἡ[μ]ιτριβεῖς κεκομμέναι δύο, χλαμύδ[ες]
v. ἐφηβικαὶ παλαιαὶ ἀχρεῖαι τέσσαρες, προ[σ]ωπίδια βομβύκινα πα-
[λ]αιὰ ἀχρεῖα τέσσαρα, ἄλλα ἐρεᾶ παλαιὰ ἀχρεῖα δύο, λινᾶ πα-
[λ]αιὰ ἀχρεῖα δεκαδύο, ἐπίκρηνον λ[ι]νοῦν παλαιόν, ἄλλα [ἄ]-
χρεῖα δύο, ἄλλο ἡμιτριβὲς κεκομμένον, ἄλλο βομβύκινον ἀχ-
ρεῖον κατατετιλμένον ἄλλο βομβύκινον ἡμιτριβὲς κεκομμέν-
[ο]ν, λημνίσκοι ξυστοὶ πράσινοι κατακεκομμένοι δύο, ἄλλος κόκκ[ι]-
[ν]ος παλαιὸς κατακεκομμένος, στρόφοι παλαιοὶ <ἐ>πίχρυσοι δύο, [ἄ]-
λλος σπα{ν}δίκινος παλαιὸς ἔχων κεραύνιον χρυσοποίκιλον, διά[ζω]-
μα ἐρεοῦν ἐπίχρυσον παλαιὸν κατακεκομμένον, ἄλλο λινο[ῦν]
καὶ ὑποκλείδιον ἡμιτριβές, ἃ [ἔφη]σεν ἀνατεθεικέναι Ἀνα<ῖ>ος, ζω[ν]α[ι]
παλαια<ὶ> δύο, ἄλλαι μείζονες παλαιαὶ δ[ύ]ο, χλάνδιον καὶ εὐπάρυ[φ]ον
[π]αιδικὰ κατακεκομμένα ἀλουργεα, παιδικ[ὰ ἄλλα] κατακεκομμέν[α..]

1 old, useless *kalaseiris*, bluish grey in the middle, with gold border
1 old, useless *himation*, bright in colour, with purple border
8 old, useless purple garments, frayed
8 old, useless *khlanides*, frayed
3 purple-dyed *himatia*, useless and frayed
1 old *karpasos* garment
1 old, useless *sindonitēs*
3 old, useless linen cloths *othonai*
2 other half-worn linen [*othonai*], frayed
4 old, useless ephebic *khlamydes*
4 old, useless silken veils (*prosōpidia*)
2 other old useless veils [*prosōpidia*] of wool
12 old useless veils [*prosōpidia*] of linen
1 old linen veil (*epikrēnon*).
2 other veils [*epikrēna*], useless.
1 other veil [*epikrēnon*], half worn out, frayed.
1 other useless silken veil [*epikrēnon*], frayed.
1 other silken veil [*epikrēnon*], half worn to pieces, frayed,
2 green cut wool ribbons (*lēmniskoi*), frayed.
1 other red ribbon [*lēmniskos*], frayed.
2 old girdles (*strophoi*) overlaid with gold.
1 other old bright red girdle [*strophos*] having a gold-inwoven thunderbolt motif.
1 old wool belt (*zōma*) overlaid with gold, old and frayed.
1 other (*zōma*) of linen with a little clasp, half worn out.

Anaios says he has dedicated 2 old belts, 1 other old larger (belt), 1 small purple *khlandion*, 1 other [*khlandion*] with a fine purple border, for children, frayed, and other items of children's clothing, frayed.

7.3.2 Ragged clothing in the Brauron clothing catalogue

In the Brauron catalogues, there are many instances of *rhakos*, a rag/ragged clothing.[11] All kinds of dedicated garments were ragged: *khitōniskos, khitōnion, khitōn, tryphēma, xenikē, himation, kandys, enkyklos, khlanis, katastikton, tarantinon, lasion, krokōtinon,* and *stuppinon*.[12]

In the year 343/342 a woman, Kallippe, is recorded as having donated a child's *himation* with a purple border, which is now a rag (*rhakos*). Likewise, another woman, Euboule, had donated a coarse *khitōnion* that is now a rag, and Pantheris had donated a *khitōniskos* with wide purple border, now a rag; Hagnodemos' wife had donated a coarse *khitōniskos*, now a rag:

IG II² 1517B.114–120

Καλλίππε ἱμάτιον παι-
δεῖ[ον] ; παραλοθργ[ες] ῥάκος ; Εὐβούλη χιτώνιον στύ-
ππινον [ῥάκος] · Πανθηρὶς χιτωνίσκον πλατυαλο-
υργῆ [ῥάκ] · Ἀγνοδήμου γυνὴ χιτωνίσκον στύππ-
ινον [ῥάκος] · Χρυσὶς χλανίδα ἀνδρεί[αν] ; Ἀριστομά-
χη χιτωνίσκον κτενω[τον] ; Μελίτη χιτωνίσκον ἀνδρεῖ[ον] ; ἡ αὐτὴ ἕτερον χιτωνίσκον ἀνδρεῖ[ον] ;

Kallippe dedicated a child's *himation* with a purple border, a rag.
Euboule dedicated a coarse *khitōnion*, a rag.
Pantheris dedicated a *khitōniskos* with wide purple border, a rag.
Hagnodemos' wife dedicated a coarse *khitōniskos*, a rag.
Chrysis dedicated a man's *khlanis*
Aristomache dedicated a spiky-bordered *khitōniskos*
Melite dedicated a man's *khitōniskos* and one more man's *khitōniskos*

One should note that while all the donors in the passage are women, they donate not just women's clothing but men's and children's too.

---

[11] Greek text from Cleland 2005, 22. My edited translation is based on Cleland 2005, with alterations.
[12] Cleland 2005, 126. Brøns 2015, 45–48. Brøns 2016, 36.

7.3.3 A ragged Tarantine dress at Tanagra

At Tanagra, only once is there a record of a ragged (*rakinos*) garment. It is a Tarantine garment (*tarantinon*) in an annual inventory of the 3rd century BCE.[13]

> Νίκωνος ἄρχοντος, ἰαραρχιόντων Εὐγίτο*γ*[ος]
> Τυχωνίω, Τιμίναο Φρουνωνίω, γραμματίδδον[τος]
> Φρούνωνος Τιμίναο, ἐπάνθετα χιτώνια· Ἐμπεδί[α]
> χιτῶνα κορικὸν γευματικὸν ἐπισανδαλίδας ἔχον-
> τα ἔξ : Πτωιοδώρα σχιστὸμ μάλινον πουρεινί-
> δας ἔχοντα ἔξ· *vacat*
> Φιλοξένα τρίβωνα ἀνδρῖον· *vacat*
> Ἀνδροκκὼ χλανιδίσκαν λευκάν· *vacat*
> Εὐφανία χιτῶνα μάλινον πουρείνια *vacat*
> σάρδια ἔχοντα ἔξ· *vacat*
> Λιουσὶς χλαμουδίσκαν· *vacat*
> Φιλοκκὼ ταραντῖνον ῥάκινον· *vacat*
> Ξενοκκὼ χλανίδας δύο, τεγίδιον λευκόν,
> λίνινος παρπόρφουρος·

With Nikōn as archon, the high priests were Eugiton son of Tychō and Timinas son of Phrounōnos; the secretary was Phrounōnos son of Timinas; Dedicated *khitōnes*:
Empedia, 1 girl's *khitōn geumatikos* having six sandal straps (?)
Ptōiodōra, 1 yellow open garment with six buttons
Philoxenā, 1 man's *tribōn*
Androkkō, 1 white *khlanidiska*
Euphania, 1 yellow *khitōn* with six Sardian buttons
Liousis, 1 small *khlamys*
Philokkō, 1 ragged *Tarantinon*
Xenokkō, 2 *khlanides*, 1 white headdress (*tegidion*), and 1 linen garment with purple borders.

7.3.4 Ragged linen clothes and textiles at the Hera sanctuary in Samos

The clothing inventory dates to the year 346/5 BCE. It first records clothes dedicated to the goddess Hera, and then, from line 31, those dedicated to Hermes.[14] Ragged clothes are described by the adjective *rakinos*. Among Hera's clothes were a ragged linen wrap (*periblēma*), a ragged purple patterned loincloth (*perizōma*),

---

13 Boeotia, ca. 260–250 BCE, *SEG* 43: 212 (B), lines 26–39. Translation from Roller 1989 (with modifications by Brøns 2016 and MLBN). Casevitz 1993 translates quite differently. See also Brøns 2015, 48–50 and Brøns 2016, 37, 393–395.
14 *IG* XII 6, 1, 261, lines 12–35. See also Brøns 2015, 52–53 and Brøns 2016, 38–39, 397–398.

and a ragged table cover (*katapetasma*), and among the clothing dedicated to Hermes an old (*palaios*) veil.

7.4 Clothing passed on from one generation to another

Some classical Greek authors give some fascinating insights into the religious importance of old clothing in the monarchical traditions of neighbouring societies. In the royal Achaemenid dynasty in Persia, items of clothing were passed down the male line from the old monarch to his successor, and this royal historic clothing emphasized the longevity of the monarchy and hence its legitimacy.

The Greek biographer Plutarch describes how King Artaxerxes II (ca. 445 to 359/8 BCE, reigned 405/4 to 358 BCE) went to a temple in Pasargadae shortly after his coronation to undergo a royal rite (τελετή) performed by the local Persian priests. It must have happened around 404 BCE. Pasargadae was the ancient capital of the Achaemenid Empire and the rite involved undressing and redressing:

> εἰς τοῦτο δεῖ τὸν τελούμενον παρελθόντα τὴν μὲν ἰδίαν ἀποθέσθαι στολήν, ἀναλαβεῖν δὲ ἣν Κῦρος ὁ παλαιὸς ἐφόρει πρὶν ἢ βασιλεὺς γενέσθαι
>
> Into this sanctuary, the candidate for initiation must pass, and after laying aside his own proper robe, must put on that which Cyrus the Elder used to wear before he became king.[15]

The ritual thus meant that Artaxerxes removed his own clothes (*stolē*) and dressed in the clothes of his ancestor, the renowned King Cyrus the Great, also called Cyrus the Elder (reigned 559–529 BCE). However, it was not Cyrus' royal dress but clothes Cyrus had worn before he became king, clothing from 560 BCE or earlier, allegedly at least 155 years old.

This dressing and undressing rite also contained a critically dangerous moment of '*kairós*' (discussed above), since it offered an opportunity to assassinate the newly crowned king: undressing is a vulnerable moment. The story as Plutarch tells it is that Artaxerxes' younger brother Cyrus aimed to overthrow his brother and take over the Achaemenid throne.[16] It was reported to Artaxerxes that his brother Cyrus would attempt to kill him in the moment of undressing (ἐκδύηται τὴν ἐσθῆτα).[17]

---

15 Plut. *Artax.* 3.2. See also Flemestad 2022, 120.
16 Plut. *Artax.* 1–2.
17 Plut. *Artax.* 3.4. κατηγόρει δὲ ὡς μέλλοντος ἐνεδρεύειν ἐν τῷ ἱερῷ, καὶ ἐπειδὰν ἐκδύηται τὴν ἐσθῆτα ὁ βασιλεύς, ἐπιτίθεσθαι καὶ διαφθείρειν αὐτόν (And he accused him of planning to lie in

The Seleucid king Antiochus III, during his visit to Babylon in 187 BCE, was presented with the 400 years old robe of Nebuchadnezzar II, according to Assyrian astronomical diaries in cuneiform. The robe had been stored in the treasury of the Marduk temple. This robe of Mesopotamian royal tradition may have helped the Seleucid monarchy legitimize its rule over Babylonia as heir of the Neo-Babylonian kings.[18]

Alexander the Great's own *khlamys* was also preserved for centuries and passed on to the next generations of rulers. It is told that Pompey wore this 200-years old *khlamys* in his triumphal procession into Rome after defeating Mithridates in 61 BCE. Pompey had taken the *khalmys* as booty from Mithridates, who had it from the inhabitants of Cos, who in turn had it from Egypt.[19]

7.5 Second-hand garments and markets

Used commodities of all kinds were traded in antiquity,[20] including garments and textiles.[21] Clothing had long time of use. Therefore it was used, re-used, recycled, sold second hand,[22] traded,[23] pawned,[24] stolen, or taken as booty. This not only illustrates its high value but also its long or many lives.

Late 5th century Athens had specialised cloth markets in the Agora: a garment market (ἱματιόπωλις ἀγορά) and a cloth or perhaps sailcloth market (σπειρόπωλις) and we can assume that they sold used as well as new items.[25] Some would purchase and wear old clothing for reasons of poverty: the hardship of some characters in Aristophanes' comedies is depicted via their poor clothing. There are also reports of clothing thieves who stole garments for their monetary value.[26] That

---

wait for the king in the sanctuary until he should put off his garment, and then to fall upon him and kill him.)
18 Madreiter 2016. Gaspa 2024, 18.
19 Appian, *Mithridatic Wars* 17.117.
20 Drexhage and Reinard 2014, 1: "Auch alte und abgenutzte, defekte und zerbrochnene sowie zerschlissene Güter waren in einer armen Gesellschaft von grossen Wert". Reinard et al. 2019. Reinard 2019.
21 Drexhage and Reinard 2014, mainly on Ptolemaic and Roman sources.
22 Xenophon, *Anabasis* 7.5.5 and 7.8.2 about selling one's own clothes to obtain cash.
23 Droß-Krüpe and Nosch 2016. Droß-Krüpe (unpublished).
24 Drexhage and Reinard 2014, 40, 44. Lagger 2006 and 2009.
25 Reuthner 2019, 245–246 with sources.
26 Aristophanes, *Assembleywomen* 670 suggests that in the ideal world, there will be no clothing thieves anymore. Demosthenes 24.114 for a thief of a ἱμάτιον. Lysias 10.10 for a clothes' thief.

monetary value can also be seen in the presence of clothing in some loan agreements.[27]

Auctions resulting from confiscations and political trials such as the *eisangellia* processes would commercialise the clothing of the condemned and their family. As a consequence of the notorious profanation-trial in 415 BCE targeting Alcibiades and his followers, inscribed lists of goods that were confiscated and sold include a woolen *ampekhonon* (cloak, I, 60), an *exōmis* (worker's clothing, VII, 107–111), a yellow wool *krokē* (I, 212), and many *himatia* (I, 189–201, 209–210, VII, 101–106).[28] In court cases and confiscations[29] as well as in disputes pertaining to property derived from inheritance,[30] clothing would find new owners and users or be resold.

Finally, clothing and textiles were taken as booty in war and conflicts to be sold or used as remuneration for soldiers. After the Persian Wars, Greece had experienced Persian and Median luxury in clothing and large amounts of Persian textiles were left behind by the Persian army in Greece or taken booty by the Greeks.[31] These fabrics and garments were probably recycled and re-used, offered as votives in sanctuaries, distributed among the Greek soldiers or sold in the market.

7.6 The lifespan of textile tools: heirlooms – loom-weights

It wasn't just clothes that could have an extended lifespan: the same could also be true of the tools used to make the clothes. For example, loom-weights can, as techno-archaeological items, give us information about weaving technology and loom technology; in archaeological contexts, they can inform about gender, and about industrial or domestic production. Loom-weights have also recently been recognised as potential sources of information about values and beliefs[32] and ethnicity.[33]

Drexhage and Reinard 2014, 13–14, 35 for Ptolemaic and Roman clothes thieves. For women cursing clothes thieves, see Chaniotis 2009 and Thomsen 2023.
27 E.g. Demosthenes 49.22 involving a loan in cash and στρώματα and ἱμάτια.
28 Reuthner 2019, 247–248. *IG* I³ 421. Pritchett 1953, 292–296. Pritchett and Pippin 1956, 203–208.
29 Demosthenes 21.133 mentions the confiscation of a *khlaina*.
30 Demosthenes 27.10. Demosthenes 36.14 on clothes inherited from a mother.
31 Reuthner 2019.
32 For images from feminine and domestic life and values on loom-weights, see Nosch and Sauvage 2023.

Time should be included as part of the historical reflections on loom-weights given their use in archaeological dating by archaeologists. New research, however, suggests that loom-weights could be heirlooms, used and kept for a very long time for both personal and practical reasons. Classical archaeologists have observed how some loom-weights dated to a certain chronological context had older decorations. They could be termed *'heirloom loom-weights'*, because they are loom-weights with a long history. One example is a pyramidal loom-weight from the Fattoria Fabrizio, a farmhouse near Metaponto. The loom-weight was uncovered in a layer from the late 4th to early 3rd century BCE, but it displays a Greek inscription with a form of the letter iota which was no longer in use after approximately 500 BCE. This loom-weight was hence an heirloom when it was used on a loom some 200 years later in the farm house.[34]

There are other cases of loom-weights from Metaponto from 4th century BCE contexts but with stamped decoration of a much earlier date (probably the late 7th to 5th centuries BCE), termed 'heritage stamps'. Lin Foxhall suggests that the stamps were heirlooms handed down in the family's female line from generation to generation and that these stamps were used to mark loom-weights each time a new set was produced. The loom-weights should not be seen simply as the backcloth to some interesting texts: they represent textile tools with a pedigree and can carry a long history on the distaff side of society within a domestic and productive context.

---

33 See discussions of Minoan loom-weights in Cutler 2021, and the attempts to distinguish between Greek and indigenous Italic loom-weights in Southern Italy in Quercia and Foxhall 2012. See also Landenius Enegren 2015. Nosch and Sauvage 2023.
34 Foxhall forthcoming.

8 Clothing for life chapters, life stages and lifetime

8.1 Clothing for life stages and ages

We have seen that clothing might pass down the generations. It could also be used to mark time within generations, and the life stages of its wearer. The main categories of clothing terminology concern gender and life stages expressed in age or size. Ages or life stages (*hēlikiai*)[1] were largely based on transitions and phases rooted in the number seven. Here is the male version:
- Little boy, *paidion*, up to 7 years
- Child, *pais*, up to 14 years
- Youth, *meirakion*, up to 21 years
- Young man, *neāniskos*, up to 28 years
- Adult man, *anēr*, up to 49 years
- Aged man, *presbytēs*, up to 56 years
- Old man, *gerōn*, 56 years and more.

Adolescent boys in Athens gained civil status at the age of 16 when they were registered in their phratry and at 18 when registered in their deme; at the age of 20 they could take part in the Assembly.[2] Young men also passed through the ritual of the *ephēbeia* (see ch. 9.1).

Female life stages could be denoted by terms including *parthenos*, *korē* and *nymphē*, *gynē* and *alokhos*.[3] The *parthenos* was physically mature but unmarried and probably 11–14 years old.[4] The *nymphē* denoted a girl, a young woman, a bride and a married wife until the first child was born.[5] In the marriage, a woman was called *gynē* and *alokhos*. In addition to the social division of female life stages came the biological markers of menstruation around the age of

---

[1] Singer 2022, 41–42 referring to the 'Hippocratic' text *Hebdomads*, as well as Aristotle, *Politics* 7.17 1336b40–1337a1.
[2] Reeder 1995, 27–28.
[3] On girls in Archaic and Classical Greece, see Brelich 1969, especially chapter II "Le fanculle atenesi" p. 229–311 and Calame 1977, both with inspirations from anthropological theories. More recently, see Moraw and Kieburg 2014. According to Stears 1995, Athenian grave reliefs depict three stages of female childhood: the baby, the small girl and the *parthenos*.
[4] On the *parthenos*, see Lefkowitz 1995.
[5] Reeder 1995, 22.

13–14 and the menopause at the age of 40–50 years.[6] While women could never aspire to the full civic status enjoyed by men, there were institutions that introduced girls into a more public world. Attic girls were initiated as little bears in Brauron when they were between 6–7 and 10–11 years old, and the *arrhēphoroi* (girls recruited for the manufacture of Athena's *peplos*) were also of the same age of ca. 7–11 years.[7] Even if this was a task for only a few girls, the *arrhēphoria* may represent a parallel to the boys' *ephēbeia*.[8]

Textiles mark the ages and life stages. Female life ages and cycles were marked by the veil (*kalyptra, krēdemnon*) and the belt (*zōnē*).[9] Both the veil and the belt are woven, worn, dedicated to divinities and offered at each life stage of a girl or woman and veils and belts symbolised female life cycles.[10]

Clothing terminology functions as a chronological marker based on ages for clothing for children and adults. Moreover, several terms for clothing have both a regular form and a diminutive form ending in *-ion* mirroring the ages of young adults, e.g. the *khlamys* and the smaller *khlamydion*.[11] This may refer to a smaller size garment or to the age of the wearer. In some cases the diminutive form clearly designates children's clothing, as is the case of the upper-body garment *khlaniskion*. The main garment term *khlanis* is used for adults.[12]

Clothing thus references the age and size of the wearer. Special clothing was made for children, probably mostly as miniature versions of adult clothing. There are records in temple inventories of *paideios* clothing, for children/boys,[13] and there is *korikon* clothing, 'for girls'.[14]

---

[6] Amundsen and Diers 1970. Aristotle, *Historia animalium* 585b: παύεται δὲ ταῖς γυναιξὶ ταῖς μὲν πλείσταις τὰ καταμήνια περὶ τετταράκοντα ἔτη, αἷς δ᾽ ἂν ὑπερβάλῃ τὸν χρόνον τοῦτον διαμένει μέχρι τῶν πεντήκοντα ἐτῶν, καὶ ἤδη τινὲς ἔτεκον· πλείω δὲ χρόνον οὐδεμία. (The menses cease in most women at about forty years, but wherever they exceed this time they continue up to fifty years, and there have been some who gave birth; but none has continued longer.).

[7] On girls and women's life stages, see Calame 1977, I, 63–70, and the chapter "Les âges de la vie" in Brulé 1987, 333–378. Sourvinou 1971 also discusses girls' ages.

[8] Burkert 1966, 13–15.

[9] According to Llewellyn-Jones 2003, 213, 216, there was a *zōnē*, a waist sash, first worn by girls at puberty and then dedicated to Artemis immediately before their wedding.

[10] See in particular Llewellyn-Jones 2003, 215–258: "From parthenos to gynē: veiling and the female life cycle".

[11] Cleland et al. 2007, 34: "probably referring to the short chlamys worn by ephebes."

[12] Cleland 2005, 66–67, 111.

[13] Cleland 2005, 91, note 1 and 121. The *paideion* garments in Brauron are a *khitōniskos*, a *khitōnion*, a *himation* and a *khlaniskion*.

[14] Tanagra, *SEG* 43:212 (B) line 29. See ch. 7.3.3.

There is, however, another layer of complexity. The clothing term *khitōniskos* is a diminutive form of *khitōn*,[15] but it has gained a meaning as a specific garment, not clothing in small size or clothing for children. The *khitōniskos* appears so frequently in the Brauron catalogues in connection with adults that this garment term cannot be an indication of clothing for a younger age or a smaller size but is instead an indication of a slightly different garment type: it seems to be a shorter *khitōn*, perhaps just reaching the thighs, while the regular *khitōn* may have been of knee-length.[16] At least 46 *khitōniskoi* are recorded in Brauron, of which six are attributed to a person: three to men, two to children, and one to a woman: it is evidently a unisex and uni-age garment.[17]

8.2 A girl is born in wool

Textiles and wool were gendered female and associated with women from the moment they were born and throughout their lives. Hence, the birth of a baby girl was signalled by wool of the front door, a sign of how she would spend much of her life. Hesychius explains:

στέφανον ἐκφέρειν· ἔθος ἦν, ὁπότε παιδίον ἄρρεν γένοιτο παρὰ Ἀττικοῖς, στέφανον ἐλαίας τιθέναι πρὸ τῶν θυρῶν· ἐπὶ δὲ τῶν θηλειῶν ἔρια διὰ τὴν ταλασίαν

To display a wreath: it was tradition among people of Attica to put an olive wreath on the front door when a baby boy war born, and to put wool on the front door if the baby was female.[18]

8.3 Clothing for the end of a lifetime

The dead in antiquity were always buried dressed. The shroud was usually called *endyma* but Penelope describes Laertes' shroud as a *pharos*, mantle (*Od.* 19.143).[19]

That clothing the dead is crucial can be deduced from Herodotus' story about Melissa, the murdered wife of the tyrant Periander of Corinth. Melissa appeared to him in a vision and complained that she was cold and had been buried naked

---

15 Cleland 2005, 91.
16 Cleland 2005.
17 Cleland 2005, 62–63, 91–92.
18 My translation.
19 van Wees 2005a, 18 on textiles for the end of life in the Homeric epics. Wagner-Hasel 2000, 199–203; 2020, 257–262; 2022.

because her burial clothes had not been burnt in the funerary ceremony (or perhaps on the pyre with her).²⁰

> ῥιγοῦν τε γὰρ καὶ εἶναι γυμνή· τῶν γάρ οἱ συγκατέθαψε ἱματίων ὄφελος εἶναι οὐδὲν οὐ κατακαυθέντων·
>
> for she was cold (she said) and naked; for the clothes Periander had buried with her had never been burnt, and availed her nothing

In response, Periander took clothes from all the women of Corinth as a renewed offering. This shows the importance of textiles in the cult of the dead, but also, of course, Periander's wickedness.

Dark-coloured clothing was associated with death and mourning.²¹ The goddess Demeter dressed in a dark *kalymma* after the loss of her daughter. She wore a veil (*krēdemna*) over her hair and a dark *kalymma* on her shoulders. Even if the translator quoted below uses the term cloak, the *kalymma* is probably rather a veil reaching from the head to the shoulders. In the second passage Demeter is veiled (*kekalymmena*) and wears a dark *peplos* (*Homeric Hymn to Demeter* 40–42 and 180–183):

> ὀξὺ δέ μιν κραδίην ἄχος ἔλλαβεν, ἀμφὶ δὲ χαίταις
> ἀμβροσίαις κρήδεμνα δαΐζετο χερσὶ φίλῃσιν·
> κυάνεον δὲ κάλυμμα κατ' ἀμφοτέρων βάλετ' ὤμων,
>
> Bitter pain seized her heart, and she rent the covering around her divine hair with her dear hands: her dark cloak she cast down from both her shoulders and sped,
>
> ἣ δ' ἄρ' ὄπισθε φίλον τετιημένη ἦτορ
> στεῖχε κατὰ κρῆθεν κεκαλυμμένη· ἀμφὶ δὲ πέπλος
> κυάνεος ῥαδινοῖσι θεᾶς ἐλελίζετο ποσσίν.
>
> And she walked behind, distressed in her dear heart, with her head veiled and wearing a dark blue cloak which waved about the slender feet of the goddess.

We see a similar connection between dark colours and mourning in Greek tragedies.²² In Aischylos' play *Libation Bearers*, verse 10, the chorus is composed of elderly women dressed in *pharea melankhima*, black cloaks. In Euripides' play

---

20 Herodotus 3.50 and the quoted passage from 5.92 with my alteration in the translation.
21 Flemestad 2022, 23–30. Plutarch, *Consolatio as uxorem* 4.608F mentions mourning dress as ἱμάτιον πένθιμον.
22 Pollux 4.118 writes that female characters on stage wear purple garments except when staged as in mourning which means changing to dark clothing and coverlets of blue or green.

Helen (verse 1186), the protagonist changes into dark clothes (πέπλους μέλανας) when she believes that her husband Menelaus has died:

αὕτη, τί πέπλους μέλανας ἐξήψω χροὸς

You, why have you changed your white clothes for black

Epigraphical evidence suggests that black and dark clothing was not the only mourning clothes colour but also grey or even white.[23]

Some garments in Greek fiction can even cause the end of life. This was the case for the garment gifted by Medea to Jason's new wife Glauke in Euripides' *Medea*. The gift (*dōra*) consists of a thin (*leptos*) *peplos* and a crown braided in gold (*plokos khrysēlatos*). They are wedding gifts (*phernai*) (*Medea* 949, 960, 1159). But it is a poisonous *peplos* and Glauke burns to death when she dresses in it.[24]

Funerals mark a transition in time and there is some evidence to suggest that clothing and women's behavior were regulated at funerals in ancient Greece (Fig. 9).[25] Ancient sources report instructions for women's clothing at funerals by the legendary law-giver Solon. The reason for the regulations and even their historicity is debated;[26] our evidence comes from Plutarch who wrote much later. According to Plutarch (*Solon*, 21.4) women were only allowed three *himatia* to wear when attending funerals, suggesting restrictions on the public display of wealth.[27]

Ἐπέστησε δὲ καὶ ταῖς ἐξόδοις τῶν γυναικῶν καὶ τοῖς πένθεσι καὶ ταῖς ἑορταῖς νόμον ἀπείργοντα τὸ ἄτακτον καὶ ἀκόλαστον· ἐξιέναι μὲν ἱματίων τριῶν μὴ πλέον ἐχούσας κελεύσας, μηδὲ βρωτὸν ἢ ποτὸν πλείονος ἢ ὀβολοῦ φερομένην, μηδὲ κάνητα πηχυαίου μείζονα, μηδὲ νύκτωρ πορεύεσθαι πλὴν ἁμάξῃ κομιζομένην λύχνου προφαίνοντος. Ἀμυχὰς δὲ κοπτομένων καὶ τὸ θρηνεῖν πεποιημένα καὶ τὸ κωκύειν ἄλλον ἐν ταφαῖς ἑτέρων ἀφεῖλεν.

---

23 Flemestad 2022, 46–48 mentions *LSAM* 16.4–9 prescribing grey or white for men in 3rd century Aeolis.
24 Clothes were not the only textiles that might be associated with death. Precious carpets can be inauspicious, like the purple carpet (πορφυρόστρωτος, ἁλουργής and πορφύρας) that Klytaemnestra spread on the ground before her husband Agamemnon, thus presaging his fatal destiny (Aischylos, *Agamemnon* 910, 946, 957–960). Alföldi 1955, 15–55. Jenkins 1985. Bakola 2016.
25 On the regulations of dress at funerals, see Wagner-Hasel 2000, 213–217; 2001. Women behaved and dressed in specific ways at funerals, as is reported in both texts and vase paintings. See Stears 1998 and van Wees 2005a, 20–22 on women in grief in Homeric epics. Brøns 2016, 345–347, writes about clothing in funeral legislations.
26 Blok 2006.
27 Flemestad 2022, 25.

He [Solon] also subjected the public appearances of the women, their mourning and their festivals, to a law, which did away with disorder and licence. When they went out, they were not to wear more than three garments, they were not to carry more than an obol's worth of food or drink, nor a pannier more than a cubit high, and they were not to travel about by night unless they rode in a waggon with a lamp to light their way. Laceration of the flesh by mourners, and the use of set lamentations, and the bewailing of anyone at the funeral ceremonies of another, he forbade.

Figure 9: Women gathered in mourning dressed in dark but patternd clothes and cloaks. Clay plate from a burial in Athens, painted by Exekias, ca. 540 BCE. Berlin, Staatliche Museen zu Berlin, Antikensammlung, inv. F 1813.
Photo: Staatliche Museen zu Berlin, Antikensammlung (Johannes Laurentius), CC BY-SA 4.0, https://id.smb.museum/object/685984 (last access 04.07.2025).

9 Dressing for special transition points in time and status

If clothes and textiles helped mark birth and death, they were equally important in marking transitions *within* life. Peder Flemestad calls this "dress in liminal life events".[1] In their analysis of time and the sacred, Henri Hubert and Marcel Mauss spoke of 'critical dates' that mark the beginning, the end or the duration of a certain period.[2] Clothing plays a singular role in marking and materialising such critical dates, especially those marking entries, starts, exits and ends.

Not only clothes but also clothing actions – to cover, to dress, to rip off, and to undress – could be used to embody and enact the rituals and mark the transitions between various phases of a ceremony.[3] These rites of passage could be performed by dressing in a special cloak,[4] veil, or dress, or by changing wardrobe entirely.

Here I present some examples of transitions in antiquity that are expressed in changes of clothing.[5] For men, this includes the ephebic *khlamys*, investiture clothing, Alexander the Great's change of wardrobe after conquering Asia, and cloaks of transitions in Jewish traditions; for women, the wedding veil, unbelting, and the *anakalypteria* rite.

9.1 Transition clothing for young Greek male citizens: the ephebic khlamys cloak

Young male citizens known as *ephebes*[6] entered a two-year program of military service, the *ephēbeia*,[7] at the age of about 18 in Athens and other city-states.

---

[1] Flemestad 2022, 18.
[2] Hubert and Mauss 1905, 10.
[3] Quillien 2019, 77.
[4] The transition of authority from the prophet Elijah to his disciple Elisha is marked by passing on the mantle in the *Old Testament* (1 *Kings* 19:19–20). The elderly Elijah "found Eli'sha the son of Shaphat, who was plowing, with twelve yoke of oxen before him, and he was with the twelfth. Eli'jah passed by him and cast his mantle upon him. And he left the oxen, and ran after Eli'jah".
[5] On how a change of clothing in Aristophanes' comedies enables the wearer to change personality, see Robson 2005.
[6] See Chankowski 2010 and Chankowski (forthcoming) on ephebic institutions in Athens, Sparta and Macedonia, and Chaniotis 2005, 23, 28, 46–56 on ephebes in Boeotia. See also Flemestad and Nosch 2023.
[7] Chankowski 2010 and Chankowski (forthcoming).

This life chapter was marked by donning and wearing the woolen cloak called a *khlamys*.[8]

This garment was not reserved for *ephebes:* it was worn generally by men and especially by travellers, riders, and those on military service.[9] The *khlamys* cloak nonetheless gained a specific meaning as a marker of the special time in a young man's life when he served as *ephebe*.[10] They appear, as we have seen above, in inventories of clothing donated to the sanctuary at Miletus specifically as *ephebic khlamydes*. Why did the *khlamys*, a male cloak, become a signifier for a time-limited ephebic service? My colleague Peder Flemestad and I have argued that the social, political and historical contexts endowed the *khlamys* with values of the 4th century such as courage and masculinity and associated it with military victory and youth.[11]

The *ephēbeia* was a prolonged transition period between the age of boys and that of young adults, with duties specifically intended for young men.[12] The bulk of the evidence for this formal and compulsory military training comes from late Classical and Hellenistic times.[13]

The entry into ephebic service was marked by an inauguration and dressing ceremony called the ἐισιτήρια/ ἐισιτητήρια to mark this new phase of life and the beginning of military duties.[14] It has been suggested that Bacchylides' 4th dithyramb, in which Theseus[15] was dressed in a Thessalian wool *khlamys*, was composed to be performed at an Attic *ephēbeia* celebration.[16]

Metaphorically and literally, to take off a *khlamys* is denoted by the Greek verb *apotithēmi* (ἀποτίθημι) and marks the undressing and the end of ephebic identity. The undressing may have meant literally to undress completely. An inscription from Crete links the exit ritual to nudity: young men are described as

---

8 For the special used of the *khlamys* by ephebes, see Roussel 1941. Vidal-Naquet 1968, 953. Chankowski 2010, 300–305. Flemestad 2022, 146–148. Flemestad and Nosch 2023. [Arist.] *Ath. Pol.* 42.5, on the *khlamys* as ephebic dress.
9 Abrahams 1908, 55–56.
10 The *ephebe* also wore a *khiton* in wool or linen, and a loin cloth fastened by a belt, a hat and (in winter) footwear called *krepides*. See *SEG* 65.420. See also Chankowski (forthcoming). Flemestad 2022, 145. Flemestad and Nosch 2023.
11 Flemestad and Nosch 2023.
12 Chankowski 2010 and Chankowski (forthcoming).
13 Chankowski 2010, 135. In *Against Timarchos* 1.49, the Athenian orator and statesman Aischines, in a public speech given in 346/5, recalls his youth and his time as *ephebe* back in the 370s.
14 Chankowski 2010, 300–305. Henderson 2020, 105–106.
15 Wind 1972. Athanassaki 2016, 18. Nobili 2018, 23–25.
16 Merkelbach 1973, 56–60.

"completely without belts" i.e., without clothes (ἀγέαλοι πανάζωστοι).[17] The ceremony signified another moment in time, namely the end of the *ephēbeia* period marked by the exit ceremony called ἐξιτήρια / ἐξετητήρια.[18]

9.2 Transition time for a king: investiture clothing

To dress in royal robes was an important public ritual for kings, and ancient sources illustrate how dressing and undressing mark important moments in time for monarchs and monarchies. For example, donning a purple cloak for the first time marks a beginning that is coded into the institutionalized ritual of royal investiture: coronation is closely associated with the wearing of specific clothes.[19] Helmut Utzschneider describes this dressing and undressing, robing and disrobing, as *Investitur* and *Devestitur*.[20] Our known examples come from the Persian[21] or Assyrian kingdoms,[22] (see Artaxerxes' royal dress, ch. 7.4) but they are so abundant that the practice must have been known to the Greeks.

In Tyre, Alexander the Great appointed Abdalonymus king and sent him a royal outfit (βασιλικῆς ἐσθῆτος). Later, for his first appearance as King of the Tyrians, Abdalonymus dressed in a royal dress (βασιλικὴν στολήν).[23]

9.3 New clothes – new times – for Alexander the Great

Changing to a new clothing style marks a turning point in Alexander the Great's life and career. According to Plutarch, when Alexander returned to Parthia from his vast conquests in the East in the autumn of 330 BCE, he had changed his ward-

---

17 Chankowski 2010, 311–312: πανάζωστοι. *Syll.*³ 527; *I.Cret.* I.9.1; Chaniotis 1992, 195–201, n. 7.
18 Chankowski 2010, 300–305. Henderson 2020, 105–106.
19 Nosch 2021; 2022; 2025.
20 Utzschneider 1988, 172–175.
21 Nosch 2021. Flemestad 2022, 116–124 on Persian royal dress in Plutarch and other Greek and Roman authors.
22 Gaspa 2018, 21. The royal Assyrian investiture robe is termed *tillû*, which is in fact a Babylonian garment term.
23 Diod. Sic. XVII, 47, 4–5: (…) λαβὼν τὴν ἐπιτροπὴν κατήντησεν ἐπὶ τὸν ὠνομασμένον μετὰ βασιλικῆς ἐσθῆτος καὶ κατέλαβεν αὐτὸν ἔν τινι κήπῳ μισθοῦ μὲν ἀντλοῦντα, ῥάκεσι δὲ τοῖς τυχοῦσιν ἐσθῆτι χρώμενον. δηλώσας δὲ τὴν περιπέτειαν καὶ περιθεὶς τὴν βασιλικὴν στολὴν καὶ τὸν ἄλλον τὸν ἁρμόζοντα κόσμον ἀνήγαγεν αὐτὸν εἰς τὴν ἀγορὰν καὶ ἀπέδειξε βασιλέα τῶν Τυρίων.

robe: he no longer wore only the typical Macedonian *kausia* (hat) and *khlamys*, but added 'barbarian' clothes to his outfit:

Ἐντεῦθεν εἰς τὴν Παρθικὴν ἀναζεύξας καὶ σχολάζων, πρῶτον ἐνεδύσατο τὴν βαρβαρικὴν στολήν, εἴτε βουλόμενος αὐτὸν συνοικειοῦν τοῖς ἐπιχωρίοις νόμοις, ὡς μέγα πρὸς ἐξημέρωσιν ἀνθρώπων τὸ σύνηθες καὶ ὁμόφυλον, εἴτ' ἀπόπειρά τις ὑφεῖτο τῆς προσκυνήσεως αὕτη τοῖς Μακεδόσι, κατὰ μικρὸν ἀνασχέσθαι τὴν ἐκδιαίτησιν αὐτοῦ καὶ μεταβολὴν ἐθιζομένοις. οὐ μὴν τήν γε Μηδικὴν ἐκείνην προσήκατο, παντάπασι βαρβαρικὴν καὶ ἀλλόκοτον οὖσαν, οὐδ' ἀναξυρίδας οὐδὲ κάνδυν οὐδὲ τιάραν ἔλαβεν, ἀλλ' ἐν μέσῳ τινὰ τῆς Περσικῆς καὶ τῆς Μηδικῆς μειξάμενος εὖ πως, ἀτυφοτέραν μὲν ἐκείνης, ταύτης δὲ σοβαρωτέραν οὖσαν.[24]

From thence he marched into Parthia, where, during a respite from fighting, he first put on the barbaric dress, either from a desire to adapt himself to the native customs, believing that community of race and custom goes far towards softening the hearts of men; or else this was an attempt to introduce the obeisance among the Macedonians, by accustoming them little by little to put up with changes and alterations in his mode of life. However, he did not adopt the famous Median fashion of dress, which was altogether barbaric and strange, nor did he assume trousers, or sleeved kandys, or tiara, but carefully devised a fashion which was midway between the Persian and the Median, more modest than the one and more stately than the other.

Other ancient authors confirm this change in dress style but they differ as to why and in what ways Alexander changed his clothing.[25]

It seems that Alexander mixed elements of Persian and Macedonian clothing in his new hybrid royal dress. Both Plutarch and Diodorus write that Alexander avoided the sleeved *kandys* garment[26] and Persian trousers (*anaxyrides*), but wore a purple tunic decorated with a central white stripe, called a *khitōn mesoleukos* or *khitōn dialeukos*.[27] Alexander also wore the Macedonian *kausia* and a purple *khlamys* cloak.

His clothing has been subject to lively debate in the modern literature on Alexander: was it Persian, or Macedonian, or a mixture of both? Alexander knew how to link his clothing to his political objectives and to use items of clothing and decoration for strategic purposes.[28] His change of dress marks an important time of political transition within his reign.

---

24 Plut. *Alex.* 45, 1–3.
25 Curt. 6.6,1–5. Arr. *Anab.* 4.7.4 (who uses the term *kitaris*). Athenaeus XII 535 f. and 537 f. Blum 1998, 191–193. Ritter 1965, 47–49.
26 Flemestad 2022, 119–120.
27 Plut. *Alex.* 45.2; Plut. *Mor.* 329F–330D (with reference to Eratosthenes of Cyrene). Diod. Sic. 17.77.4–5.
28 See the discussion of Alexander's wardrobe in Fredericksmeyer 1986. Blum 1998, 191–196. Nosch 2021; 2022; 2025. Flemestad 2022, 137–159.

9.4 Passing the cloak and passing the office and responsibility

The Jewish officer Jonathan[29] was appointed as high priest in Jerusalem in 153 BCE and donned the high priest's robes[30] as a sign of his investiture. His dress is called *hagia stolē* (1 *Macc.* 10.21) or *hieratikē stolē* (Josephus, *AJ* 13.46).

1 *Macc.* 10.21

Καὶ ἐνεδύσατο Ἰωνάθαν τὴν ἁγίαν στολὴν τῷ ἑβδόμῳ μηνὶ ἔτους ἑξηκοστοῦ καὶ ἑκατοστοῦ ἐν ἑορτῇ σκηνοπηγίας καὶ συνήγαγε δυνάμεις καὶ κατεσκεύασεν ὅπλα πολλά.

So Jonathan put on the holy robes in the seventh month of the one hundred and sixtieth year, at the feast of tabernacles, and he recruited troops and equipped them with arms in abundance.

Josephus, *AJ* 13.46

Δεξάμενος δὲ ὁ Ἰωνάθης τὴν ἐπιστολὴν ἐνδύεται μὲν τὴν ἱερατικὴν στολὴν τῆς σκηνοπηγίας ἐνστάσης

On receiving this letter, Jonathan, at the time of the festival of Tabernacles, put on the high-priestly robe

In these passages, the holy robe illustrates the moment of transition into a new role.

9.5 Veiling and unveiling the bride and the Anakalypteria ritual in Athens

> Le port d'un voile et son enlèvement rythment la vie sexuelle des jeunes filles[31]

Clothing could also be critical in the different stages of the lives of women. For example, veiling means covering a girl or woman's head, hair, and sometimes face with a piece of cloth, a veil. Alternatively, a section of clothing, an upper garment or cloak, is pulled up to cover her head, hair or face. Both the veil itself and the act of veiling have significant meanings in female life.

---

29 1 *Macc.* 10.16–20. Josephus, *AJ* 13.44–45.
30 For the traditional garb of the high priest, see *Exodus* 28.4–5 and Bender 2008, 228–242.
31 Gherchanoc 2006, 267.

The veiling and unveiling of the bride is an important moment in the wedding ritual of ancient Greece.[32] It was a "ritualised enactment of her separation from her old status prior to the assumption of her new",[33] marking a transition in time and status.[34] A girl would be first unveiled and then veiled again as a married woman in the nuptial ritual of the *Anakalypteria*, and then unveiled again by her new husband (Fig. 10).[35] In the days before the wedding, the bride-to-be would make offerings (*proaulia*) to Artemis of personal items, including locks of hair and clothing.[36]

While *Anakalypteria* refers to an unveiling, scholars disagree regarding what actually took place, and where and when it happened in the wedding ceremony. Was the bride unveiled in her paternal home immediately before the wedding or in her husband's home, or did it occur in the wedding procession or at the wedding dinner, or in the bedroom on the wedding night? The sources are many but scattered and in disagreement.[37] A compromise suggestion has been put forward by Lloyd Llewellyn-Jones who believes that there were a series of unveiling events at a wedding, first in public and with the wedding guests, and finally in the bedroom. Florence Gherchanoc also distinguished two unveilings: the public unveiling and the private unveiling.[38] She concludes that the veil was a significant textile accessory for a girl in the marriage ritual as it marked a time and transition of status.[39]

---

32 Cairns 2002, 80, with bibliography and discussion of marriage, veiling, modesty and shame. The wedding is also a time of the exchange of gifts, often clothing, between the husband and wife and their families: textiles thereby form a physical manifestation of a social bond.
33 Cairns 2002, 76. Cairns emphasizes the many other meanings of veiling for both men and women, beyond the wedding ritual.
34 Gherchanoc 2006, 257: "le voile apparaît, ainsi, comme une pièce importante dans le processus de construction du lien marital, à la fois signe et garant de la valeur de la jeune fille (pudeur, beauté, rang etc.) et sur lequel se joue le geste de prise de possession et d'acceptation ou non du *gamos*."
35 On the ritual of *anakalypteria*, see Swalec 2016, 167 with bibliography.
36 Gherchanoc 2006, 240–241, 243–244. On page 244: "les *parthenoi* abandonnent leur voile de vierge pour un autre qui signale qu'elles sont nubiles ou sur le point d'être mariées."
37 Avagianou 1991, 135: "The anakalypteria is best interpreted as a ceremony that took place after the bride and groom had spent the night together." See Gherchanoc 2006, 250–251 for a presentation of the various views and bibliography. In Attic red-figure pottery, more than 90% of the wedding scenes depict the procession between the bride's father's house and the groom's, according to Oakley 1995, 63.
38 Gherchanoc 2006.
39 Gherchanoc 2006, 257: "le voile apparaît, ainsi, comme une pièce importante dans le processus de construction du lien marital, à la fois signe et garant de la valeur de la jeune fille (pudeur,

Figure 10: The moment of *Anakalypteria*, the unveiling ceremony, when a bride's veil is lifted. Behind her stands a *peplos*-clad attendant or perhaps her mother. A flying Eros offers her a ribbon. The bride modestly looks down but her groom looks directly at her. A snapshot of a crucial moment. Loutrophoros, 430–425 BCE by the Phiale Painter. Boston, Museum of Fine Arts, inv. 10.223. Photo: Museum of Fine Arts, public domain, https://collections.mfa.org/objects/153799 (last access 04.07.2025).

In Sparta, too, married women would wear a veil, but the ritual of *Anakalypteria* was not practiced, and instead the bride's long hair was cut short.[40] Perhaps unveiling and the cropping of women's hair had similar transformative meanings. In any case, we cannot assume that the *Anakalypteria* was a generalised wedding ritual in ancient Greece.

9.6 Belting and unbelting

Like the veil, the female belt is an accessory that marks transitions and essential moments. Unbelting means undressing and is a metaphor for sexual encounters and loss of virginity.[41] A belt in ancient Greek can be designated by many terms, such as ζώνη (*zōnē*), ζωστήρ (*zōstēr*), ζῶμα (*zōma*) or ἅμμα (*hamma*). The

---

beauté, rang etc.) et sur lequel se joue le geste de prise de possession et d'acceptation ou non du *gamos*."
40 Cartledge 1981, 91 note 44, 101. Flemestad 2022, 21–23. Plutarch, *Lycurgus* 15.4–6 on loosening the belt of a bride in Sparta.
41 Schmitt-Pantel 1977; 2019, 337. Delalande et al. 2024, 18–19.

zōnē, a woven belt, had a special transitional meaning for women. Surprisingly, belts rarely appear as donated clothing items in temple inventories[42] but we see them in other sources. Troizen had a ritual belt offering by young girls to Athena Apatouria[43] which is well attested in epigrams (regrettably mostly of uncertain date). They describe women dedicating their belts (*zōnē*) in gratitude for a happy life and the delivery of healthy babies.[44] An epigram by Antipater of Sidon has a tombstone questioning a deceased woman (*Anthologia Palatina* VII, 164):[45]

α. Φράζε, γύναι, γενεήν, ὄνομα, χθόνα.
β. Καλλιτέλης μενό σπείρας, Πρηξὼ δ' οὔνομα, γῆ δὲ Σάμος.
α. Σῆμα δὲ τίς τόδ' ἔχωσε;
β. Θεόκριτος, ὁ πρὶν ἄθικτα ἡμετέρας λύσας ἅμματα παρθενίης.
α. Πῶς δ' ἔθανες;
β. Λοχίοισιν ἐν ἄλγεσιν·
α. Εἰπὲ δὲ ποίην ἦλθες ἐς ἡλικίην.
β. Δισσάκις ἑνδεκέτις.
α. Ἦ καὶ ἄπαις;
β. Οὐ, ξεῖνε· λέλοιπα γὰρ ἐν νεότητι Καλλιτέλη, τριετῆ παῖδ' ἔτι νηπίαχον.

A. "Tell me, lady, thy parentage, name and country."
B. "Calliteles begat me, Praxo was my name, and my land Samos."
A. "And who erected this monument?"
B. "Theocritus who loosed my maiden belt, untouched as yet."
A. "How didst thou die?"
B. "In the pains of labour."
A. "And tell me what age thou hadst reached."
B. "Twice eleven years."
A. "Childless?"
B. "No, stranger, I left Calliteles behind me, my baby boy."

Praxo's husband had loosened her belt (*hamma*) on their wedding night. She had given birth to a son, but she died at childbirth, probably because of another pregnancy at the age of 22.

---

42 Brøns 2016, 70–73.
43 Pausanias 2.33.1. Schmitt-Pantel 1977; 2019, 349–350.
44 *Anthologia Palatina* V, 200, 217, 285. VI, 59, 201, 202, 210, 272, 276, VII, 164, 182.
45 With alteration by MLBN.

10 Annual and cyclic times in festivals for textile work

Let us move from the significance of clothes in the life stages of individuals to their significance in the religious lives of whole communities. The religious world was structured around an annual ritual cycle of textile tasks (including dressing rituals) undertaken in the service of sanctuaries and divinities. This mirrored the annual ritual cycles of domestic or agricultural textile tasks. Some of these rituals were clustered into festivals (mainly reserved for women), and these festivals formed part of the annual calendar that helped organize both religious and civic life.[1] The literature on this topic is vast. I cannot cover all the aspects and discussions but will focus entirely on aspects of time and textiles exclusively within the festivals.[2] I refer to significant works in the notes.

10.1 Festivals for weaving Athena's peplos in Athens

In Athens, several religious festivals mark the process of weaving the annual gift for the goddess Athena: a *peplos* to clothe the life-size statue of Athena Polias standing in the Erechtheion temple on the Acropolis.

The *Chalkeia* festival was held in honour of Athena Ergane and marked the time of the year when young girls, *arrhēphoroi*, began weaving the *peplos*.[3] The lexicographers use the Greek verb *diazein* to mark the weaving.[4] Daughters of the respected Praxiergidai family,[5] assisted by the little *arrhēphoroi* and female

---

[1] See Brelich 1969, 312–438. Mikalson 1975 discusses and systematises how two Attic calendar systems co-existed, a political and a sacred one, two systems which have, moreover, often been studied separately by epigraphists, ancient historians and scholars of ancient religion. Mikalson merges the two calendars and concludes that it was considered irregular to host political meetings in the Ekklesia on the same days as religious festivals. This is an interesting observation since women, who were not active in political life, played a significant role in the festivals related with textiles. For an introduction to religious festivals, see Parke 1977. Dillon 2001. Sourvinou-Inwood 2011. Walter 2024.

[2] On the topic of textiles in the religious practices of Greece, Rome and ancient near eastern cultures, see Brøns and Nosch 2017.

[3] Deubner 1956, 35. Parke 1977, 38. Barber 1992, 113. Clements 2017 givea a complete overview of the lexicographical, epigraphical and iconographical sources.

[4] *Suda*: Χαλκεῖα · ἑορτὴ ἀρχαία (...) ἐν ᾗ καὶ ἱέρειαι μετὰ τῶν ἀρρηφόρων τὸν πέπλον διάζονται.

[5] Robertson 2004.

textile workers (*ergastinai*) were tasked with the weaving.⁶ There were two or four *arrhēphoroi* and the *ergastinai* were probably adult women with textile skills.⁷ Priestesses of Athena Polias helped set up the loom and the warp.⁸ The *Chalkeia* festival took place annually on the last day of the month of *Pyanepsion* (October-November). The weaving would then take nine months, the same timespan as a full human pregnancy.

The *Arrhēphoria* festival celebrated weaving⁹ and the *arrhēphoroi* girls and it probably took place in the month of *Skirophorion* (see below).¹⁰

The woven *peplos* was an important part of the ritual cycle of life in Athens. The city's highest officers, the nine archons, selected a board of officials, *athlothetai*, who supervised its weaving.¹¹ The Council (*boulē*) had earlier had the authority to make decisions about the patterns (*paradeigmata*) of the *peplos*, writes Aristotle, apparently an important yet contested task, which could potentially lead to corruption:¹²

Ἔκρινεν δέ ποτε καὶ τὰ παραδείγματα καὶ τὸν πέπλον ἡ βουλή, νῦν δὲ τὸ δικαστήριον τὸ λαχόν· ἐδόκουν γὰρ οὗτοι καταχαρίζεσθαι τὴν κρίσιν.

---

6 There was an ongoing discussion in late antiquity about who actually did the weaving. According to Apollodorus in his now lost work Περὶ θεῶν, it was young girls but other authors and scholiasts believed that older married women also helped weave. See Vian 1948 for a comparison of sources. Burkert 1966, 3–4 discusses the number of *arrhēphoroi*.
7 Brelich 1969, 231–232, 268. Neils 1992, 17.
8 Brulé 1987, 99. Neils 1992, 17.
9 Deubner 1956, 9–16 associated this festival with agriculture but Burkert 1966, 9–10 argued convincingly against this. See also Brelich 1969, 231–232. Mikalson 1975, 165–181. Parke 1977, 156–169. I note that ancient and modern authors are more interested in the nocturnal and secret rituals than exploring the spinning and weaving of the *arrhēphoroi*. See for example Calame 1977, I, 236: "Ces jeunes filles étaient au nombre de quatre. Choisies parmi les meilleures familles d'Athènes, deux d'entre elles se consacraient au tissage du *péplos* offert à Athéna aux Panathénées; les deux autres accomplissaient le rite nocturne des Arrhéphories. Au cours de ce rite, les jeunes filles descendaient dans un souterrain situé dans un sanctuaire d'Aphrodite dite *au jardins*, un sanctuaire que les archéologues sont parvenus à identifier sur les pentes Nord de l'Acropole. Ce souterrain menait à une source où elles apportaient dans un coffret d'osier, des objets qu'il leur était interdit de voir. Elles en ramenaient d'autres qu'un de nos témoignages identifie avec des gâteaux en forme de serpents et de *phalloi*." Note the presence of braided baskets as in the myth of baby Erichthonios.
10 Mikalson 1975, 167: "The evidence does suggest strongly that the state Arrhephoria are to be dated to Skirophorion 3 but it is not conclusive."
11 Brulé 1987, 99. Aleshire and Lambert 2003, 71. Arist. *Ath. Pol.* 60,1–3: τὸν πέπλον ποιοῦνται.
12 *Ath. Pol.* 49.3. Plutarch (*Demetr.* 10.4 and 12.2.) states that the Athenians decided after 292 BCE to include images of Demetrius Poliorcetes and Antigonus in the peplos tapestry weave among the images of gods.

At one time the Council used also to judge the patterns [for the peplos], but now this is done by the jury-court selected by lot, because the Council was thought to show favouritism in its decision.

The figures depicted on the *peplos* connected mythological time with historical time and the present: they displayed the myths that united Athens and Athena and other divinities, or they were images of foundational mythical battles of the past which helped form the identity of Athens. As the chorus leader declares in Aristophanes' comedy *The Knights* (verses 565–566):

ΚΟΡΥΦΑΙΟΣ
εὐλογῆσαι βουλόμεσθα τοὺς πατέρας ἡμῶν, ὅτι ἄνδρες ἦσαν τῆσδε τῆς γῆς ἄξιοι καὶ τοῦ πέπλου

Chorus Leader
We want to praise our forebears for being gentlemen worthy of this land and the peplos.

The *Panathenaia* was the festival during which the finished *peplos* was finally offered to Athena, the protector of Athens and patroness of weaving.[13] It took place in the 23rd to 30th days in the month of *Hekatombaion*, which was the first month of the Athenian year (July–August).[14] Quite appropriately, 28 *Hekatombaion* was also the supposed date of Athena's birthday.

Athenians gathered in a procession from the Dipylon Gate to the Acropolis to present the goddess with the newly woven *peplos*. The procession appears on the east frieze on the Parthenon temple, an idealised visualisation of the mid-5th century procession and its participants.[15] The Praxiergidai family's women had the special duty to dress the statue, according to a decree from 470–460 BCE.[16]

There is scholarly disagreement about whether the *peplos* offering took place yearly or only at the 'Greater Panathenaia' celebrated every four years.[17] Some scholars believe that the ritual weaving was limited to the Greater Panathenaic festivals only;[18] against this, Elizabeth Barber and John Mansfield argued that

---

[13] Deubner 1956, 22–34. Brelich 1969, 314–348. Barber 1992. Neils 1992. Reuthner 2006, 295–323.
[14] Mikalson 1975, 34. Neils 1992, 14.
[15] Blundell 1998, 58–59 with bibliography. It appears that *ergastinai* are depicted with long hair and the young *arrhēophori* of 7–11 years carry stools on their heads, see Blundell 1998, 63–64. Sourvinou-Inwood 2011, 284–307.
[16] *IG* I^3 7. Robertson 2004 associates this decree to the Panathenaic festival but Sourvinou-Inwood 2011, 149 connects it to the Plynteria.
[17] Blundell 1998, 9 on the four-year cycle.
[18] Brelich 1969, 269, 343, 321: "la consegna del nuovo peplo alla dea avveniva nella festa penteterica e non in quella annuale." See Aleshire and Lambert 2003, 72 who argue that the annual weaving rite was only established at the end of the 4th century BCE according to Diod. Sic. 20.46.

the annual weaving of a life-sized *peplos* for Athena by local girls and women was, at some point in time, supplemented by the production of a much larger and elaborate 'sail-*peplos*' woven by professional male weavers.[19] The latter occurred every four years at the Greater Panathenaia festival and so added another time dimension to the ritual.[20]

The festival continued in Hellenistic times in Athens and two decrees dated around 100 BCE stipulate that the girls participating in the making of the *peplos* were given awards and wreaths for their fine textile work.[21] It seems that by then the ritual had expanded – now about 120 girls participated – and it was organised as an annual weaving ritual. It had also introduced some clothing regulations of white clothes (*esthētes*) and a donation of a cloak (*himation*), as a fragmentary decree notes.[22]

In conclusion, the Panathenaic festival followed a number of different temporalities – its annual schedule based on the calendar year, a longer four year schedule for the Great Panathenaic festival, the hints of biological time in the nine months 'gestation' of the weaving of the *peplos*, and the 'social' time of the goddess Athena's birthday in the *Hekatombaion* month. There is also a very specific historical date associated with the festival: 556/555 BCE, when the festival was supposedly reformed, though this date has now been questioned.[23] Finally, the Panathenaic was also structured via the participation and collaboration of women of different age-groups: the young *arrhēphoroi* aged 7–11, the *parthenoi* of the Praxiergidai family, the more experienced adult *ergastinai* and priestesses of Athena Polias.

10.2 Festivals for washing Athena's peplos in Athens

There were two further festivals honouring Athena Polias, the *Plynteria* and the *Kallynteria*, which celebrated the washing of her statue and clothing and the

---

19 Vian 1948 with relevant sources. Barber 1992, 113–114 with references. Sourvinou-Inwood 2011, 267.
20 Barber 1992, 113. Neils 1992, 14.
21 Aleshire and Lambert 2003. Robertson 2004, 139–147. Sourvinou-Inwood 2011, 178, 207–207, believes that this decree *IG* II² 1060+1036 fr.b.3 pertains to the *Plynteria* festival and not the *Panathenaic* or *Arrhephoria* festivals.
22 *IG* II² 1060+1036. Aleshire and Lambert 2003. Robertson 2004, 139–141.
23 The date is accepted by Sourvinou-Inwood 2011, 337. However, Robertson 2004, 155–161 offers the intriguing interpretation that the Panathenaic festival was an innovation of the 5th century, created as an ambitious political and cultural unifying initiative for Athenians.

cleaning of her sanctuary.[24] These purification festivals were for women only. The two festivals took place on 25–28 *Thargelion* (May-June).[25]

One scholar has theorised an entanglement of weaving, laundering and clothing: I will in this section mainly follow Christiane Sourvinou-Inwood's interpretations which offer the most comprehensive view of the role of clothing and textiles in the *Plynteria* and *Kallynteria* festivals.[26]

The *Plynteria* name is based on πλυνεῖν, to wash (clothes). The *Plynteria* began on the 25 Thargelion when the priestess undressed the statue of Athena Polias and passed her *peplos* to women of the Praxiergidai family.[27] The Athena Polias sanctuary was then closed off and the Praxiergidai covered the statue in a cloth for reasons of modesty and respect. The covering was perhaps a *khitōn*, as one is mentioned in an inscription about the festival, serving as a kind of intermediate dress while her *peplos* was being washed.[28] If this is correct, the Praxiergidai had to deliver a *khitōn* annually. A decree from between 470 and 460 BCE states that they had to deliver a *khitōn* of a certain value (2 mnai) or pay a fine (1 mna).[29] Having replaced the *peplos* with a *khitōn*, the women descended from the Acropolis in a procession to the sea carrying the statue.

Meanwhile, some of the Praxiergidai, with the special title *Plyntides*, washed the statue's *peplos*. This took place either on the Acropolis,[30] or, as I would suggest, in a river or spring near the sea. Clothes would normally not benefit from being washed in salt water, but there were freshwater streams near the beach, similar to

---

24 Deubner 1956, 17–21. Parke 1977, 152–155, 186. Dillon 2001, 133. Sourvinou-Inwood 2011, 135–224.
25 Mikalson 1975, 164. The exact date is based on studies of political meetings on other days of the month: the 25–28th never hosted meetings.
26 Sourvinou-Inwood 2011. She operates with concepts of time stemming from anthropology, 'normal time' and 'abnormal time'. I feel reluctant to follow her emphasis on *Greekness* in rituals and mentality.
27 *IG* I³ 7. Robertson 2004. Sourvinou-Inwood 2011, 145–148.
28 *IG* I³ 7. Robertson 2004. Sourvinou-Inwood 2011, 145–148, 178. Sourvinou-Inwood 2011, 150: "This *chiton*, since it was not the *peplos* normally worn by the statue, would be abnormal, and therefore appropriate for marking the abnormality of that period, part of the rites performed by the Praxiergidai while the temple was in 'abnormal' time and state (...)."
29 *IG* I³ 7. Robertson 2004 associates this decree to the Panathenaic festival, Sourvinou-Inwood 2011, 149 to the Plynteria. It is tempting to speculate that the Praxiergidai had a special workshop for this ritual weaving (like the *arrhēphoroi* and *ergastinai*) where they would annually prepare a *khitōn* and with available female labour – it was probably financially more attractive to make the *khitōn* themselves than to pay a fine and the weaving could associate the Praxiergidai closer with the cult.
30 Sourvinou-Inwood 2011, 177.

those I imagine Nausikaa and her maids washed their laundry in the *Odyssey* book 6.

Once it had arrived at the sea, the statue was washed in seawater by the *Loutrides* of the Praxiergidai family and then clothed in the clean *peplos* and taken to a local shrine for the night.

Animals were sacrificed at the *Plynteria* festival, according to the ritual calendar of Thorikos dated ca. 430 BCE,[31] and perhaps also a *pharos* mantle was sacrificed to Athena at the same occasion, according to a sacrificial calendar from Athens dated around 400 BCE.[32] There is mention of a *himation* in another inscription, and Sourvinou-Inwood suggests this was what the statue was wrapped in after its bath. It was during the *Plynteria* that Alcibiades returned to Athens, and it was mentioned *en passant* in the reports of his return that the Athena stature was veiled/covered up (*katakekalymmena*) during the entire festival.[33]

Early in the following day, by torchlight, the statue was transported back to the Acropolis and reinstalled in the sanctuary.[34]

The washing and laundering of the *Plynteria* would take two days. It was followed immediately, on 27–28 Thargelion, by the *Kallynteria* festival.[35] Even if it is tempting to translate καλλύνειν as adorning and making beautiful as in κοσμεῖν, the aim of the *Kallynteria* was mainly to clean and sweep the shrine, and perhaps to re-decorate it.[36]

10.3 Clothes and Athena in the Panathenaia, Plynteria and Kallynteria

The manufacture of Athena's *peplos* is well documented in various sources and thoroughly discussed by modern scholars. The scattered references to other textile-related items in the festivals – fleece, *pharos*, *himation*, *khitōn* – have received

---

31 In lines 52–53 is stated that a selected lamb has to be offered at the *Plynteria* festival in the month of Skirophorion, see Lupu 2009. Rasmussen 2023.
32 Lambert 2002, 374: "From the mention of a φᾶρος 'cloak' (7), and 'pure' or 'clean' somethings (8), it seems that these contributions had to do with the state *Plynteria*, a festival entailing washing/cleaning of a statue of Athena at Phaleron (probably the old wooden one in the shrine of Athena Polias) and/or its clothes, which involved the genos Praxiergidai and which is dated by Photios to this day, 29 Thargelion."
33 Plutarch, *Alc.* 34.1. Xenophon, *Hell.* 1.4.12.
34 Sourvinou-Inwood 2011, 192.
35 Sourvinou-Inwood 2011, 193–224.
36 Sourvinou-Inwood 2011, 156.

less attention.³⁷ Christiane Sourvinou-Inwood offers to integrate them into a ritual narrative where each of them plays a role. Indeed, the *himation* and *pharos* may have been essential annually donated pieces for the statue of Athena:

> I suggest that it is likely that, as part of the same ritual stressing of the cyclical nature of the rite, one year's clean cloth that covered the statue as it came out of the sea, eventually became next year's 'dirty' cloth that covered up the statue before it was purified.³⁸

All three festivals, *Panathenaia*, *Plynteria* and *Kallynteria* honoured Athena Polias. They are all three:

> part of a nexus of renewal that began with a 'dirty' robe and concluded with a new robe at the Panathenaia.³⁹

If Sourvinou-Inwood's theory above is correct, we would have two annual systems of clothing the statue, one via donations from a specific family and another via collective weaving. This textile-based interpretation enables Sourvinou-Inwood to hypothesise two mythological layers in the *Plynteria* and *Kallynteria* festivals: if Kekrops's daughters, Pandroses, Heste and Aglauros, were the first weavers, and if Aglauros was the first priestess of Athena, then Aglauros may have introduced the tradition of weaving a wool *peplos* for the goddess.⁴⁰ The *khitōn* could instead be a relic of the statue's clothing before the wool *peplos* tradition supposedly initiated by Aglauros. The ritual therefore may have two clothing layers, an earlier 'ur-*khitōn*' replaced in mythological time by a *peplos*. The older *khitōn* layer would be observable only on a few days of the year. This interpretative model matches the chronology of the historical clothing terminology where *khitōn* is attested earlier than *peplos* (cf. ch. 6).

It is also a merit of Sourvinou-Inwood's interpretation that it views the production of ritual textiles within the *chaîne opératoire*, not just assuming that it starts with weaving. She endeavours to include wool purification, combing and spinning in the ritual as well,⁴¹ and suggests that the wool for the next year's *pe-*

---

37 Robertson 2004, 120–121 discusses the fleece (*koidion*) and *khitōn* (doubted by Roberson).
38 Sourvinou-Inwood 2011, 178.
39 Sourvinou-Inwood 2011, 203.
40 Sourvinou-Inwood 2011, 158: "The reclothing of the statue with the clean peplos would also have been partially evocative of Aglauros first establishing the woollen peplos as the statue's normal dress."
41 Sourvinou-Inwood 2011, 205–212.

plos was distributed, washed and purified during the *Plynteria* festival.⁴² Not incidentally, this was also the month of shearing the sheep.

10.4 The festival of veils and wool?

Right at the beginning of Aristophanes' comedy *Assemblywomen* (verses 17–18), a woman declares:

> ἀνθ' ὧν συνείσει καὶ τὰ νῦν βουλεύματα ὅσα Σκίροις ἔδοξε ταῖς ἐμαῖς φίλαις.
>
> Therefore thou shalt know likewise the whole of the plot that I have planned with my friends, the women, at the festival of the Scirophoria.

The *Skirophoria* was held in last month of the Attic year, *Skirophoriōn* (σκιροφοριών).⁴³ It was celebrated on one day, the 12th or 13th day of the month.⁴⁴ It honoured Athena Skiras for whom there was a shrine near Phaleron. There a variety of theories on the etymology of the festival's name but it may be connected with a σκίρον, a sunshade or canopy held over the priests and priestesses during the festival.⁴⁵ It may also refer to the ritual veiling of a statue, or women veiling themselves or being veiled but this is speculation.⁴⁶ The festival involved a procession from Athens to the shrine by the sea. According to a lexicographer the *Skirophoria* also featured a 'fleece of Zeus'.⁴⁷ Both this and the procession to the sea recall elements of the *Plynteria*, so there seem two parallel festivals with elements in common taking place two weeks apart.⁴⁸

10.5 Time of textiles in religious festivals outside Athens

There is scattered yet consistent evidence that other cities and sanctuaries outside Attica hosted festivals involving ritual weaving, and those weaving rituals had a

---

42 Sourvinou-Inwood 2011, 208–209.
43 Deubner 1956, 40–49. Mikalson 1975, 165–181. Parke 1977, 156–169. Dillon 2001, 124–125. Sourvinou-Inwood 2010, 172–174.
44 Aristophanes, *Eccl.* 834. Mikalson 1975, 170. Parke 1977, 160.
45 The etymology is questioned by Deubner 1956, 48–49.
46 It may also derive from the name of the month.
47 Robertson 2004, 121–122 for sources and bibliography.
48 Sourvinou-Inwood 2011, 174.

significant time dimension in their annual nature. Other festivals celebrated the annual dressing and undressing of statues.[49] These festivals are attested in most parts of the Greek-speaking world and women play a prominent or exclusive role in all of them.

In Amyklai in Laconia lay a sanctuary, probably dedicated to Apollo's daughters, where young girls served as priestesses. In a special room, the *Khitōn*, women wove a *khitōn* for Apollo each year:[50]

ὑφαίνουσι δὲ κατὰ ἔτος αἱ γυναῖκες τῷ Ἀπόλλωνι χιτῶνα τῷ ἐν Ἀμύκλαις, καὶ τὸ οἴκημα ἔνθα ὑφαίνουσι Χιτῶνα ὀνομάζουσιν.

Each year the women weave a khitōn for the Apollo at Amyclae, and they call Khitōn the chamber in which they do their weaving.

There was also a *Hyakinthia* festival in Laconia, a Spartan equivalent of the Panathenaic festival in Athens, celebrating the annual donation to Apollo of a *khitōn* made by local girls.[51] It is possible that the two Laconian festivals of ritual weaving were in fact one and the same.[52] The poet Alcman also writes about a donation of a mantle, *pharos*, to the goddess Orthia in Laconia (*Partheneion* fr. 1, 60).

In Olympia, there was a festival where sixteen respectable women functioned as cult officials and wove a new *peplos* for Hera every four years.[53] They also oversaw annual festivals and could conclude peace treaties and arbitrate in conflicts between cities.

In Boeotia, a Daidala festival was celebrated. It included the annual dressing of a statue of Daidale, a proxy for Hera.[54] After a series of rituals, a wooden statue and its clothes were burnt on an altar. The women participants probably wove the *peplos* for the statue.

Halae in East Locris saw the ritual weaving of a cloak for Athena by women called *petamnyphanteirai*, weavers of **petamn-*, cf. *petasma*.[55]

---

49 See examples in Dillon 2001, 135–136. Reuthner 2006, 291–295. Sourvinou-Inwood 2011, 179–192. Brøns 2016, 183–268.
50 Pausanias 3.16.2. Amendment by MLBN in translation. See also Brelich 1969, 142–143.
51 Calame 1977, 308–318. Brulé 1987, 396.
52 Brelich 1969, 147 and note 89 assumes that the ritual weaving for Apollo at Amyklai took place during the *Hyakinthia* festival.
53 Brelich 1969, 452. Scheid and Svenbro 2003, 17–20. Brulé 1987, 396. Blundell 1998, 20–21. Gartziou-Tatti 2019. Pausanias 5.16.2: διὰ πέμπτου δὲ ὑφαίνουσιν ἔτους τῇ Ἥρᾳ πέπλον αἱ ἓξ καὶ δέκα γυναῖκες (Every fourth year there is woven for Hera a robe by the Sixteen women)
54 Blundell 1998, 22–26.
55 Robertson 2004, 150 note 97 with references. Robertson argues that Locris was the origin of the *peplos* weaving, integrated into the Panathenaic festival.

In Argos there was, according to Callimachos' *Hymn V: On the Bath of Pallas*, a ritual bathing of a statue of Athena. Argos also had a Hera cult with ritual weaving and with multiple references to the female sphere, such as heroines, nymphs, queen Amyone and others.[56]

Finally, some pastoral festivals appear to have been rooted in the seasonal requirements of textile production, such as the annual shearing of sheep in late spring /early summer and purification rites associated with shepherding. One imagines that annual festivals may have taken place around the times of the flax harvest, fibre processing and wool shearing, especially in the countryside.[57] However, there are no sources on this topic from ancient Greece, perhaps because many ancient written sources relate to urban life. Such festivals are, however, attested in Roman sources,[58] Mary Beard rightly warns, however, that even if there are some traditional agricultural temporalities associated with festivals, they cannot explain their full ritual meaning, especially in urban settings.[59]

10.6 The cyclic time of textile production in religious festivals

To summarise in the case of Athens for which we have most evidence, festivals with textile-related content were part of cyclic cult, and women played an essential role in all of them. Textile-related festivals in Attica occurred throughout the

---

56 Callimachos, *Aetia* Book 3, 66 (= Oxyrhynchus papyrus; Meletius, *On the Nature of Man*): "Heroines, descendants of the daughter of Iasus. Water nymph of Poseidon, nor is it right for those who must weave the holy cloak of Hera to stand by the weavers' rods before sitting upon the holy rock around which you flow, and pouring your water over their heads. Queen Amymone and dear Physadea, Hippe and Automate, hail most ancient dwelling places of the nymphs, and may you flow on, shining Pelasgian girls."
The editor explains that Pelasgian here refers to Argive. See also Dillon 2001, 132.
57 In Locris was a month called *Pokios* from *pokos*, 'fleece', and according to Chantraine, s.v. πέκω, it was the month of sheep shearing. Nilsson 1920, 175, 234, 287, gives examples from his comparative ethnographical and terminological research of months connected with flax: an inscriptional calendar dated ca. 600 CE from Gezer includes a month for pulling the flax; the Chuvash people, a Turkic ethnic group, named a month the 'flax month'; the time around October was 'time of flax-preparing' in East Slavic languages.
58 The Roman *Parilia* festival for the purification of sheep on April 21 marks an agricultural event and the foundation of Rome. On this day, shepherds cleaned out sheep pens and purified their space to protect the flocks. See Beard 1987.
59 Beard 1987, 2: "For by locating the 'meaning' of the rituals in the primitive community of peasant farmers, the traditional approaches make it hard to understand the practice of those rituals in the complex urban society of the historical periods, several centuries later."

year but most were held in summer. The year started in late *Hekatombaion* (July–August) with the Panathenaic festival and the offering of a *peplos* to Athena Polias. Then in the *Pyanepsion* month (October–November), the *Chalkeia* festival celebrated Athena Ergane and marked the warping and the beginning of weaving of the *peplos*. The weaving would take nine months so that the *peplos* was completed for the Panathenaic festival of the following summer. The month of *Thargelion* (May–June) had the *Plynteria* and *Kallynteria* festivals celebrating the cleaning of Athena's statue and clothing. The *Arrhēphoria* festival perhaps celebrated weavers and probably took place in the month of *Skirophorion* (June–July). The *Skiraphoria* festival took place in the same month and included a textile in the form of a canopy, sunshade or veil (σκίρον) and wool.

Scholars generally struggle to discern a coherent pattern from the religious calendar which involved the annual production of a *peplos*, different cycles of diverse festivals and divergent chronologies. The complexity is vast, and perhaps there was never a consistent system. Robertson, who proposes a chronological difference between the older *Plynteria* and *Kallynteria* festivals and the Panathenaic festival as an innovation, offers a model that illustrates the complexity:

> The two customs, old and new, can be reconciled if, every fourth year at the Callynteria, near the end of the following May, the Panathenaic *peplos* – which has been folded up and laid away in the interval – is now ceremonially draped on the statue, taking the place of the one that has been washed. (...). At the Plynteria and Callynteria of the next three years it is washed and placed again on the statue in the good old way. In the fourth year, however, which is another Panathenaic year, it is washed and removed and laid away permanently, and the new *peplos* of the past July is placed in the statue. Twice in the same cycle – in the year following the Panathenaic year and again in the second year after that – a new mantle is both presented and placed on the statue at the Callynteria, and at the same time the previous mantle is removed and laid away permanently. Very likely this is meant to reinforce the twining of the two customs.[60]

Let us consider this cyclical calendar from the perspective of textile production with the *chaîne opératoire* in mind: it seems surprising to start the *peplos* manufacture by warping and weaving, factoring out the long processes of fibre preparation, spinning and the dyeing of yarns. Yarn is required for warping, and for a tapestry weave as complex as Athena's *peplos* with images of the battle of Giants, many different yarns would need to be prepared. So, where is the time allocated for these tasks? It is tempting to suggest that a new round of fibre work and spinning began immediately after the offering of a finished *peplos* at the Panathenaic festival in *Hekatombaion* (July–August), or perhaps even earlier at the *Arrephoria*

---

60 Robertson 2004, 149.

festival in the *Skirophorion* month (June–July) when new *arrhēphoroi* girls were recruited and may have been given the tasks. We know from a late decree dated around 100 BCE that girls received praise for having worked the wool (ἐργάζεσθαι τὰ ἔρια),[61] which, if understood literally, would include fibre work, combing and spinning before weaving. This would potentially make the months from June to November the time of spinning and fibre preparation, so that the yarn was ready for warping at the *Chalkeia* festival. In this way, the same girls and women would follow through all the processes from fleece to yarn and finally to the finished *peplos*. My model has the advantage of reflecting the experience of craftspersons that it is an advantage that the wool combers and spinners know for what purpose the yarn is spun and have the final result in mind. Sourvinou-Inwood proposes a slightly different model for the organisation of work and division of labour: to ensure continuity and coherence, one cohort of ritual textile workers would weave a *peplos* and then spin the yarn so it was ready for the next cohort, who would then weave with these yarns before spinning the yarn for the *peplos* the year after.[62] This interpretation has the advantage of emphasising continuity and collaboration, but it ignores some of the practicalities and preferences of textile craft. I believe weavers would prefer to finish their own tapestry and would identify with it, doing their best to make their piece unique, from the spun yarns to the last knots.[63]

In conclusion, there are some questions which it would be welcome to have answers to. Did the four known weaving-related festivals stem from a common tradition, taking inspiration from each other, or did they develop independently?[64] Was ritual weaving exceptional in Greek religion or much more practiced than the ancient written sources suggest? As festivals and rituals for women, they may be underrepresented in the source material. We saw that the frequency of ritual weaving in Athens – every year or every four years, or both – is debated

---

61 Aleshire and Lambert 2003, 75–76. They understand "working wool" as weaving.
62 Sourvinou-Inwood 2011, 212: "Though it may appear logical in our eyes that it should be those maidens who would use the wool who should receive it, in ritual logic a practice in which one year's group of Ergastinai received and washed the wool for next year's weaving would have been ritually significant: it would have helped convey the notion of continuity and the cyclic nature of the enterprise."
63 Sourvinou-Inwood 2011, 213: "each year-crop would take over and continue the weaving begun by its predecessors, receive the new wool and wash it, complete the peplos and process at the Panathenaia, and then at some point spin the wool and then, after the Chalkeia, begin the weaving of next year's peplos that would be completed by their successors, after they themselves had finished their service and been honored."
64 Brelich 1969, 322 and note 38. Sourvinou-Inwood 2011, 281–286 emphasise that the Panathenaic and Plynteria festivals belong together.

among scholars. The annual nature of ritual weaving in Laconia and Boeotia would strengthen the argument of an annual weaving ritual at Athens, while the ritual weaving for Hera in Olympia every four year would support the argument for longer pauses between the weaving rituals. I would suggest that weaving took place annually, at every Panathenaic festival, and plausibly on a grander scale every four years for the Great Panathenaic festival. This would best explain the other Attic textile-related festivals, especially the annual *Chalkeia* warping festival which only makes sense if followed by weaving.

These festivals combined the short timespan of the celebration day or days with annual cycles and even longer timespans.

11 Woven lifetime – textiles as time capsules of memories in Greek tragedy

In ancient Greek literature, textiles and clothing, in particular, were a means of establishing, strengthening and confirming family and emotional ties. Family history was woven into the social fabric in the form of dowry textiles from the wife's family and the domestic household textiles of beds and living spaces: cushions, mattresses, blankets and curtains, rugs and carpets, or woven ornamental heritage wall-hangings with in-woven motifs. On a much smaller and more intimate scale, it could be in the form of a little girl's first sample of weaving with carefully selected yarns, designs and motifs.

Such fabrics sometimes play a significant role in Greek tragedy as tokens of memory and of family bonds because they bridge time. Children could be reunited with their parents or brothers with their sisters through textiles, even after many years. In four tragedies of the 5th century BCE – *Libation Bearers* by Aischylos, and *Ion*, *Electra* and *Iphigenia in Tauris* by Euripides – recognition scenes used textiles as tokens of identity across time.

11.1 The reunion of brother and sister through a tapestry

The *Oresteia*, a trilogy by Aischylos performed in 458 BCE, is a family drama set in the aftermath of the Trojan War. It tells of the murder of Agamemnon by his wife Klytemnestra following his return from Troy, and the events that unfold subsequently. Agamemnon's son Orestes returns home from exile years afterwards in order to kill his mother in revenge and Aischylos describes how Orestes is reunited with his sister Electra.

Aischylos tells the story as follows: Electra sits mourning at her father's grave and does not recognize Orestes as her brother. She is puzzled, however, by a lock of hair recently deposited on the grave because it resembles her own. She then wonders about a footprint which also resembles her own.[1] The final and decisive proof of Orestes' identity, however, is a textile (*hyphasma*):[2] Orestes shows Electra

---

[1] It is amusing to follow the very serious and academic discussions about the validity of the foot size as proof of identity, see Lloyd-Jones 1961. Fitton Brown 1961. Burkert 1963. Solmsen 1967. Roux 1974. Jouanna 1977.

[2] Jouanna 1977, 190: "Les deux premiers signes n'ont pas en fait la même fonction que le troisième. Les deux premiers ne sont que des indices qui préparent l'arrivée d'Oreste; le troisième est une preuve que le personnage arrivé est bien Oreste." As Wilamowitz-Möllendorf 1901,

his most precious possession (cf. Fig. 11), a piece of tapestry with a motif of a wild animal woven into it that Elektra herself had woven for him as a little girl.³ In the following passage, Orestes addresses his sister (Aischylos, *Libation Bearers* 225–234):

> Ὀρέστης
> αὐτὸν μὲν οὖν ὁρῶσα δυσμαθεῖς ἐμέ· κουρὰν δ' ἰδοῦσα τήνδε κηδείου τριχὸς ἰχνοσκοποῦσά τ' ἐν στίβοισι τοῖς ἐμοῖς ἀνεπτερώθης κἀδόκεις ὁρᾶν ἐμέ. σκέψαι τομῇ προσθεῖσα βόστρυχον τριχὸς σαυτῆς ἀδελφοῦ σύμμετρον τῷ σῷ κάρᾳ. ἰδοῦ δ' ὕφασμα τοῦτο, σῆς ἔργον χερός, σπάθης τε πληγὰς ἠδὲ θήρειον γραφήν.

> Orestes: So when you see me in person you're reluctant to recognize me – whereas when you saw this cut lock of mourning, [picking the lock of hair up from the tomb] and when you were examining the tracks of my feet, your heart took wing and you imagined you could see me. [Handing the lock to Electra, and slinging his travelling hat behind his neck] Put the lock of hair next to the place it was cut from, and take a look: it's your own brother's, and it matches that of your own head. And look at this piece of weaving, the work of your hands, the strokes of the batten and the picture of a beast.

11.2 The refusal to recognise a brother from his clothing

A generation later, in another Greek tragedy, *Electra*, Euripides copies Aischylos' recognition scene with a certain irony. In his play, Electra has been married off to a peasant and lives a simple life outside the palace. Her mourning of her father's death and her anger against her mother have led Electra to wear rags and refuse to wash. She exclaims (Euripides, *Electra* 184–185):

> σκέψαι μου πιναρὰν κόμαν καὶ τρύχη τάδ' ἐμῶν πέπλων
>
> Look at my filthy hair and these tatters that are my clothes

This reference to her ragged and old clothes is repeated later in the play (verses 503–504).⁴

147, noted dryly: "er bewirkt die Identifikation durch ein Beweisstück, das auch ein Rationalist gelten lassen muss: sein Mantel ist von Elektra selbst gearbeitet."
3 Lloyd-Jones 1961, 171, assumes that Orestes had intentionally brought the woven cloth with him to prove his identity. Solmsen 1967, 36, suggests that Orestes wears a garment woven by Electra. Roux 1974, 42, 46, assumes that the fabric is embroidered. All these interpretations are possible but not directly supported by the text. The idea that the *hyphasma* is a piece of embroidery is, however, difficult to reconcile with the passage's references to weaving and the *kerkis* and the fact that embroidery was an uncommon textile technique in ancient Greece.
4 Note the uncertainties about this passage.

Figure 11: Orestes and Elektra before their family fell apart or after their reunification. He is naked and she is well-dressed. Copy of original from 1st century BCE to 1st century CE. Plaster cast, circa 1900. Ithaca, Cornell Cast Collection, inv. Sage no. 97.
Photo: © Cornell Cast Collection, https://digital.library.cornell.edu/catalog/ss:173020 (last access 04.07.2025).

11.2 The refusal to recognise a brother from his clothing

Ἠλέκτρα
τί δ', ὦ γεραιέ, διάβροχον τόδ' ὄμμ' ἔχεις; μῶν τἀμὰ διὰ χρόνου σ'ἀνέμνησαν κακὰ <τηλουρὸς οἶκος καὶ πέπλων ἐμῶν ῥάκη>;

Electra: Why, old sir, is your face wet with tears? Has <the sight of this lonely dwelling and my ragged clothing> after so long a time reminded you of my troubles?

An old palace servant brings Electra news that her brother Orestes might be back but she rejects the possible evidence that this is the case. She argues that colour of hair or size of feet are not valid proofs of a biological tie. She points out that she was too young to weave when Orestes escaped, and that even if she had woven a garment for him at the time, it would now be too small for him. This is all clearly a caricature of Aischylos' recognition scene. Here is the relevant passage where Electra addresses the old servant (verses 524–544):[5]

Ἠλέκτρα
οὐκ ἄξι' ἀνδρός, ὦ γέρον, σοφοῦ λέγεις, εἰ κρυπτὸν ἐς γῆν τήν δ'ἂν Αἰγίσθου φόβῳδοκεῖς ἀδελφὸν τὸν ἐμὸν εὐθαρσῆ μολεῖν. ἔπειτα χαίτης πῶς συνοίσεται πλόκος, ὁ μὲν παλαίστραις ἀνδρὸς εὐγενοῦς τραφείς, ὁ δὲ κτενισμοῖς θῆλυς; ἀλλ' ἀμήχανον. πολλοῖς δ' ἂν εὕροις βοστρύχους ὁμοπτέρους καὶ μὴ γεγῶσιν αἵματος ταὐτοῦ, γέρον.

Πρέσβυς
σὺ δ' εἰς ἴχνος βᾶσ'ἀρβύλης σκέψαι βάσιν εἰ σύμμετρος σῷ ποδὶ γενήσεται, τέκνον.

Ἠλέκτρα
πῶς δ' ἂν γένοιτ' ἂν ἐν κραταιλέῳ πέδῳ γαίας ποδῶν ἔκμακτρον; εἰ δ' ἔστιν τόδε, δυοῖν ἀδελφοῖν ποὺς ἂν οὐ γένοιτ' ἴσος ἀνδρός τε καὶ γυναικός, ἀλλ' ἄρσην κρατεῖ.

Πρέσβυς
οὐκ ἔστιν, εἰ καὶ γῆν κασίγνητος μόλοι, κερκίδος ὅτῳ γνοίης ἂν ἐξύφασμα σῆς, ἐν ᾧ ποτ' αὐτὸν ἐξέκλεψα μὴ θανεῖν;

Ἠλέκτρα
οὐκ οἶσθ', Ὀρέστης ἡνίκ' ἐκπίπτει χθονός, νέαν μ' ἔτ' οὖσαν; εἰ δὲ κἄκρεκον πέπλους, πῶς ἂν τότ' ὢν παῖς ταὐτὰ νῦν ἔχοι φάρη, εἰ μὴ ξυναύξοινθ' οἱ πέπλοι τῷ σώματι;

Electra: What you say, old sir, is unworthy of a wise man if you imagine that my brave brother would come to this land in secret because he feared Aegisthus. Furthermore, how should his hair be like mine since his was grown in the wrestling schools of young noblemen while mine is feminine and combed? It is impossible. You will find that many people possess locks that are similar, old man, who are not of the same blood.

Old man: Step into his footprint and see whether the mark of his boot agrees with your foot, my child.

---

5 Lines 517–544 are perhaps an interpolation.

Electra: But how could a footprint be made on ground well-stoned? And if there is one, the feet of siblings will not be of equal size when one is male and the other female: the male will be larger.

Old man: But if in fact your brother should come to this land, is there not some bit of your weaving by which you could recognize him, weaving in which I spirited him away from death?

Electra: Do you not know that when Orestes went into exile I was still a child? And even if I had been weaving clothes, how could a man who was a child at that time be wearing the same garments unless his clothing were to grow with his body?

It will be a scar that reveals Orestes' identity to Electra (verse 572), Euripides thereby recalling the Homeric recognition of Odysseus's scar by his wet-nurse.

11.3 A second reunion of a brother and a sister by means of pieces of tapestry

In Euripides' play *Iphigenia in Tauris*, performed in 405 BCE, the recognition scene involves Orestes and his other sister Iphigenia. Orestes believes Iphigeneia has been slain by their father Agamemnon before his departure for Troy, but instead she has survived and lives as a priestess of Artemis in Tauris. The siblings do not recognize each other until Orestes describes two pieces of tapestry that Iphigenia had woven as a child and which he remembers from his childhood in Argos. The tapestries depict crucial events in their family history such as the conflict between their father Atreus and their uncle Thyestes over a golden lamb. They thereby illustrate the family's history and legitimacy as well as the biological ties and relationship between the siblings Orestes and Iphigenia. In this passage, Orestes tries to convince Iphigeneia that he really is her brother and eventually succeeds thanks to the memories stored in the weave of the tapestries (verses 798–817):

Ἰφιγένεια
ξέν', οὐ δικαίως τῆς θεοῦ τὴν πρόσπολον χραίνεις ἀθίκτοις περιβαλὼν πέπλοις χέρα.

Ὀρέστης
ὦ συγκασιγνήτη τε κἀκ ταὐτοῦ πατρὸς Ἀγαμέμνονος γεγῶσα, μή μ' ἀποστρέφου, ἔχουσ' ἀδελφόν, οὐ δοκοῦσ' ἕξειν ποτέ.

Ἰφιγένεια
ἐγώ σ' ἀδελφὸν τὸν ἐμόν; οὐ παύσῃ λέγων; τό τ' Ἄργος αὐτοῦ μεστὸν ἥ τε Ναυπλία.

Ὀρέστης
οὐκ ἔστ' ἐκεῖ σός, ὦ τάλαινα, σύγγονος.

11.3 A second reunion of a brother and a sister by means of pieces of tapestry

Ἰφιγένεια
ἀλλ' ἡ Λάκαινα Τυνδαρίς σ' ἐγείνατο;

Ὀρέστης
Πέλοπός γε παιδὶ παιδός, οὗ 'κπέφυκ' ἐγώ.

Ἰφιγένεια
τί φής; ἔχεις τι τῶνδέ μοι τεκμήριον;

Ὀρέστης
ἔχω· πατρῴων ἐκ δόμων τι πυνθάνου.

Ἰφιγένεια
οὔκουν λέγειν μὲν χρὴ σέ, μανθάνειν δ' ἐμέ;

Ὀρέστης
λέγοιμ' ἂν ἀκοῇ πρῶτον Ἠλέκτρας τάδε· Ἀτρέως Θυέστου τ' οἶσθα γενομένην ἔριν;

Ἰφιγένεια
ἤκουσα· χρυσῆς ἀρνὸς ἦν νείκη πέρι.

Ὀρέστης
ταῦτ' οὖν ὑφήνασ' οἶσθ' ἐν εὐπήνοις ὑφαῖς;

Ἰφιγένεια
ὦ φίλτατ', ἐγγὺς τῶν ἐμῶν χρίμπτῃ φρενῶν.

Ὀρέστης
εἰκώ τ' ἐν ἱστοῖς ἡλίου μετάστασιν;

Ἰφιγένεια
ὕφηνα καὶ τόδ' εἶδος εὐμίτοις πλοκαῖς.

Iphigenia: Stranger, it is not right for you to defile the servant of the goddess, putting your arms about her inviolate clothing!

Orestes: Sister, born from the same father Agamemnon, do not turn away from me: you have your brother though you never expected to have him again!

Iphigenia: I have my brother? Won't you stop this talk? It is Argos and Nauplia that hold him.

Orestes: Poor woman, your brother is not there.

Iphigenia: But did the Spartan daughter of Tyndareus bear you?

Orestes: Yes, to Pelops' grandson, my father.

Iphigenia: What? Do you have some proof of this for me?

Orestes: I have: ask me something about our father's house.

Iphigenia: Should you not rather speak, while I listen?

Orestes: I will tell you first what I heard from Electra. Do you know of the strife that occurred between Atreus and Thyestes?

Iphigenia: I have heard about it: the quarrel concerned a golden lamb.

Orestes: Then do you remember weaving this tale upon cloth of fine thread?

Iphigenia: Dear man, how near you touch my memory!

Orestes: And do you remember weaving the story of the sun's change of course?

Iphigenia: This story too I wove in the lovely tapestry.

11.4 A reunion of a mother and her son through a tapestry

Euripides narrates another story in which textiles transcend time and generations. The tragedy *Ion* was performed ca. 418 BCE and involves the foundling child Ion, who grew up as a temple servant in Delphi. He was the product of Apollo's encounter with the mortal princess Creusa.

At the beginning of the tragedy, we learn that the baby had been found wrapped in soft and luxurious textiles (*khlidē*) (verse 26). The god Hermes had rescued the infant in his cradle (*aggos*) and baby-clothes (*sparganon:* a strip of cloth for swaddling), and had brought him to Apollo's temple at Delphi (verse 32). Hermes declares that he had brought the woven (*plektos*) basket (*kytos*) (verse 37). In the story, therefore, the baby is wrapped, protected and cared for in woven and plaited baskets and fabrics, and there is probably also a literary reference to baby Erichthonios in his basket (cf. ch. 2.2).

Later in the tragedy, a woman (Creusa), tells him she is his mother, and Ion learns that the temple still holds the textiles he was wrapped in when he was found as a baby. The woman claims that among them is a tapestry with motifs that she, his birth mother, had woven when she was a young girl. The textiles, along with an olive branch, were intended to prove his identity as the true descendant and successor of the king of Athens. Ion is still reluctant to believe the story of his alleged mother.

Creusa tries to convince Ion that she is his mother by describing the items, textiles and swaddling clothes[6] she had wrapped him in as a baby and that had been stored for all these years in the temple: *peploi* (verse 955) and cloths she had woven as a young girl (*parthenōn hyphasmata*), of which one piece is unfinished (*ou teleon*). She recalls that this was an exercise or weaving sample she had made for her weaving training (*ekdidagma kerkidos*) and that it was her maiden

---

[6] Thomson 1972, 48: "In ancient Greece the new born child was wrapped in swaddling bands and adorned with amulets such as necklaces and rings. These articles were known collectively as *gnorísmata*, or tokens, because they were sufficiently distinctive to identify the child." See also Martin 2015.

loom work (*histōn partheneuma tōn emōn*). She also gives some precise textile technical details, for example, the in-woven motif of a Gorgon head in the middle of the warp (*en mesoisin ētriois*).[7] *Ion*, verses 1417–1425:

Κρέουσα
σκέψασθ᾽ ὃ παῖς ποτ᾽ οὖσ᾽ ὕφασμ᾽ ὕφην᾽ ἐγώ.

Ἴων
ποῖόν τι; πολλὰ παρθένων ὑφάσματα.

Κρέουσα
οὐ τέλεον, οἷον δ᾽ ἐκδίδαγμα κερκίδος.

Ἴων
μορφὴν ἔχον τίν᾽· ὥς με μὴ ταύτῃ λάβῃς.

Κρέουσα
Γοργὼ μὲν ἐν μέσοισιν ἠτρίοις πέπλων.

Ἴων
ὦ Ζεῦ, τίς ἡμᾶς ἐκκυνηγετεῖ πότμος;

Κρέουσα
κεκρασπέδωται δ᾽ ὄφεσιν αἰγίδος τρόπον.

Ἴων
ἰδού· τόδ᾽ ἔσθ᾽ ὕφασμα θέσφαθ᾽ ὡς εὑρίσκομεν.

Κρέουσα
ὦ χρόνιον ἱστῶν παρθένευμα τῶν ἐμῶν.

Creusa: See, all of you, the weaving I wove as a girl.

Ion: What kind of weaving? Maidens weave many things.

Creusa: One piece is not finished: you could call it my shuttle's apprentice work.

Ion: And its design? Don't try to trick me here!

Creusa: In the middle of the warp it has a Gorgon.

Ion: O Zeus, what is this fate that tracks me down?

Creusa: And it is fringed with serpents like an aegis.

Ion: [Holding it up] See! Here is the weaving! I find you speak the truth!

Creusa: O maiden loomwork, woven so long ago!

By means of the old textiles, woven perhaps twenty to twenty-five years earlier, Ion finds his birth mother and his identity, and the world is put right.

---

7 Loeb translation with a few alterations by MLBN.

To sum up: the four plays, *Libation Bearers* by Aischylos and *Electra*, *Ion* and *Iphigenia in Tauris* by Euripides, are divided by approximately 50 years yet mirror a common *topos* of recognition via weaving done by a girl in her childhood. In each of the plays, the textiles are about 10–20 years of age. It seems that Aischylos' play was so commonly known that two generations later, Euripides could caricature Aischylos' recognition scene and the audience would know the reference and why this was funny.[8] In *Libation Bearers*, the recognition scene sets off the plot and comes at the beginning of the play, in *Electra* and in *Iphigenia in Tauris* it is in the middle, while in *Ion*, the recognition scene is touched upon right at the start and again at the end of the play. In all four tragedies, the recognition sets off the narrative and gives the story a new twist.[9] In *Libation Bearers*,[10] *Ion* and *Iphigenia in Tauris*, it is a woven piece of cloth (*hyphasma*) that is key to the plot, not necessarily a garment. In the parody scene in *Electra*, it is garments (*peploi*), hence the mockery about whether *Orestes* could still fit into clothes made for him years earlier.

---

[8] Note that the authenticity of the recognition scenes in *Libation Bearers* and *Electra* have been questioned, especially for stylistic reasons. See the discussion in Lloyd-Jones 1961. Fitton Brown 1961 defends the authenticity of the passages.

[9] Scholars disagree about how far Orestes is depicted as having arrived with the intention of using a woven 'proof' of his identity or whether it is implied that this happened by accident. Lloyd-Jones 1961, 171: "Orestes goes on to produce a piece of cloth woven by Electra herself, which he had brought with him as a proof of his identity."

[10] *Pace* Fitton Brown 1961, 368, who calls the *hyphasma* in *Libation Bearers* a garment: "Orestes goes on to tell Electra to fit the lock to the place from which it was cut, and as further proof he shows her a garment she wove for him before his exile. (...) All Aeschylus implies is that when Orestes was sent away from home he was so nearly full-grown that seven years later he could still wear the same garment (whichever it was)." Likewise Thomson 1966, vol. I, 34: "[he] offers proof – a garment she wove for him before he left home."

12 Dress changes

Studies of ancient dress are closely linked to ideas within classical archaeology and art history of sequences and developments. Generally, there is scholarly agreement that dress practices changed slowly, over long periods of time. Ancient dress is articulated around concepts of types and typologies that scaffold chronologies over time. A testimony of this is Margarete Bieber's systematic study from 1934 *Entwicklungsgeschichte der griechischen Tracht.*

Significant changes have been noted in the dress of men and women in ancient Greek sculpture and in depictions of dress on pottery. This poses the methodological challenge of determining how far art reflected everyday reality. A few ancient texts describe abrupt dress changes, but the underlying tenet in ancient history is to consider dress changes as slow and mirroring cultural or political changes more than fashion, with the notable exception of the Athenian politician and 'fashionista' Alcibiades. Dress changes are mostly perceived as coming from outside (the East) and are seen as politically motivated. Let us explore some of the developments that occurred over time.

12.1 The change from peplos to khitōn in women's clothing in Archaic Greece

Female dress is depicted in ancient sculpture, in vase painting and is discussed in ancient texts. It undergoes clear changes in the Archaic and Classical periods.

In Greek sculpture, the dress of female figures changed in the 6th century from a long garment pinned on the shoulders to a garment stitched or buttoned on the shoulders.[1] This was probably the same change described by Herodotus (5.87–88) who speaks of a radical and sudden alteration in dress among Athenian women. This shift marks a time shift, as the pinned wool dress sometimes called a *peplos* fell out of use around the middle of the 6th century BCE, and instead women began to wear the Ionian linen *khitōn*. According to Herodotus, this was not due to a simple change of fashion, but was brought about by a political act connected to a tragic event: in a catastrophic battle on the island of Aegina, all Athenian soldiers were killed, except one. This lone soldier made it back to Athens, but was then brutally attacked by the widows of his dead comrades who stabbed him to death with their dress-pins (Hdt. 5.87):

---

[1] Lee 2003, 122.

κομισθεὶς ἄρα ἐς τὰς Ἀθήνας ἀπήγγελλε τὸ πάθος· πυθομένας δὲ τὰς γυναῖκας τῶν ἐπ' Αἴγιναν στρατευσαμένων ἀνδρῶν, δεινόν τι ποιησαμένας κεῖνον μοῦνον ἐξ ἁπάντων σωθῆναι, πέριξ τὸν ἄνθρωπον τοῦτον λαβούσας καὶ κεντεύσας τῇσι περόνῃσι τῶν ἱματίων εἰρωτᾶν ἑκάστην αὐτέων ὅκου εἴη ὁ ἑωυτῆς ἀνήρ.

It would seem that he made his way to Athens and told of the mishap; and when this was known (it is said) to the wives of the men who had gone to attack Aegina, they were very angry that he alone should be safe out of all, and they gathered round him and stabbed him with the dress-pins of their garments, each asking him "where her man was".

There was outrage across Greece and as a consequence, the Athenian authorities decided to punish the Athenian women by forbidding them to wear a dress held by dress-pins (Hdt. 5.88).

Καὶ τοῦτον μὲν οὕτω διαφθαρῆναι, Ἀθηναίοισι δὲ ἔτι τοῦ πάθεος δεινότερόν τι δόξαι εἶναι τὸ τῶν γυναικῶν ἔργον. ἄλλῳ μὲν δὴ οὐκ ἔχειν ὅτεῳ ζημιώσωσι τὰς γυναῖκας, τὴν δὲ ἐσθῆτα μετέβαλον αὐτέων ἐς τὴν Ἰάδα· ἐφόρεον γὰρ δὴ πρὸ τοῦ αἱ τῶν Ἀθηναίων γυναῖκες ἐσθῆτα Δωρίδα, τῇ Κορινθίῃ παραπλησιωτάτην· μετέβαλον ὦν ἐς τὸν λίνεον κιθῶνα, ἵνα δὴ περόνῃσι μὴ χρέωνται. ἔστι δὲ ἀληθέι λόγῳ χρεωμένοισι οὐκ Ἰὰς αὕτη ἡ ἐσθὴς τὸ παλαιὸν ἀλλὰ Κάειρα, ἐπεὶ ἥ γε Ἑλληνικὴ ἐσθὴς πᾶσα ἡ ἀρχαίη τῶν γυναικῶν ἡ αὐτὴ ἦν τὴν νῦν Δωρίδα καλέομεν.

Thus was this man done to death; and this deed of their women seemed to the Athenians to be yet more dreadful than their misfortune. They could find, it is said, no other way to punish the women; but they changed their dress to the Ionian fashion; for till then the Athenian women had worn Dorian dress, very like to the Corinthian; it was changed, therefore, to the linen tunic, that so they might have no dress-pins to use. But if the truth be told, this dress is not in its origin Ionian, but Carian; for in Hellas itself all the women's dress in ancient times was the same as that which we now call Dorian.

The authorities in Argos and Aegina stipulated that dress-pins should be halved in length and that dress-pins should be dedicated to sanctuaries (Hdt. 5.88):

τοῖσι δὲ Ἀργείοισι καὶ τοῖσι Αἰγινήτῃσι καὶ πρὸς ταῦτα ἔτι τόδε ποιῆσαι νόμον εἶναι παρὰ σφίσι ἑκατέροισι τὰς περόνας ἡμιολίας ποιέεσθαι τοῦ τότε κατεστεῶτος μέτρου, καὶ ἐς τὸ ἱρὸν τῶν θεῶν τουτέων περόνας μάλιστα ἀνατιθέναι τὰς γυναῖκας

As for the Argives and Aeginetans, this was the reason of their even making a law for each of their nations that their dress-pins should be made half as long again as the measure then customary, and that dress-pins in especial should be dedicated by their women in the temple of those goddesses

These passages are often used to underpin textually the change from the *peplos* to the *khitōn* as was observed in Greek sculpture around 550 BCE. However, as Mirelle Lee observed, these passages never use the dress term *peplos*.² Herodotus instead speaks of clothing as *himatia*, *khitōns* and *esthēta*, in the form of Dorian, Carian or Ionian clothing. Therefore, while the equation of the *peplos* with the old Dorian female dress is a plausible interpretation, it is not demonstrated in the sources. An additional methodological challenge is that the sculpture of dressed women comes from many places and many different dates in Greece while Herodotus' text has a narrow scope of Athens, Argos and Aegina.

12.2 From khitōn and back to peplos in the 5th century BCE: dress of the 'good old days'

In early Classical sculpture around 480–450 BCE, the pinned (Dorian) *peplos* type reappeared as female dress.³ This goes unnoticed in Herodotus and Thucydides, despite the fact that they would have witnessed it in their own lifetime.⁴ The reason is probably that the return to the *peplos* did not happen in daily life, for real women, but in cult, art, and sculpture, a symbolic return of an old garment type which conveyed nostalgia about a past 'ideal' world.

The early Classical *peplophoros* figure is, according to Mirellie Lee, "an iconographic construct of a female figure wearing a historical garment that was remembered from earlier times, perhaps through its continued ritual use."⁵ Modern scholars believe that the return of the *peplos* only happened in art and not in the Athenian women's wardrobes, not least because dress-pins are rarely found in excavations and also rarely attested in iconography.⁶ Laura Gawlinski calls such dress "fossilized fashion," since it uses dress types that were no longer worn by the general population.⁷ The *peplos* became a ceremonial garment to wear when remembering the 'good old days'.⁸

---

2 Lee 2003, 123. Lee 2005, 57.
3 Lee 2003, 118, the *peplos* being "the hallmark of the Severe style of Greek art, appearing both in sculpture and painting in the decades after the Persian Wars, roughly 480–450 B.C.". See also Lee 2005, 55–58, with examples of changes in female dress in sculpture and also references to cases where dress is not altered: the dress change was not as radical as sometimes assumed.
4 Lee 2005, 57.
5 Lee 2005, 59.
6 Lee 2003, 138; Brøns 2014; Brøns 2016, 421–430.
7 Gawlinksi 2017, 164–167. She gives the example of the dress of the *kanephoros*, literally "the basket bearer", a girl or woman identified in cult iconography carrying a basket on the head and wearing a *peplos*.
8 Lee 2003, 139.

Female clothing must therefore be understood in its wider 'rhetorical' context, which had historical, regional and social meanings. When examining a piece of dress such as the *peplos*, we must carefully consider what meanings were meant to be communicated by it.[9] Further, dress in iconography does not necessarily represent what women actually wore but what the artist felt that women *ought* to be wearing. Mireille Lee concludes that

> the simple pinned garment was remembered from earlier times (perhaps through its continued use in ritual contexts?) and applied to heroic and mythological figures in the art of the fifth century as a means of marking them as historical.[10]

It represents, therefore, an ideological statement rather than a change of dress, one that, moreover, reflects a view of women as being repositories of tradition.

12.3 A new look: the change to more modest male dress in the 5th century BCE

Thucydides (1.6.3–5) states that Athenian men changed dress in the early 5th century from the luxurious long linen *khitōn* to the more modest Lacedaemonian-style wool *himation*.

> ἐν τοῖς πρῶτοι δὲ Ἀθηναῖοι τόν τε σίδηρον κατέθεντο καὶ ἀνειμένη τῇ διαίτῃ ἐς τὸ τρυφερώτερον μετέστησαν. καὶ οἱ πρεσβύτεροι αὐτοῖς τῶν εὐδαιμόνων διὰ τὸ ἁβροδίαιτον οὐ πολὺς χρόνος ἐπειδὴ χιτῶνάς τε λινοῦς ἐπαύσαντο φοροῦντες καὶ χρυσῶν τεττίγων ἐνέρσει κρωβύλον ἀναδούμενοι τῶν ἐν τῇ κεφαλῇ τριχῶν· ἀφ' οὗ καὶ Ἰώνων τοὺς πρεσβυτέρους κατὰ τὸ ξυγγενὲς ἐπὶ πολὺ αὕτη ἡ σκευὴ κατέσχεν. μετρίᾳ δ' αὖ ἐσθῆτι καὶ ἐς τὸν νῦν τρόπον πρῶτοι Λακεδαιμόνιοι ἐχρήσαντο καὶ ἐς τὰ ἄλλα πρὸς τοὺς πολλοὺς οἱ τὰ μείζω κεκτημένοι ἰσοδίαιτοι μάλιστα κατέστησαν.

> But the Athenians were among the very first to lay aside their arms and, adopting an easier mode of life, to change to more luxurious ways. And indeed, owing to this fastidiousness, it was only recently that their older men of the wealthier class gave up wearing tunics of linen and fastening up their hair in a knot held by a golden grasshopper as a brooch; and this same dress obtained for a long time among the elderly men of the Ionians also, owing to their kinship with the Athenians. An unpretentious costume after the present fashion was

---

9 Lee 2005, 59, with earlier references. Lee 2005, 63: "The *peplophoros* may be seen as the embodiment of these traditional values: she is sober, modest in dress, restrained in gesture, a 'good woman' who occupies herself with weaving traditional garments such as the *peplos*. The *peplophoros* is a domesticated woman, her clothed body, tamed."
10 Lee 2003, 139.

first adopted by the Lacedaemonians, and in general their wealthier men took up a style of living that brought them as far as possible into equality with the masses.

This is clearly a statement about modesty and morality and a critique of conspicuous consumption by Athenian citizens.[11] Dress serves here as a marker of political orientation.[12] Some scholars have emphasised Thucydides' point that the change was a sign of a radical shift in the social fabric of the city and a stronger adherence to democracy,[13] though others have connected it to a cultural reaction against eastern and Persian dress styles within the wider context of the Greek-Persian wars.[14]

Thucydides recalls an older and more luxurious dress style that earlier generations of wealthy men had favoured: Ionian style linen clothes and jewellery. If Thucydides remembers seeing men in this dress style in his own time, it must have been in the early 5th century, worn by men born in the middle of the 6th century.[15]

The passage thus reveals wardrobe shifts of three generations of men, from the early warrior dress to a more sophisticated, Ionian-inspired civil dress for the few, and finally to a less conspicuous and simpler dress.

---

11 In the scholarly literature, the perceived gap between the Ionian *khitōn* and the 'Dorian' *peplos* or *himation* was widened by the use of historical linguistics emphasising a Semitic origin for the *khitōn*: see Lee 2003, 120, 132–133. Studniczka 1886, vii: "Der orientalische Leinenrock (…) verbreitete sich auch zu anderen Stämmen und drohte, ähnlich wie die französische Kleidung in moderner Zeit, zu allgemeiner Herrschaft zu gelangen, als die Perserkriege mit dem Bewusstsein des Gegensatzes zwischen hellenischem und barbarischem Wesen auch den Sinn für nationale Tracht belebten und die Wiederaufnahme der auch sonst in abgeschlosseneren Gegenden, besonders aber bei den strengeren Vertretern des dorischen Stammes rein bewahrten und desshalb nach ihm benannten ursprünglichen Kleidung veranlassten."
12 For notions of local Greek ethnic distinction, see Flemestad 2022, 13–14. Hallmann 2023, 493–494 observed changes in men's dress in Late Period Egypt (ca. 747–322 BCE) with Bronze Age dress styles reintroduced and reinvented in the 1st millennium BCE.
13 Geddes 1987.
14 Lee 2003, 120: "The reappearance of the Dorian garment in art of the early 5th century is often explained as a symbol of renewed panhellenic sentiment following the Persian Wars." Lee 2005, 56. See especially Miller 2013 on the emulation of Persian dress style by Greeks and by peoples in Asia Minor.
15 "It is conceivable that the adoption of more elaborate and exotic attire was indeed a new phenomenon around 600 BC". van Wees 2005b, 50.

12.4 Dress changes or fashion changes?

As seen above, Laura Gawlinski speaks of the *peplos* as "fossilized fashion". This raises the question of whether fashion and fashion changes existed in ancient Greece in the sense understood today. Did people change clothes and wardrobes because of taste, status, innovations and wealth, or only for reasons of functionality? Traditionally, scholars have considered fashion a modern, capitalist and western phenomenon, but this has been challenged and fashion phenomena are now explored more broadly, both geographically and across time.[16] In ancient history we have been reluctant to speak of fashion in Greece for many reasons, including a focus on other topics, a certain conservative view of the ancient economy, and the challenges created by our sources.[17] Below I survey two older studies that use fashion as analytical tool to examine dress in ancient Greece.

Max von Boehn published *Antike Mode* in 1927, written for the wider German public.[18] Boehn stated that men adopted new fashion before women.[19] He spoke explicitly of Ionian fashion (*Mode*), in contrast to Dorian traditional dress. He characterized Ionian dress by fashionable pleats and folds and linen garments, in contrast to conservative, 'primitive' woolen dress.[20] He thereby uses fashion to differentiate ethnic groups in antiquity.

---

[16] Craik 1993. Welters and Lillethun 2018.
[17] Droß-Krüpe and Nosch 2016. My own definition of fashion is that it is tied to capitalism, colonial economies, a growing middle class, global trade and consumption, and dress changes in antiquity are due to cultural or political changes and not fashion changes.
[18] Boehn 1927, 18–19: "Die Ionische Mode büßte ihre Anziehungskraft durch die Perserkriege ein. Sie waren von einem großen nationalen Aufschwung begleitet, der sich naturgemäß, wir brauchen ja nur an ähnliche Erscheinungen zu denken die sich in Deutschland 1813, 1870, und 1914 wiederholten, in einer Stellungname gegen den Anzug des Feindes äußerte. Nun auf einmal fühle man, daß die Tracht des fremden Unterdrückers dem eigenen Wesen nicht entsprach und die Reaktion, die gegen die ionische Mode einsetzt, in Athen zuletzt, hat zwar nicht die Stoffe, aber die Schnitte gründlich beseitigt. Die nationale Reform ging von Sparta aus und wurde auch in Attika von völkisch gesinnten unterstützt. Der reiche Athener Kimon gab die fremde Prunktracht auf, um ein gutes Beispiel zu geben. Die dorische Art sich zu kleiden, die ja auch während der Herrschaft der ionischen Mode nur zurückgedrängt und nicht beseitigt worden war, erhält wieder ein gewisses Übergewicht, die Schlichtheit im äußeren Auftreten, welche die Dorier lieben, wird guter Ton und trotz der Abneigung gegen Sparta, mit der die Athener auf die Welt kamen, wird im peloponnesischen Krieg und nachher gerade altspartanische Einfachheit auch in Attika Mode, das bis dahin der Vorplatz des Ionismus gewesen war."
[19] Boehn 1927, 11: "Die Männer sind der neuen Mode zuerst erlegen".
[20] Boehn 1927, 12–13, 17.

Another study of fashion and trends in ancient Greek clothing was written by Detlef Rössler.[21] Rössler suggests identifying the Greek term *tropos* as 'fashion'.[22] He introduced time as a key difference between men's and women's clothing in antiquity: changes in women's clothing was a function simply of time, while changes in men's clothes depended, for Rössler, on social and political position.[23] Rössler advanced the idea that fashion appears as a result of the dismantling of democratic institutions in 5th and 4th centuries BCE city-states. Men were no longer participating in the city-state matters but were either at war or would follow demagogues.[24] A disengagement with democratic norms, particularly from the time of the Peloponnesian War, led to a desire for greater differentiation in men's dress, according to Rössler.[25] Foreign luxurious clothing fuelled a desire to dress extravagantly, a trend led by men such as Alcibiades.[26] Rössler finds evidence in Aristophanes of clothing considered old fashioned.[27] Another explanation of the appearance of fashion was according to him the increased trade and specialization of textile occupations and manufacturers of accessories.[28]

Nevertheless, Rössler eventually concludes that despite the costume changes that he can document in iconography and ancient textiles, ancient Greece did

---

21 Rössler 1974, 1540: "'Mode'-Tendenzen". Rössler's paper is remarkable in several ways. He wrote it as part of a prestigious collective scholarly publication in DDR in the early 1970s.
22 Rössler 1974, 1556.
23 Rössler 1974, 1542: "Weniger als die der Frauen unterlag die Männerkleidung in der Zeit der Poliskrise typologische Wandlungen. Die zweifellos vorhandene, den Denkmälern ablesbaren Unterschiede waren hier in viel geringeren Maß als in der Frauentracht **zeitbedingt**: In ihnen drückte sich vor alle, eine soziale Differenzierung aus." (my emphasis)
24 Rössler 1974, 1555.
25 Rössler 1974, 1540: "Alles das berechtigt uns, scheint mir, von 'Mode'-Tendenzen zu sprechen, die in Griechenland seit dem Peloponnesischen Krieg bemerkbar wurden und sich im 4. Jahrhundert noch verstärkten". Rössler 1974, 1546: "Gerade während des Peloponnesischen Krieges scheint das Tragen gemusterte Gewänder wieder in stärkeren Maße 'modern' geworden zu sein."
26 Rössler 1974, 1550: "Alkibiades war in seiner Jugend der Prototyp eines solches Gecken. Er ging im Langen, bis auf die Füße hängenden Gewand durch die Stadt, sah sich nach Salbenhändlern um, trug einen milesischen Mantel und Purpurkleider." Rössler 1974, 1555.
27 Rössler 1974, 1556. Aristophanes, *The Knights* 1330, in the caricature of a personified Demos-figure wearing old-fashioned clothes: "resplendent in his old-time costume." ἀρχαίῳ σχήματι λαμπρός·
28 Rössler 1974, 1549: "die beginnende Konzentration in manufakturartigen *Ergasterien*." Rössler 1974, 1556: "Spezialisierung und Konzentration im Bereich der Kleiderproduktion."

not have fashion as part of their clothing practice but did have 'trends' that gave impulses to new ways of dressing.[29]

Summing up, fashion as an explanation for dress changes has not gained solid ground in ancient history and other models of explanation are preferred such as trade and politics, or influence from other ethnic groups. This is both due to the disciplinary gap between fashion studies and ancient history but also to the fundamental debates about how to define fashion. Moreover, the question of fashion in antiquity is central to the ongoing debates of how to define the ancient economy, as open or closed, primitive or modern, based on household economy or on capitalism, and situated in a consuming or producing city.[30] Fashion tends to be emphasised by the historians who understand the ancient economy as modern and based on industry, trade and production. Yet, as we have seen, the evidence for dress changes is consistently present in the ancient sources but interpreted in many different ways.

---

29 Rössler 1974, 1554–1555: "Wir haben die meisten dieser Neuerungen unter dem Begriff ‚Modetendenzen' zusammengefasst, weil es sich bei ihnen zum Teil um vorübergehende, also zeitlich abgegrenzte, in jeden Fall aber um Erscheinungen handelt, die – zumindest in diese Ausprägung – den Griechen bis dahin fremd waren. Freilich, zu einer ‚Mode', ist es wie im ganzen Entwicklungsablauf der griechischen Tracht, so auch in dieser Zeit nicht gekommen. Es blieb bei einzeln Ansätzen, bei ‚Tendenzen'."
30 Wagner-Hasel 2011, 203–209. Droß-Krüpe and Nosch 2016.

13 Conclusion – following the threads up to today

In this book, I have surveyed instances of how time and textiles interrelate in ancient Greece. In summary, for textiles and clothing, our reference points are rarely historical dates, years, times of the day, or other points on a linear time scale. Rather, for a woven fabric, there is a beginning and an end and there is an interaction with cultural, physical and social temporalities: the time of the day, daylight, weather, social occasions, and memory of the past. Seasons are an important temporality for textile production as well as for clothing. Overall, textiles enable a longer historical time perspective, the *longue durée*.

I have surveyed the 'metabolism' of garments of antiquity, the relative pace at which a garment might be consumed by wear or the environment; I observed that it could be remarkably slow. Clothing and textiles can be kept for a long time, for reasons of poverty or tradition, or because of emotional bonds. This fact was used on stage in Greek tragedies to visualise and express time and feelings through clothing:

> Euripides makes the time stop: Electra seems to wear the same outfit she wore when her father died, Orestes is wearing the garment she wove when he was only a little baby.[1]

In ancient Greece's polytheist system of beliefs, threads, clothing and weaving are entangled with divinities and heroes and a complex cosmology. Athena was the goddess of weaving in a simplified version of the division of labour in the pantheon. Yet, as we have seen, thread, fabrics, and weaving connect many other divinities and mythological figures, including Pandora, the Moirai, Arachne, Pandrosos, Aglauros, and Erichthonios.

In the Panathenaic festival and in the other weaving festivals, time and textiles converge. The concrete weaving of a *peplos* or a *khitōn* establishes and materialises the intimate bond of sacred space and notions of time.

The time of textiles is rhythm, duration, frequency, periodicity and repetition, as expressed in textile production processes, in dressing rituals, and in weaving festivals.

Rarely does the cyclic and ritual time of weaving intersect with political, historical and linear time. One exception is the weaving in the sanctuary of Hera in Olympia where sixteen respectable local women were appointed to weave and to

---

1 Milanezi 2005, 85 note 13.

act as peace-weavers and arbitrators in a concrete historical political conflict taking place at a specific time in history.

The inventories of clothing in sanctuaries bring time, textiles and women together. The meticulous recording of these worn, old, ragged and frayed garments shows that these textiles were valued and meaningful. It shows that in a sanctuary context, the passage of time does not necessarily diminish the value of garments, even when turned into rags, with their significance and value perhaps even increasing.[2]

One might compare that with the following comment by design scholars about modern clothes: "while some of our clothes wear out before we have tired of them, many of them are 'retired' because of fashion obsolescence. Here a garment's symbolic properties age long before it falls apart physically".[3]

It looks as if the situation was the opposite in ancient Greece: textiles would not 'retire' but be re-used and recycled as long as possible; a garment's symbolic value would increase with age, at least where religion and family history were concerned.

When ancient authors write about old clothes, it is mostly in a negative way to signal someone's low social class or outright poverty.[4] The Greek words for rags even sound like tear:

> In their phonetic structure, *rhakos, tryché, lakis, rhakoma,* and *sparganon* are onomatopoeic of decaying fabrics: their liquids and gutturals mimic the sound of tearing in the interrupted action of decay.[5]

But rags can also be signs of clothing time and clothing life, and in Greek theatre, rags may have a gendered association to women.[6]

Ancient Greek literature illustrates how women use textiles to express what they care for: from the swaddling clothes of babies, some with in-woven motifs, to the shroud of a father-in-law – making textiles was a *love language*.

---

2 The tradition of keeping ancient textile relics continued in the Christian church. Items of clothing that holy men and women had left behind were often regarded as having magical properties. The close skin contact, sweat and blood of saints made textiles a particularly powerful medium of memory, emotion and veneration. The tunic of the canonized French monarch Louis IX, kept in Notre Dame Cathedral, is said to date from the 13th century. In Trier there is a tunic of Christ, supposedly the very tunic that the Roman soldiers cast lots for after the crucifixion.
3 Fletcher and Tham 2004, 258.
4 Milanezi 2005, 75.
5 Milanizi 2005, 76.
6 Milanezi 2005, 75.

Textiles preserve family history and dynastic legacy over generations and even centuries. One can imagine how the walls of the Mycenaean and Trojan palace halls were covered in figurative tapestries, passed down from generation to generation, in particular by the female members of the ruling family. Each tapestry manifested how much time the women had spent on it.

Dress terms change over time in antiquity. It is worth noting that dress in antiquity was identified by ethnic markers, such as Dorian, Ionian, Corinthian, Carian, and Persian. Passages about dress in Athens by Herodotus (5.87–88) and Thucydides (1.6.3–5) have been instrumental in forming modern ideas of ancient Greek ethnic dress types and setting them in a chronological sequence (with Dorian as the older and Ionian the more recent). Scholars of the 19th century attributed a more positive value to the Dorian style of dress that they considered older and more 'authentic' than Ionian.[7] This chronological sequencing and ranking is questioned by dress scholars today, who have especially deconstructed earlier interpretations of the *peplos*.[8] I should add that the idea of an older Dorian *peplos* and *himation* versus a younger Ionian *khitōn* is not supported by studies of textile terminology because the term *khitōn*, *ki-to* in Mycenaen Greek, is attested much earlier than the *peplos*, *esthētes* or *himation*.[9]

Time and textiles are not just bound to the past. In ancient sources, weaving is an activity for the future and for future generations. So let us return to the Homeric poems for some examples. While in captivity in Troy (*Il.* 3.125–128), Helen weaves scenes of the Trojans and the Achaeans fighting. In her tapestry, she records her contemporary history, as she chooses to depict it, but her aim is the future: to narrate (her view of) the war and how it should be remembered.

Penelope, the Homeric weaver par excellence (cf. Fig. 12), weaves for an event which lies in the future: the day her father-in-law passes away (*Od.* 19.138–145). She declares:

κοῦροι, ἐμοὶ μνηστῆρες, ἐπεὶ θάνε δῖος Ὀδυσσεύς,
μίμνετ' ἐπειγόμενοι τὸν ἐμὸν γάμον, εἰς ὅ κε φᾶρος
ἐκτελέσω—μή μοι μεταμώνια νήματ' ὄληται—
Λαέρτῃ ἥρωϊ ταφήϊον, εἰς ὅτε κέν μιν
μοῖρ' ὀλοὴ καθέλῃσι τανηλεγέος θανάτοιο:

---

7 Studniczka 1886, vi: "Die elementaren Formen der classischen Tracht, die auch späterhin unter dem Namen der dorischen ihren vorgeschichtlichen Charakter bewahrte, hatte der edle Arierstamm als Erbgut seiner Völkerfamilie mit nach Hellas gebracht, die Chlaina der Männer und den Peplos der Frauen."
8 Lee 2003, 123–147, highlighting J. J. Winckelmann's role in propagating the chronological and value-based ranking of Dorian and Ionian dress styles and cultural differences more generally.
9 Nosch 2016.

> Although Odysseus is dead, postpone
> requests for marriage till I finish weaving
> this sheet to shroud Laertes when he dies.
> My work should not be wasted, or the people
> in Argos will reproach me, if a man
> who won such wealth should lie without a shroud.

Penelope's weaving functions as a premonition of another future event: her marriage to a suitor (*Od.* 19.137):

> οἱ δὲ γάμον σπεύδουσιν: ἐγὼ δὲ δόλους τολυπεύω.
>
> The suitors want to push me into marriage, but I spin schemes.

Starting to weave means planning the future and envisioning a result that will last for the coming generation, and it is to the next generation that I wish to turn in my epilogue.

Figure 12: *Penelope Unraveling Her Work at Night.* Silk embroidered with silk thread. By Dora Wheeler (1856–1940), 1886. New York, The Metropolitan Museum of Art, Object Number: 2002.230.
Photo: © The Metropolitan Museum of Art, https://www.metmuseum.org/art/collection/search/16951 (last access 04.07.2025).

Epilogue. The long time of textiles, the short time of a T-shirt

We give witness to our age and our time through our clothing. Even if we believe our clothes to be timeless, they will look outdated in 20 years. Nothing signals time like clothes.

The brilliant anthology *Time in Fashion* explores how time affects textile makers[1] and textile consumers, and how fashion shapes modalities of time:

> Few phenomena embody the notion of time as well as fashion. Rooted in the 'now', it creates its own past through the process of rapid style change. Fast-moving, it is always on the verge of becoming something else. Uniquely poised between the past and the future, fashion has a curious affinity with unorthodox models of time.[2]

There is a remarkable tension between the linear, industrial production time of fabric and clothing and how fashion is configured as seasonal and cyclical when commodified and commercialised.[3] Fashion is temporal and the time of fashion becomes visible through its configuration as cyclical, seasonal and fast-moving. The fashion year is typically divided into two seasons of spring/summer and fall/winter. Spring/summer begins in January and ends in June. Autumn/winter begins in July and lasts until December.[4] In between these two seasons are pre-spring, pre-summer, pre-fall and pre-winter.[5] This seasonal model is following Europe, North America and China since it reflects climate and summer clothes of the northern hemisphere alone. But on a global fashion market, it is summer twice a year. This traditional, seasonal timing collapsed in the late 1990s when *fast fashion* companies began producing clothing globally for approximately 52 so-called *micro-seasons* lasting about one week each.[6]

The modern acceleration of consumption is enabled by falling prices, overproduction, low salaries and an ever-narrowing profit margin. A T-shirt available

---

1 Norbert Elias' 1988 essay *Über die Zeit* considers time and time organisation as a political tool and cultural construct. Time has a "disziplinierende Funktion".
2 Evans and Vaccari 2020b, 3.
3 Evans and Vaccari 2020a.
4 Illustrating, of course, the domination of the northern hemisphere in the fashion world.
5 In addition, there are artificial seasons such "resort" or "cruise": vacation time means shopping time.
6 Evans and Vaccari 2020b, 18: Fast fashion is "cheap, disposable and mass produced garments, made for western consumers in non-western factories, with scant regard for ethics or sustainability" according to Caroline Evans and Alessandra Vaccari.

in any store around the world is the result of a delicate web of global collaboration, trade and politics.[7] From cotton fields in Texas or Turkmenistan to spinning mills in Türkiye or China, textile sweatshops in Southeast Asia, printing houses in North America and second-hand markets in Africa – a T-shirt travels thousands of kilometres around the planet in its life.[8] Fast fashion's business model requires frictionless global trade, inexpensive long-distance transportation, and cheap, flexible labor. Production efficiency follows the tenets of *Taylorism* (sic!) and constantly aims at reducing time and accelerating production. In antiquity, spinning and weaving were the most time-consuming processes, today it is the sewing of garments: a worker in a Bangladeshi garment factory sews a t-shirt in 3 minutes and 43.38 seconds today.[9]

Overproduction, coupled with a low level of recycling, presents a constant challenge to the environmental sustainability and green transition of the textile industry. Producing one pair of jeans requires 7000 litres of water,[10] and washing synthetic clothes releases half a million tons of plastic micro fibres into the oceans annually. An average Scandinavian consumer buys nine t-shirts per year and tends to throw them away before they are the slightest worn out. Greenpeace found that on average we only keep our clothes for 3 years before discarding them. Research in the Netherlands documented that a piece of clothing stayed for an average of 3.4 years in a Dutch wardrobe, was worn on the body for a total of 44 days, and was worn 2.4 to 3.1 days between washings.[11] A survey in Germany showed that respondents owned on average 95 pieces of clothing (not including underwear and socks) and 19% of their clothes remained unused or worn very little, and they owned the clothes ca. three years before discarding or donating them.[12] Wear per garment is the lowest in world history.[13] This is a late 20th-century novelty. Nowadays it is quite rare for a garment to last a lifetime, or even until the next season, either because it becomes unfashionable or because the quality of the fabric, tailoring and stitching is so poor that the clothing has little durability.[14] Previously, for thousands of years, clothing was expensive, worth repairing and maintaining, long-lasting and full of memories. We still experience

---

7 Rivoli 2014.
8 Tranberg Hansen 2000.
9 Howlader et al. 2015, quoted from Evans and Vaccari 2020a, 67–69.
10 Wahnbaeck and Groth 2015.
11 Fletcher and Tham 2004, 264.
12 Wahnbaeck and Groth 2015. Survey of more than 1000 respondents conducted in 2015.
13 Black 2012.
14 Frankopan et al. 2022 with references.

this temporal tension in our wardrobes as the constant offer of new clothes versus our personal reluctance to change style abruptly.

What does the timeliness of our wardrobe and garments mean in a time of climate- and biodiversity crisis? The 2018 UN Environment Program Report estimates that 2–8% of global carbon emissions come from the textile industry and that the industry has a major impact on the global wastewater challenge. Most of us as consumers, most fashion designers and most of the clothing industry are at a loss as to how to change to more sustainable clothing. A blanket solution for many is to turn to more durable clothing.[15] Durable clothing is perhaps not a viable solution alone, given that our clothes are discarded rapidly for reasons other than just wear and tear, often accumulated in land-fills or dumps of the global south, and given that washing and laundry is a major source of energy consumption, water consumption and the diffusion of microplastics.[16] More fine-grained and diverse strategies must be put in place. Indeed, we need to reduce, reuse, repurpose, resale and recycle our clothes[17] to use them for a much longer time.

---

[15] Fletcher and Tham 2004, 260.
[16] Fletcher and Tham 2004, 264: "An LSC of a woman's polyester blouse performed by Franklin Associates (1993) for the American Fiber Manufacturers Association, assumed that a blouse is worn 40 times in its life and is worn twice between washings (i.e. 20 times in its life). This study went on to reveal that the waste majority (85%) of energy consumed in a garment's life is as a result of laundering."
[17] Nielsen and Skjold 2024.

Ancient sources

All ancient sources are abbreviated according to the *Oxford Classical Dictionary*, 4th edition. See https://classics.oxfordre.com/staticfiles/images/ORECLA/OCD.ABBREVIATIONS.pdf (last access 04.07.2025).

I have quoted the English translations from the following editions:

Aischylos

Oresteia: Agamemnon. Libation-Bearers. Eumenides. Edited and translated by Alan H. Sommerstein. LCL 146. Cambridge: Harvard University Press, 2009.

Anthologia Palatina

The Greek Anthology. Vol. 2. Translated by William R. Paton. LCL 68. Cambridge: Harvard University Press, 1917.
The Greek Anthology. Vol. 3. Translated by William R. Paton. LCL 84. Cambridge: Harvard University Press, 1917.

Aristophanes

Birds. The Complete Greek Drama. Translated by Eugene O'Neill. New York: Random House, 1938.
The Birds. Translated by John H. Frere. London: William Pickering, 1839.
Ecclesiazusae. The Complete Greek Drama. Translated by Eugene O'Neill. New York: Random House, 1938.
Knights. Edited and translated by Jeffrey Henderson: LCL 178. Cambridge: Harvard Univeristy Press, 1998.

Aristotle

Politics. Translated by Harris Rackham. LCL 264. Cambridge: Harvard University Press, 1944.
History of Animals. Translated by Arthur L. Peck. LCL 437. Cambridge: Harvard University Press, 1964.
The Athenian Constitution. Translated by Harris Rackham. LCL 285. Cambridge: Harvard University Press, 1935.

Callimachos

Aetia. Iambi. Lyric Poems. Edited and translated by Dee L. Clayman. LCL 421. Cambridge: Harvard University Press, 2022.
Hecale. Hymns. Epigrams. Edited and translated by Dee L. Clayman. LCL 129. Cambridge: Harvard University Press, 2022.

Debate Between Grain and Sheep

The Electronic Text Corpus of Sumerian Literature Project. Faculty of Oriental Studies, University of Oxford (https://etcsl.orinst.ox.ac.uk/cgi-bin/etcsl.cgi?text=t.5.3.2#).

Diodorus

Diodorus Siculus. With a translation by Charles H. Oldfather. LCL 279. London: Heinemann, 1933.

Euripides

Suppliant Women. Electra. Heracles. Edited and translated by David Kovacs. LCL 9. Cambridge: Harvard University Press, 1998.
Electra. Translated by Edward P. Coleridge. In: *Euripides. The Complete Greek Drama*. Edited by Whitney J. Oates and Eugene O'Neill, Jr., vol. 2. New York: Random House, 1938.
Iphigenia in Taulis. Translated by Robert Potter. In: *Euripides. The Complete Greek Drama*. Edited by Whitney J. Oates and Eugene O'Neill, Jr., vol. 1. New York: Random House, 1938.
Euripidis Fabulae, vol. 2. Translated by Gilbert Murray. Oxford: Clarendon, 1913.
Helen. Edited and translated by David Kovacs. LCL 11. Cambridge: Harvard University Press, 2002.
Ion. Edited and translated by David Kovacs. LCL 10. Cambridge: Harvard University Press, 1999.

Galen

Ian Johnston, Niki Papavramidou, *Galen on the Pulses. Medico-historical Analysis, Textual Tradition, Translation*. Berlin/Boston: De Gruyter, 2024.
Singer Peter N. (ed.), Galen. *Writings on Health. Thrasybulus and Health (De Sanitate Tuenda)*. Cambridge: Cambridge University Press, 2023.

Gilgamesh

Sophus Helle (ed.), *Gilgamesh. A New Translation of the Ancient Epic with Essays on the Poem, its Past, and its Passion*. New Haven: Yale University Press, 2021.

Herodotus

Historiae. With an English translation by Alfred D. Godley. LCL 117. London: 1920.

Hesiod

Barry B. Powell, The Poems of Hesiod. Theogony, Works and Days, and The Shield of Herakles. Oakland: University of California Press, 2017.

Hesychius

Hesychii Alexandrini Lexicon. Vol. I [Alpha – Delta]. Edited by Kurt Latte and Ian Cunnigham. Berlin/New York: De Gruyter, 2018.
Hesychii Alexandrini Lexicon. Vol. II. [1) Epsilon – Iota. 2) Kappa – Omicron]. Edited by Ian Cunningham. Berlin/Boston: De Gruyter, 2020.
Hesychii Alexandrini Lexicon. Vol. III [Pi – Sigma]. Edited by Peter Allan Hansen and Kurt Latte. Berlin/New York: De Gruyter, 2005.

Homer

The Odyssey. Translated and edited by Emily Wilson. New York: W. W. Norton and Company, Inc., 2020.
The Odyssey. Rendered into English prose for the use of those who cannot read the original. Translated by Samuel Butler. Revised over several years by Timothy Power and Gregory Nagy for the public domain edition. London: A. C. Fifield, 1900.
The Odyssey. Vols. 1–2. With an English translation by Augustus T. Murray. LCL 104–105. London: Heinemann, 1919.
The Iliad. Vols. 1–2. With an English translation by Augustus T. Murray. LCL 170–171. London: Heinemann, 1925.

Homeric Hymns

Hesiod, the Homeric Hymns and Homerica. With an English translation by Hugh G. Evelyn-White. LCL 57. London: Heinemann, 1914.

Hyginus

The Myths of Hyginus. Translated and edited by Mary Grant. Lawrence: University of Kansas Publications, 1960. (www.theoi.com [last access 04.07.2025])
Peter K. Marshall. *Fabulae.* Munich: K. G. Saur, 2002.

Josephus

Jewish Antiquities. Vol. I. With an English translation by Henry St. J. Thackeray. Vol. II. With an English translation by Henry St. J. Thackeray and Ralph Marcus. Vols. III–VII. With an English translation by Ralph Marcus. Vols. VIII–IX. With an English translation by Louis H. Feldman. LCL 242, 490, 281, 326, 365, 489, 410, 433, 456. Cambridge: Harvard University Press, 1930.1934.1937.1943.1963.1965.
The Jewish War. 3 vols. With an English Translation by Henry St. J. Thackeray. LCL 203, 487, 210. Cambridge, Harvard University Press, 1927–1928.

1 Maccabees

English translation by George Themelis Zervos. In: *New English Translation of the Septuagint.* New York: Oxford University Press, 2007.

Pausanias

Pausanias' Description of Greece. Vol. 2. With an English Translation by William H. S. Jones and Henry A. Ormerod. LCL 188. London: Heinemann, 1918.
Pausanias' Description of Greece. Vol. 3. With an English Translation by William H. S. Jones and Henry A. Ormerod. LCL 272. London: Heinemann, 1933.

Pherekydes

Hermann Sadun Schibli, *Pherekydes of Syros.* Oxford: Clarendon Press, 1990.

Philo

On Dreams. With an English translation by. F. H. Colson and G. H. Whitaker. LCL 275. Cambridge: Harvard University Press, 1929.

Plato

Cratylus. With an English Translation by Harold N. Fowler. LCL 167. Cambridge: Harvard University Press, 2021.
Laws. Vols. 1–2. With an English translation by Robert G. Bury. LCL 187 and 192. Cambridge: Harvard University Press, 1926.

Pliny the Elder

Natural History. Vol. 2. Translated by Harris Rackham. LCL 352. Cambridge: Harvard University Press, 1942.

Plutarch

Plutarch's Lives. With an English Translation by Bernadotte Perrin. LCL 99. London: Heinemann, 1919.

Sophocles

Antigone. The Women of Trachis. Philoctetes. Oedipus at Colonus. Edited and translated by Hugh Lloyd-Jones. LCL 21. Cambridge: Harvard University Press, 1994.

The Old Testament

World English Bible. Revision of the American Standard Version by Rainbow Missions, Inc. 1901.

Thucydides

History of the Peloponnesian War, Volume I, Books 1–2. Translated by Charles F. Smith. LCL 108. London: Heinemann, 1919.

Bibliography

Abrahams, Ethel Beatrice. 1908. *Greek Dress. A Study of the Costumes Worn in Ancient Greece. From Pre-Hellenic Times to the Hellenistic Age.* London: John Murray.
Adovasio, James M., Soffer, Olga and Klíma, Bohuslav. 1996. "Upper Palaeolithic Fibre Technology. Interlaced Woven Finds from Pavlov I, Czech Republic, c. 26,000 Years Ago", *Antiquity* 70, 526–534.
Aleshire, Sara and Lambert, Stephen. 2003. "Making the *Peplos* for Athena. A New Edition of *IG* II^2 1060 + *IG* II^2 1036", *Zeitschrift für Papyrologie und Epigraphik* 142, 65–86.
Alföldi, Andreas. 1955. "Gewaltherrscher und Theaterkönig. Die Auseinandersetzung einer attischen Ideenprägung mit persischen Repräsentationsformen im politischen Denken und in der Kunst bis zur Schwelle des Mittelalters", in Kurt Weitzman (ed.), *Late Classical and Mediaeval Studies in Honor of Albert Mathias Friend, Jr.*, 15–55. Princeton: Princeton University Press.
Amundsen, Darrel W. and Diers, Carol Jean. 1970. "The Age of Menopause in Classical Greece", *Human Biology* 42 no. 1, 79–86.
Andersson Strand, Eva. 2012. "The Textile Chaîne Opératoire. Using a Multidisciplinary Approach to Textile Archaeology with a Focus on the Ancient Near East", *Paléorient* 38 no. 1/2, 21–40.
Andersson Strand, Eva and Mannering, Ulla. 2021. "Sailmaking. A Gigantic Collective Undertaking", in Jeanette Varberg and Peter Pentz (eds.), *The Raid. Join the Vikings*, 29–44. Copenhagen: National Museum of Denmark.
Andersson, Eva and Nosch, Marie-Louise. 2003. "With a Little Help from my Friends: Investigation Mycenaean Textiles with the help from Scandinavian Experimental Archaeology", in Karen Polinger Foster and Robert Laffineur (eds.), *METRON. Measuring the Aegean Bronze Age. Proceedings of the 9th International Aegean Conference, Yale University, 18–21 April 2002*, Aegaeum 24, 197–205 and table XLV.
Andersson Strand, Eva and Nosch, Marie-Louise. eds. 2015. *Tools, Textiles and Contexts. Investigating Textile Production in the Aegean and Eastern Mediterranean Bronze Age*, Ancient Textiles Series 21. Oxford/Havertown: Oxbow.
Apparudai, Arjun. ed. 1986. *The Social Life of Things. Commodities in Cultural Perspective.* New York: Cambridge University Press.
Athanassaki, Lucia. 2016. "Political and Dramatic Perspectives on Archaic Sculptures. Bacchylides' *Fourth Dithyramb* (Ode 18) and the Treasury of the Athenians in Delphi", in Vanessa Cazzato and André Lardinois (eds.), *The Look of Lyric. Greek Song and the Visual. Studies in Archaic and Classical Greek Song, vol.* 1, Mnemosyne Supplements. Monographs on Greek and Latin Language and Literature 391, 16–49. Leiden/Boston: Brill.
Avagianou, Aphrodite. 1991. *Sacred Marriage in the Rituals of Greek Religion*, European University Studies, Series 15. Classics 54. Berne/Berlin/Frankfurt/New York/Paris/Vienna: Peter Lang.
Baert, Barbara. 2016. "Kairos or Occasion as Paradigm in the Visual Medium. *Nachleben*, Iconography, Hermeneutics", *Antwerp Royal Museum Annual* 2013–2014, 193–251.
Bakola, Emmanuela. 2016. "Textile Symbolism and the 'Wealth of the Earth'. Creation, Production and Destruction in the 'Tapestry Scene' of Aeschylus' *Oresteia* (*Ag.* 905–978)", in Giovanni Fanfani, Mary Harlow and Marie-Louise Nosch (eds.), *Spinning Fates and the Song of the Loom. The Use of Textiles, Clothing and Cloth Production as Metaphor, Symbol and Narrative Device in Greek and Latin Literature*, Ancient Textiles Series 24, 115–136. Oxford/Havertown: Oxbow.
Baldry, Harold Caparne. 1952. "Who Invented the Golden Age?", *The Classical Quarterly* 2 no. 1/2, 83–92.

Ball, Rashid. 1979. "Generation Dating in Herodotus", *The Classical Quarterly* 29 no. 2, 276–281.
Barber, Elizabeth. 1991. *Prehistoric Textiles. The Development of Cloth in the Neolithic and Bronze Ages with Special Reference to the Aegean.* Princeton: Princeton University Press.
Barber, Elizabeth. 1992. "The Peplos of Athena", in Jenifer Neils (ed.), *Goddess and Polis. The Panathenaic Festival in Ancient Athens*, 103–117. Princeton: Princeton University Press.
Bartol, Krystyna. 2006. "The Lost World of Inventors. Athenaeus' Sentimental Heurematography", *Palamades. A Journal of Ancient History* 1, 85–98.
Beard, Mary. 1987. "A Complex of Times. No More Sheep on Romulus' Birthday", *Proceedings of the Cambridge Philological Society. New Series* 33, 1–15.
Bender, Claudia. 2008. *Die Sprache des Textilen. Untersuchungen zu Kleidung und Textilien im Alten Testament*, Beiträge zur Wissenschaft vom Alten und Neuen Testament 177. Stuttgart: Kohlhammer.
Bender Jørgensen, Lise, Rast-Eicher, Antoinette and Wendrich, Willeke. 2023. "Earliest Evidence for Textile Technologies", *Paléorient* 49 no. 1, 213–228.
Bergfjord, Christian, Karg, Sabine, Rast-Eicher, Antoinette, Nosch, Marie-Louise, Mannering, Ulla, Allaby, Robin G., Murphy, Brigit M. and Holst, Bodil. 2010. "Comment on '30,000-Year-Old Wild Flax Fibers'", *Science* 328, 1634.
Bergren, Ann L. T. 1983. "Odyssean Temporality. Many (Re)Turns", in Carl A. Rubino and Cynthia W. Shelmerdine (eds.), *Approaches to Homer*, 38–73. Austin: University of Texas Press.
Bieber, Margarete. 1934. *Entwicklungsgeschichte der griechischen Tracht von der vorgriechischen Zeit bis zur römischen Kaiserzeit.* Berlin: Gebr. Mann.
Black, Sandy. 2012. *The Sustainable Fashion Handbook.* London: Thames & Hudson.
Bloch, Maurice. 1977. "The Past and The Present in the Present", *Man* 12 no. 2, 278–292.
Blok, Josine H. 2006. "Solon's Funerary Laws. Questions of Authenticity and Function", in Josine H. Blok and André P. M. H. Lardinois (eds.), *Solon of Athens. New Historical and Philological Approaches*, Mnemosyne Suppl. 272, 197–247. Leiden/Boston: Brill.
Blondell, Ruby. 2005. "From Fleece to Fabric. Weaving Culture in Plato's Statesman", in David Sedley (ed.), *Oxford Studies in Ancient Philosophy* 28, 23–75. Oxford: Oxford University Press.
Blum, Hartmut. 1998. *Purpur als Statussymbol in der griechischen Welt*, Antiquitas, Reihe 1, Abhandlungen zur alten Geschichte, Bd. 47. Bonn: R. Habelt.
Blundell, Sue. 1986. *The Origins of Civilization in Greek and Roman Thought.* London/Sydney/Dover, New Hampshire: Croom Helm.
Blundell, Sue. 1998. "Marriage and the Maiden. Narratives on the Parthenon," in Sue Blundell and Margaret Williamson (eds.), *The Sacred and the Feminine in Ancient Greece*, 47–70. London/New York: Routledge.
Boehn, Max von. 1927. *Antike Mode.* Munich: Bruckmann.
Bourdieu, Pierre. 1963. "The Attitude of the Algerian Peasant Towards Time", in Julian Pitt-Rivers (ed.), *Mediterranean Countrymen. Essays in the Social Anthropology of the Mediterranean*, 55–72. Paris/Den Haag: Mouton and Co.
Bourdieu, Pierre. 1980. *Le sens pratique.* Paris: Editions de Minuit.
Brelich, Angelo. 1969. *Paides e parthenoi*, Incunabula graeca XXXVI. Rome: Edizioni dell'Ateneo.
Brøns, Cecilie. 2014. "Representation and Realities. Fibulas and Pins in Greek and Near Eastern Iconography", in Mary Harlow and Marie-Louise Nosch (eds.), *Greek and Roman Textiles and Dress. An Interdisciplinary Anthology*, Ancient Textiles Series 19, 60–94. Oxford/Havertown: Oxbow.

Brøns, Cecilie. 2015. "Textiles and Temple Inventories. Detecting an Invisible Votive Tradition in Greek Sanctuaries in the Second Half of the First Millennium BC", in Jane Fejfer, Mette Moltesen and Anette Rathje (eds.), *Tradition. Transmission of Culture in the Ancient World*, Acta Hyperborea 14, 43–83. Copenhagen: Museum Tusculanum Press.

Brøns, Cecilie. 2016. *Gods and Garments. Textiles in Greek Sanctuaries in the 7th–1st Centuries BC*, Ancient Textiles Series 28. Oxford/Havertown: Oxbow.

Brøns, Cecilie. 2019. "Geschlechtsspezifische Gaben. Kleiderweihungen in griechischen Heiligtümern", in Beate Wagner-Hasel and Marie-Louise B. Nosch (eds.), *Gaben, Waren und Tribute. Stoffkreisläufe und antike Textilökonomie. Akten eines Symposiums (9./10. Juni 2016 in Hannover)*, 163–189. Stuttgart: Franz Steiner Verlag.

Brøns, Cecilie and Nosch, Marie-Louise. eds. 2017. *Textiles and Cult in the Ancient Mediterranean*. Ancient Textiles Series 31. Oxford/Havertown: Oxbow.

Brulé, Pierre. 1987. *La fille d'Athènes. La religion des filles à Athènes à l'époque classique. Mythes, cultes et société*, Annales Littéraires de l'Université de Besançon 363. Paris: Les Belles Lettres.

Burkert, Walter. 1963. "A Note on Aeschylus Choephori 205 ff.", *The Classical Quarterly* 13 no. 2, 177.

Burkert, Walter. 1966. "Kekropidensage und Arrhephoria. Vom Initiationsritus zum Panathenäenfest", *Hermes* 94 no. 1, 1–25.

Busana, Maria Stella, Francisci, Denis and Lena, Agnese. 2024. "Which Tool for Which Fiber? Experimental Spinning Tests Using Bone, Glass and Amber Instruments", in Francesca Coletti, Christina Margariti, Vanessa Forte and Stella Spantidaki (eds.), *Multidisciplinary Approaches for the Investigation of Textiles and Fibres in the Archaeological Field*, Interdisciplinary Contributions to Archaeology 139–158. Cham: Springer.

Cairns, Douglas L. 1996. "Off with her ΑΙΔΩΣ'. Herodotus 1.8.3–4", *The Classical Quarterly* 46 no. 1, 78–83.

Cairns, Douglas L. 2002. "The Meaning of the Veil in Ancient Greek Culture", in Lloyd Llewellyn-Jones (ed.), *Women's Dress in the Ancient Greek World*, 73–93. London: Duckworth.

Calame, Claude. 1977. *Les chœurs de jeunes filles en Grèce ancienne. I. Morphologie, fonction religieuse et sociale. II. Alcman*, Filologia e critica 20–21. Rome: dell'Ateneo and Bizarri.

Carr, Karen. 2000. "Women's Work. Spinning and Weaving in the Greek House", in Dominique Cardon and Michel Feugère (eds.), *Archéologie des textiles. Des Origines au Ve Siècle. Actes du Colloque de Lattes, Octobre 1999*, Monographies instrumentum 14, 163–166. Montagnac: Éditions Monique Mergoil.

Cartledge, Paul. 1981. "Spartan Wives. Liberation or Licence?", *The Classical Quarterly* 31 no. 1, 84–105.

Chaniotis, Angelos. 1992. *Die Verträge zwischen kretischen Poleis ab der hellenistischen Zeit*. Stuttgart: Franz Steiner Verlag.

Chaniotis, Angelos. 2005. *War in the Hellenistic World. A Social and Cultural History*, Ancient World at War Series. Malden/Oxford/Victoria: Blackwell.

Chaniotis, Angelos. 2009. "From Woman to Woman. Female Voices and Emotions in Dedications to Goddesses", in Clarisse Prêtre (ed.), *Le donateur, l'offrande et la déesse. Systèmes votifs dans les sanctuaires de déesses du monde grec*. Kernos Suppl. 23, 51–68. Presses universitaires de Liège.

Chankowski, Andrzej S. 2010. *L'éphébie hellénistique. Étude d'une institution civique dans les cités grecques des îles de la Mer Égée et de l'Asie Mineure*. Paris: De Boccard.

Chankowski, Andrzej S. Forthcoming. "The Diffusion of Youth Training in the Hellenistic World. The Role of the Athenian Model", in Davide Amendola and Shane Wallace (eds.), *Beyond*

Athenocentrism. Greek Cities' Responses to Athenian Institutional and Judicial Legacy in the So-Called "Hellenistic Polis Convergence", University of Dublin, 15*th*–16*th* June 2021.

Chantraine, Pierre. 1968. *Dictionnaire étymologique de la langue grecque. Histoire des mots.* Paris: Klincksieck.

Ciccarelli, Elena and Perilli, Assunta. 2017. "Tracing the Thread. Spinning Experiments with Etruscan Spindle Whorl Replicas", in Margarita Gleba and Romina Laurito (eds.), *Contextualising Textile Production in Italy in the 1st Millennium BC*, Origini 40, 155–164. Rome: Gangemi Editore SPA.

Cleland, Liza. 2005. *The Brauron Clothing Catalogues. Text, Analysis, Glossary and Translation*, BAR International Series 1428. Oxford: BAR Publishing.

Cleland, Liza, Davies, Glenys and Llewellyn-Jones, Lloyd. 2007. *Greek and Roman Dress. From A to Z*, The Ancient World from A to Z. London/New York: Routledge.

Clements, Jacquelyn H. 2017. "Weaving the Chalkeia. Reconstruction and Ritual of an Athenian Festival", in Cecilie Brøns and Marie-Louise Nosch (eds.), *Textiles and Cult in the Ancient Mediterranean*, Ancient Textiles Series 31, 36–48. Oxford/Havertown: Oxbow.

Cole, Susan Guettel. 1998. "Domesticating Artemis", in Sue Blundell and Margaret Williamson (eds.), *The Sacred and the Feminine in Ancient Greece*, 27–43. London/New York: Routledge.

Conard, Nicholas J. and Malina, Maria. 2016. "Außergewöhnliche neue Funde aus den aurignacienzeitlichen Schichten vom Hohle Fels bei Schelklingen", *Archäologische Ausgrabungen Baden-Württemberg 2015*, 60–66.

Coughlin, Sean and Lewis, Orly. 2020. "Pneuma and the Pneumatist School of Medicine", in Sean Coughlin and Orly Lewis (eds.), *The Concept of Pneuma after Aristotle*, Berlin Studies of the Ancient World 61, 203–236. Berlin: Edition Topoi.

Craik, Jennifer. 1993. *The Face of Fashion. Cultural Studies in Fashion*. London/New York: Routledge.

Cutler, Joanne E. 2021. *Crafting Minoanisation. Textiles, Crafts Production and Social Dynamics in the Bronze Age Southern Aegean*, Ancient Textiles Series 33. Oxford/Havertown: Oxbow.

Dakoronia, Fanouria and Gounaropoulou, Lucretia. 1992. "Artemiskult auf einen neuen Weihrelief aus Achinos bei Lamia", *Mitteilungen des Deutschen Aarchäologischen Instituts. Athenische Abteilung* 107, 217–227.

Del Freo, Maurizio, Nosch, Marie-Louise and Rougemont, Françoise. 2010. "The Terminology of Textiles in the Linear B Tablets, including Some Considerations on Linear A Logograms and Abbreviations", in Cécile Michel and Marie-Louise Nosch (eds.), *Textile Terminologies in the Ancient Near East and Mediterranean from the Third to the First Millennia BC*, Ancient Textiles Series 8, 338–373. Oxford and Oakville: Oxbow.

Delalande, Juliette, Enfrein, Barthélémy and Mézière, Dimitri. 2024. "Le vêtement antique et sa panoplie de métaphores", in Juliette Delalande, Barthélémy Enfrein, Michel Jabin, Dimitri Mézière, Floriane Sanfilippo and Pauline Rates (eds.), *Himation. Métaphores du vêtement dans l'Antiquité classique et tardive*, 11–28. Lyon: Ausonius Éditions. (https://una-editions.fr/himation-introduction [last access 04.07.2025]).

Deubner, Ludwig. 1956. *Attische Feste*. Berlin: Akademie-Verlag.

Dillon, Matthew. 2001. *Girls and Women in Classical Greek Religion*. London: Routledge.

Dimova, Bela, Harris, Susanna and Gleba, Margarita. 2021. "Naval Power and Textile Technology. Sail Production in Ancient Greece", *World Archaeology* 53 no. 5, 762–778.

Doyle, Andrea. 2016. "The Cloak of Deianeira or the Shirt of Nessus?", in Giovanni Fanfani, Mary Harlow and Marie-Louise Nosch (eds.), *Spinning Fates and the Song of the Loom. The Use of Textiles, Clothing and Cloth Production as Metaphor, Symbol and Narrative Device in Greek and Latin Literature*, Ancient Textiles Series 24, 137–160. Oxford/Havertown: Oxbow.

Drewsen, Anne, Harlow, Mary, Mannering, Ulla and Nosch, Marie-Louise. 2024. "In the Beginning …", in Ulla Mannering, Marie-Louise Nosch and Anne Drewsen (eds.), *The Common Thread. Collected Essays in Honour of Eva Andersson Strand*, New Approaches in Archaeology 3, 3–7. Turnhout: Brepols.

Drexhage, Hans-Joachim and Reinard, Patrick. 2014. "Vom Wert der Dinge. Verschlissene, getragene und ausgebesserte Kleider und Textilien im papyrologischen Befund. Überlegungen zum Verwertungskreislauf und Second-Hand-Mark", *Marburger Beiträge zur Antiken Handel* 32, 1–70.

Driessen, Jan. 1990. *An Early Destruction in the Mycenaean Palace at Knossos. A New Interpretation of the Excavation Field-Notes of the South-East Area of the West Wing*, Acta Archaeologica Lovaniensia, Monographiae 2. Leuven: Leuven University Press.

Driessen, Jan. 1999. "The Northern Entrance Passage at Knossos. Some Preliminary Observations on Its Potential Role as 'Central Archives'", in Sigrid Deger-Jalkotzy, Stefan Hiller and Oswald Panagl (eds.), *Floreant Studia Mycenaea. Akten des 10. Internationalen Mykenologischen Colloquiums in Salzburg vom 1. Mai – 5. Mai 1995*, Veröffentlichungen der Mykenischen Kommission 18, 205–226. Vienna: Verlag d. ÖAW.

Driessen, Jan. 2000. *The Scribes of the Room of the Chariot Tablets at Knossos. Interdisciplinary Approach to the Study of a Linear B Deposit*, Suppl. Minos 15. Salamanca: Ediciones Universidad de Salamanca.

Driessen, Jan and Mouthuy, Ophélie. 2022. "The Late Minoan II–IIIA2 Kingdom of Knossos as Reflected by Its Linear B Archives", in Anna Lucia D'Agata, Luca Girella, Eleni Papadopoulou and Davide G. Aquini (eds.), *One State, Many Worlds. Crete in the Late Minoan II–IIIA2 Early Period. Proceedings of The International Conference Held at Khania, Megalo Arsenali, 21st–23rd November 2019*, Studi Micenei ed Egeo-Anatolici, Nouva Serie, Supplemento 2, 71–84. Rome: Edizioni Quasar.

Droß-Krüpe, Kerstin. "Bitte nicht Wegwerfen! Nutzung und Zirkulation von Gebrauchtkleidung in der Antike" (unpublished lecture).

Droß-Krüpe, Kerstin and Nosch, Marie-Louise. 2016. "Textiles, Trade and Theories. How Scholars Past and Present View and Understand Textile Trade in the Ancient Near East and the Mediterranean in Antiquity", in Kerstin Droß-Krüpe and Marie-Louise Nosch (eds.), *Textiles, Trade and Theories. From the Ancient Near East to the Mediterranean*, Kārum – Emporion – Forum. Beiträge zur Wirtschafts-, Rechts- und Sozialgeschichte des östlichen Mittelmeerraums und Altvorderasiens 2, 293–329. Münster: Ugarit-Verlag.

Droß-Krüpe, Kerstin and Paetz gen. Schieck, Annette. 2014. "Unravelling the Tangled Threads of Ancient Embroidery. A Compilation of Written Sources and Archaeologically Preserved Textiles", in Mary Harlow and Marie-Louise Nosch (eds.), *Greek and Roman Textiles and Dress. An Interdisciplinary Anthology*, Ancient Textiles Series 19, 207–235. Oxford/Havertown: Oxbow.

Ejstrud, Bo, Andresen, Stina, Appel, Amanda, Gjerlevsen, Sara and Thomsen, Birgit. 2011. *From Flax to Linen. Experiments with Flax at Ribe Viking Centre*. Esbjerg: Maritime Archaeology Programme.

Elias, Norbert. 1988. *Über die Zeit. Arbeiten zur Wissenssoziologie* II. Frankfurt a. M.: Suhrkamp.

Evans, Caroline and Vaccari, Alessandra. eds. 2020a. *Time in Fashion. Industrial, Antilinear and Uchronic Temporalities*. London: Bloomsbury.

Evans, Caroline and Vaccari, Alessandra. 2020b. "Time in Fashion. An Introductory Essay", in Caroline Evans and Alessandra Vaccari (eds.), *Time in Fashion. Industrial, Antilinear and Uchronic Temporalities*, 3–36. London: Bloomsbury.

Fanfani, Giovanni, Harlow, Mary and Nosch, Marie-Louise. eds. 2016. *Spinning Fates and the Song of the Loom. The Use of Textiles, Clothing and Cloth Production as Metaphor, Symbol and Narrative Device in Greek and Latin Literature*, Ancient Textiles Series 24. Oxford/Havertown: Oxbow.

Fedi, Mariaelena, Barone, Serena, Coletti, Francesca and Liccioli, Lucia. 2024. "Radiocarbon for the Dating of Fibres and Textiles. The Case Study of a Silk Double Knitted Fabric from Pompeii", in Francesca Coletti, Christina Margariti, Vanessa Forte and Stella Spantidaki (eds.), *Multidisciplinary Approaches for the Investigation of Textiles and Fibres in the Archaeological Field*, Interdisciplinary Contributions to Archaeology, 123–137. Cham: Springer.

Firth, Richard and Nosch, Marie-Louise. 2012. "Spinning and Weaving Wool in Ur III Administrative Texts", *Journal of Cuneiform Studies* 64, 65–82.

Fisher, Elizabeth. 1979. *Woman's Creation. Sexual Evolution and the Shaping of Society*. New York: Anchor Books.

Fitton Brown, Antony D. 1961. "The Recognition-Scene in *CHOEPHORI*", *Revue des Études Grecques* 74, 363–370.

Flemestad, Peder. 2022. *Order and Adornment. The Role of Dress in Plutarch*. Lund University.

Flemestad, Peder, Harlow, Mary, Hildebrandt, Berit and Nosch, Marie-Louise. 2017. "Observations on the Terminology of textile tools in Diocletian's Edict of Maximum Prices", in Salvatore Gaspa, Cécile Michel and Marie-Louise Nosch (eds.), *Textile Terminologies from Orient to the Mediterranean and Europe, 1000 BC to 1000 AD*, 256–277. Lincoln: Zea Books.

Flemestad, Peder and Nosch, Marie-Louise. 2023. "En khlamys-klædt efeb? klæder skaber folk", *AIGIS suppl.* VII, 1–17 (https://www.igl.ku.dk/aigis/THN60/khlamys.pdf [last access 04.07.2025]).

Fletcher, Kate and Tham, Mathilda. 2004. "Clothing Rhythms", in Ed van Hinte (ed.), *Eternally Yours. Time in Design. Product, Value, Sustenance*, 254–274. Rotterdam: 010 Publishers.

Foxhall, Lin. Forthcoming. "Material Values. Emotion and Materiality in Ancient Greece", in Angelos Chaniotis and Pierre Ducrey (eds.), *The Role of Emotions in Classical Antiquity*. Stuttgart: Franz Steiner Verlag.

Foxhall, Lin and Luraghi, Nino. 2010. "Introduction", in Lin Foxhall, Hans-Joachim Gehrke and Nino Luraghi (eds.), *Intentional History. Spinning Time in Ancient Greece*, 9–14. Stuttgart: Franz Steiner Verlag.

Foxhall, Lin, Gehrke, Hans-Joachim and Luraghi, Nino. eds. 2010. *Intentional History. Spinning Time in Ancient Greece*. Stuttgart: Franz Steiner Verlag.

Fränkel, Hermann. 1931. "Die Zeitauffassung in der archaischen griechischen Literatur", *Zeitschrift für Ästhetik und allgemeine Kunstwissenschaft, 4. Kongress-Bericht. Beilagenheft*, 97–118.

Frankopan, Peter, Nosch, Marie-Louise and Zhao, Feng. 2022. "The World Wide Web", in Feng Zhao and Marie-Louise Nosch (eds.), *Textiles and Dress Cultures along the Silk Roads. Collection of the Cultural Exchanges along the Silk Roads*, 362–399. Paris/Hangzhou: UNESCO.

Fredericksmeyer, Ernst A. 1986. "Alexander the Great and the Macedonian *kausia*", *Transactions of the American Philological Association* 116, 215–227.

Frontisi-Ducroux, Françoise. 2003. *L'homme-cerf et la femme-araignée*. Paris: Gallimard.

Gartziou-Tatti, Ariadni. 2019. "The Peplos of Hera and the Council of the Sixteen Women of Elis", in Elias Koulakiotis and Charlotte Dunn (eds.), *Political Religions in the Greco-Roman World. Discourses, Practices and Images*, 204–224. Newcastle upon Tyne: Cambridge Scholars Publishing.

Gaspa, Salvatore. 2018. *Textiles in the Neo-Assyrian Empire. A Study of Terminology*, Studies in Ancient Near Eastern Records 19, Boston/Berlin: De Gryuter.

Gaspa, Salvatore. 2024. "Assyrian Imperial Elites and Textile Culture of the 1st Millennium BC. Shaping Power Visions Through Textiles", *Journal of Ancient Near Eastern History* 11 no. 2, 241–324.

Gaspa, Salvatore, Michel, Cécile and Nosch, Marie-Louise. eds. 2017. *Textile Terminologies from the Orient to the Mediterranean and Europe, 1000 BC to 1000 AD*. Lincoln: Zea Books.

Gawlinksi, Laura. 2017. "Theorizing Religious Dress", in Megan Cifarelli and Laura Gawlinski (eds.), *What Shall I Say of Clothes? Theoretical and Methodological Approaches to the Study of Dress in Antiquity*, Selected Papers on Ancient Art and Architecture 3, 161–178. Boston: Archaeological Institute of America.

Geddes, Ann G. 1987. "Rags and Riches. The Costume of Athenian Men in the Fifth Century", *The Classical Quarterly* 37 no. 2, 307–331.

Genette, Gérard. 1980. *Narrative Discourse. An Essay in Method*. Ithaca: Cornell University Press.

Gherchanoc, Florence. 2006. "Le(s) voile(s) de mariage dans le monde grec. Se voiler, se dévoiler. La question particulière de *anakaluptêria*", *Mètis* N. S. 4, 239–267.

Gilligan, Ian. 2010. "The Prehistoric Development of Clothing. *Archaeological* Implications of a Thermal Model", *Journal of Archaeological Method and Theory* 17, 15–80.

Gleba, Margarita. 2017. "Tracing Textile Cultures of Italy and Greece in the Early First Millennium BC", *Antiquity* 91 no. 359, 1205–1222.

Gleba, Margarita. 2025. "Textile Cultures of Mediterranean Europe in the Early First Millennium BCE: Technology, Tradition, Aesthetics, and Identity", in Aleksandra Hallmann (ed.), *Outward Appearance vs. Inward Significance. Addressing Identities through Attire in the Ancient World. The Proceeding of the 14th Annual University of Chicago Oriental Institute Seminar, March 1–2, 2018*, ISACS 15. 419–442. Chicago: Institute for the Study of Ancient Cultures.

Gräslund, Bo. 2017. "Människans Utveckling", in Maria Sjöberg (ed.), *En Samtidig Världshistoria*, 82–93. Lund: Studentlitteratur.

Gribetz, Sarit Kattan. 2017. "Women's Bodies as Metaphors for Time in Biblical, Second Temple, and Rabbinic Literature", in Jonathan Ben-Dov and Lutz Doering (eds.), *The Construction of Time in Antiquity. Ritual, Art and Identity*, 173–204. New York: Cambridge University Press.

Gribetz, Sarit Kattan. 2020. *Time and Difference in Rabbinic Judaism*. Princeton: Princeton University Press.

Grömer, Karina and Aali, Abolfazl. 2020. "How to Make a Sassanian Tunic. Understanding Handcraft Skills based on a Find from the Salt Mine in Chehrābād, Iran", in Louise Quillien and Kalliope Sarri (eds.), *Textile Workers. Skills, Labour and Status of Textile Craftspeople Between the Prehistoric Aegean and the Ancient Near East. Proceedings of the Workshop, 10th ICAANE in Vienna, April 2016*, Oriental and European Archaeology 13, 59–74. Vienna: Verlag d. ÖAW.

Guilleux, Nicole. 2016. "Of Metaphorical Matrices and their Networks. Generally Speaking and in the Field of Textile Activities", in Giovanni Fanfani, Mary Harlow and Marie-Louise Nosch (eds.), *Spinning Fates and the Song of the Loom. The Use of Textiles, Clothing and Cloth Production as Metaphor, Symbol and Narrative Device in Greek and Latin Literature*, Ancient Textiles Series 24, 1–16. Oxford/Havertown: Oxbow.

Guilleux, Nicole. 2020. "Renouer le fil entre latin ōrdior, ōrdō, ōrnō et grec ὄρδημα, ὄρδικον, ὠρδυλευσάμην", in Claire Le Feuvre and Daniel Petit (eds.), *Onomatôn Histôr. Mélanges offerts à Charles de Lamberterie*, Collection Linguistique de la Société de Linguistique de Paris 106, 469–481. Leuven: Peeters.

Günther, Wolfgang. 1988. "Vieux et inutilisable dans un inventaire inédit de Milet", in Denis Knoepler (ed.), *Comptes et inventaires dans la cité grecque. Actes du colloque international* d'épigraphie tenu à Neuchâtel du 23 au 26 septembre 1986 en l'honneur de Jacques Tréheux, Recueil de Travaux Publiés par la Faculté des Lettres 40, 215–237. Neuchâtel-Genève: Librairie E. Droz.

Hajdas, Irka, Cristi, Carlo, Bonani, Georges and Maurer, Mantana. 2014. "Textiles and Radiocarbon Dating", *Radiocarbon* 56 no. 2, 637–643.

Hallmann, Aleksandra. 2023. *Ancient Egyptian Clothing. Studies in Late Period Private Representations*, Vol. I–II, Harvard Egyptological Studies 20.1. Leiden/Boston: Brill.

Hannah, Robert. 2009. *Time in Antiquity. Sciences of Antiquity.* London/New York: Routledge.

Hannah, Robert. 2016. "Time-Telling Devices", in Georgia L. Irby (ed.), *A Companion to Science, Technology, and Medicine in Ancient Greece and Rome*, Blackwell Companions to the Ancient World, 923–939. Chichester: Wiley and Sons.

Hardy, Bruce L., Moncel, Marie-Hélène, Kerfant, Céline, Lebon, Matthieu, Bellot-Gurlet, Ludivic and Mélard, Nora. 2020. "Direct Evidence of Neanderthal Fibre Technology and Its Cognitive and Behavioral Implications", *Scientific Reports* 10, Article number: 4889. https://doi.org/10.1038/s41598-020-61839-w.

Harlizius-Klück, Ellen. 2005. *Saum and Zeit. Ein Wörter-und-Sachen-Buch in 496 lexikalischen Abschnitten angezettelt von Ellen Harlizius-Klück.* Berlin: Edition Ebersbach.

Harlizius-Klück, Ellen. 2016. "Textile Technology", in Georgia L. Irby (ed.), *A Companion to Science, Technology, and Medicine in Ancient Greece and Rome*, Blackwell Companions to the Ancient World, 747–767. Chichester: Wiley and Sons.

Harlow, Mary and Nosch, Marie-Louise. 2014. "Weaving the Threads. Methodologies in Textile and Dress Research for the Greek and Roman World. The State of the Art and the Case for Cross-Disciplinarity", in Mary Harlow and Marie-Louise Nosch (eds.), *Greek and Roman Textiles and Dress. An Interdisciplinary Anthology.* Ancient Textiles Series 19, 1–33. Oxbow Books, Oxford.

Heizer, Robert F. 1962. "The Background of Thomsen's Three-Age System", *Technology and Culture* 3 no. 3, 259–266.

Henderson, Thomas. 2020. *The Springtime of the People. The Athenian Ephebeia and Citizen Training from Lykourgos to Augustus*, Brill Studies in Greek and Roman Epigraphy 15. Leiden: Brill.

Herrmann, Peter, Günther, Wolfgang and Ehrhardt, Norbert. 2006. *Inschriften von Milet, Teil 3. Inschriften n. 1020–1580.* Berlin/New York: De Gruyter.

Higbie, Carolyn. 2003. *The Lindian Chronicle and the Greek Creation of Their Past.* Oxford: Oxford University Press.

Höpflinger, Anna-Katharina. 2019. "Between Regulation, Identification, and Representation. Clothing and Nudity from the Perspective of the Study of Religion", in Christoph Berner, Manuel Schäfer, Martin Schott, Sarah Schulz and Martina Weingärtner (eds.), *Clothing and Nudity in the Hebrew Bible*, Vetus Testamentum, 5–18. London/New York/Oxford: Bloomsbury TandT Clark.

Howlader, Ramij, Islam, Monirul, Sajib, Tanjibul Hasan, Prasad, Ripon Kumar. 2015. "Practically Observation of Standard Minute Value of T-Shirt", *International Journal of Engineering and Computer Science* 4 no. 3, 10685–10689.

Hubert, Henri and Mauss, Marcel. 1905. "Étude sommaire de la représentation du temps dans la religion et la magie", in Henri Hubert and Marcel Mauss, *Mélanges d'histoire des religions* 1905, 1–29. Paris: Librairie Félix Alcan.

Hurcombe, Linda. 2014. *Perishable Material Culture in Prehistory. Investigating the Missing Majority.* London: Routledge.

Ingold, Tim. 2000. "Making Culture and Weaving the World", in Paul Graves-Brown (ed.), *Matter, Materiality and Modern Culture*, 50–71. London: Routledge.

Jenkins, Ian D. 1985. "The Ambiguity of Greek Textiles", *Arethusa* 18 no. 2, 109–132.

Johnston, Ian Hugh and Papavramidou, Niki. 2024. *Galen on the Pulses. Medico-Historical Analysis, Textual Tradition, Translation*, Medicine in the Medieval Mediterranean 10. Berlin/Boston: De Gruyter.

Jouanna, Jaques. 1977. "Notes sur la scène de la reconnaissance dans les *Choéphores* d'Eschyle (v. 205–211) et sa parodie dans l'*Electre* d'Euripide (v. 532–537)", in *Mélanges offerts à Léopold Sédar Senghor. Langues, Littérature, Histoire Anciennes*, 185–200. Dakar: Les nouvelles éditions africaines.

Kania, Katrin. 2015. "Soft Yarns, Hard Facts? Evaluating the Results of a Large-Scale Hand-Spinning Experiment", *Journal for Archaeological and Anthropological Sciences* 7, 113–130.

Kearns, Emily. 1998. "The Nature of Heroines", in Sue Blundell and Margaret Williamson (eds.), *The Sacred and the Feminine in Ancient Greece*, 96–110. London/New York: Routledge.

Kerkhoff, Manfred. 1973. "Zum antiken Begriff des Kairos", *Zeitschrift für Philosophische Forschung* 27 no. 2, 256–274.

Kilian, Klaus. 1974. *Fibeln in Thessalien von der mykenischen bis zur archaischen Zeit*, Prähistorische Bronzefunde Abteilung XIV, 2. Munich: C. H. Beck.

Kilian-Dirlmeier, Imma. 1984. *Nadeln der frühhelladischen bis archaischen Zeit von der Peloponnes*, Prähistorische Bronzefunde Abteilung XIII, 8. Munich: C. H. Beck.

Kleingünther, Adolf. 1933. *ΠΡΩΤΟΣ ΕΥΡΕΤΗΣ. Untersuchungen zur Geschichte einer Fragestellung*, Philologus Supplementband XXVI, Heft 1. Leipzig: Dietrich.

Knapp, Bernard A. 1992. "Archaeology and *Annales*. Time, Space, and Change", in Bernard A. Knapp (ed.), *Archaeology, Annales, and Ethnohistory*, 1–22. Cambridge: Cambridge University Press.

Kolonas, Lazaros, Sarri, Kalliope, Margariti, Christina, Vanden Berghe, Ina, Skals, Irene and Nosch, Marie-Louise. 2017. "Heirs of the Loom? Funerary Textiles from Stamna (Aitolia, Greece). A Preliminary Analysis", in Michael Fotiadis, Robert Laffineur, Yannos Lolos and Andreas Vlachopoulos (eds.), *Hesperos. The Aegean Seen from the West. Proceedings of the 16th International Aegean Conference, Ioannina, 18–21 May 2016*, Aegaeum 41, 533–544. Leuven: Peeters.

Kubler, George. 1962. *The Shape of Time. Remarks on the History of Things*. New Haven/London: Yale University Press.

Kvavadze, Eliso, Bar-Yosef, Ofer, Belfer-Cohen, Anna, Boaretto, Elisabetta, Jakeli, Nino, Matskevich, Zinovi, Meshveliani, Tengiz. 2009. "30,000 Years Old Wild Flax Fibres. Testimony for Fabricating Prehistoric Linen", *Science* 325, 1359.

Lagger, Ursula. 2006. "Kleiderdiebstahl. Kein Kavaliersdelikt", in Monika Frass et al. (eds.), *Akten des 10. Österreichischen Althistorikertages. Salzburg, 11.11.–13.11.2004*. Diomedes Sonderband, 91–101. Vienna: Phoibos-Verlag.

Lagger, Ursula. 2009. "Auch Kleider machen Diebe. Diebstahl im antiken Athen", in Karl-Franzens-Universität Graz (ed.), *ERSTAUSGABE. Veröffentlichungen junger WissenschafterInnen der Karl-Franzens-Universität Graz, Volume* 2, 65–78. Graz: Uni-Press Graz.

Lambert, Stephen. 1997. "The Attic Genos Salaminioi and the Island of Salamis", *Zeitschrift für Papyrologie und Epigraphik* 119, 85–106.

Lambert, Stephen. 2002. "The Sacrificial Calendar of Athens", *Annual of the British School at Athens* 97, 353–399.

Landenius Enegren, Hedvig. 2015. "Loom Weights in Archaic South Italy and Sicily. Five Case Studies", *Opuscula. Annual of the Swedish Institutes at Athens and Rome* 8, 123–155.
Lane, Melissa S. 2009. *Method and Politics in Plato's 'Statesman'*, Cambridge Classical Studies. Cambridge: Cambridge University Press.
Le Guin, Ursula K. 1986. *The Carrier Bag Theory of Fiction*. N. Pub.
Lee, Mireille M. 2003. "The *Peplos* and the 'Dorian Question'", in Alice A. Donohue and Mark D. Fullerton (eds.), *Ancient Art and Its Historiography*, 118–146. Cambridge: Cambridge University Press.
Lee, Mireille M. 2005. "Constru(ct)ing Gender in the Feminine Greek *Peplos*", in Liza Cleland, Mary Harlow and Lloyd Llewellyn-Jones (eds.), *The Clothed Body in the Ancient World*, 55–64. Oxford/Oakville: Oxbow.
Lefkowitz, Mary R. 1995. "The Last Hours of the Parthenos", in Ellen D. Reeder (ed.), *Pandora. Women in Classical Greece*, 32–38. Baltimore/Princeton: Walters Art Gallery/Princeton University Press.
Lefkowitz, Mary R. and Fant, Maureen B. 2016. *Women's Life in Greece and Rome. A Source Book in Translation*. London: Bloomsbury.
Lemonnier, Pierre. 1983. "L'Étude des systèmes techniques, une urgence en technologie culturelle", in Geneviève Bédoucha (ed.), *Techniques et Culture, 1, "Actes de la table ronde 'Technologie culturelle (Ivry, novembre 1982)"*, 11–34. Paris: Editions de la Maison des Sciences de l'Homme.
Leroi-Gourhan, André. 1964. *Le geste et la parole, I: Technique et langage*. Paris: A. Michel.
Lewis, Orly. 2023. "The Mechanics of Galen's Theory of Nutrition", in Maria Gerolemou and George Kazantzidis (eds.), *Body and Machine in Classical Antiquity*, 262–295. New York: Cambridge University Press.
Lewy, Heinrich. 1895. *Die semitischen Fremdwörter im Griechischen*. Berlin: Gaertners.
Llewellyn-Jones, Lloyd. 2003. *Aphrodite's Tortoise. The Veiled Woman of Ancient Greece*. Swansea: Classical Press of Wales.
Lloyd-Jones, Hugh. 1961. "Some Alleged Interpolations in Aeschylus' *Choephori* and Euripides' *Electra*", *The Classical Quarterly* 11 no. 3–4, 171–184.
Longhi, Vivien. 2020. *Krisis ou la décision génératrice. Épopée, médecine hippocratique, Platon*, Cahiers de Philologie. Les Textes 36. Villeneuve d'Ascq: Presses Universitaires du Septentrion.
Losfeld, George. 1991. *Essai sur le costume grec*. Paris: De Boccard.
Loznjak Dizdar, Daria. "The Appearance of Fibulae in the Late Bronze Age. Creativity in the Crafting of the First Clothes Fasteners in the South of the Carpathian Basin", in Joanna Sofaer (ed.), *Considering Creativity: Creativity, Knowledge and Practice in Bronze Age Europe*, 143–151. Oxford: Archeopress.
Lupu, Eran. 2009. *Greek Sacred Law. A Collection of New Documents*, 2nd edition. Religions in the Graeco-Roman World 152. Leiden: Brill.
Madreiter, Irene. 2016. "Antiochos the Great and the Robe of Nebuchadnezzar. Intercultural Transfer between Orientalism and Hellenocentrism", in Saana Svärd and Robert Rollinger (eds.), *Cross-Cultural Studies in Near Eastern History and Literature. The Intellectual Heritage of the Ancient and Mediaeval Near East* 2, 111–136. Münster: Ugarit-Verlag.
Manessy-Guitton, Jaqueline. 1977. "La navette et la lyre, variations sur le thème *Kerk-* ", in *Mélanges offerts à Léopold Sédar Senghor. Langues, littérature, histoire ancienne*, 235–253. Dakar: Les nouvelles éditions africaines.

Mannering, Ulla. 2017. "Textiles and Clothing Traditions in Early Iron Age Denmark", in Margarita Gleba and Romina Laurito (eds.), *Contextualising Textile Production in Italy in the 1st Millennium BC*, Origini 40, 113–128. Rome: Gangemi Editore SPA.

Mannering, Ulla, Possnert, Göran, Heinemeier, Jan and Gleba, Margarita. 2010. "Dating Danish Textiles and Skins from Bog Finds by Means of ^{14}C AMS", *Journal of Archaeological Science* 37, 261–268.

Martin, Günther. 2015. "Weben und Wahrheit. Die Hermeneitik von Geweben in Euripides' Ion", in Henriette Harich-Schwarzbauer (ed.), *Weben und Gewebe in der Antike. Materialität – Repräsentation – Episteme – Metapoetik/Texts and Textiles in the Ancient World. Materiality – Representation – Episteme – Metapoetics*. Ancient Textiles Series 23, 109–132. Oxford: Oxbow Books.

Mauss, Marcel. 1936. *Les techniques du corps*, Journal de Psychologie XXXII, 3–4.

Merkelbach, Reinhold. 1973. "Der Theseus des Bakchylides (Gedicht für ein attisches Ephebenfest)", *Zeitschrift für Papyrologie und Epigraphik* 12, 56–62.

Mertens, Dieter. 1991. "Schnurkonstruktionen", in Adolf Hoffmann, Ernst-Ludwig Schwandner, Wolfram Hoepfner and Gunnar Brands (eds.), *Bautechnik der Antike: Internationales Kolloquium in Berlin vom 15.–17. Februar 1990*, Diskussionen zur archäologischen Bauforschung 5, 155–160. Mainz am Rhein: Ph. von Zabern.

Meyer, Richard. 1901. "Principien der wissenschaftlichen Periodenbildung. Mit besonderer Rücksicht auf die Litteraturgeschichte", *Euphorion. Zeitschrift für Litteraturgeschichte*, Achter Band, 1–42.

Michel, Cécile and Nosch, Marie-Louise, eds. 2010. *Textile Terminologies in the Ancient Near East and Mediterranean from the Third to the First Millennia BC*, Ancient Textiles Series 8. Oxford/Havertown: Oxbow.

Mikalson, Jon D. 1975. *The Sacred and Civil Calendar of the Athenian Year*, Princeton Legacy Library. Princeton/London: Princeton University Press.

Milanezi, Silvia. 2005. "Beauty in Rags. On Rhakos in Aristophanic Theatre", in Liza Cleland, Mary Harlow and Lloyd Llewellyn-Jones (eds.), *The Clothed Body in the Ancient World*, 75–86. Oxford/Oakville: Oxbow.

Miller, Kassandra. 2023. *Time and Ancient Medicine. How Sundials and Water Clocks Changed Medical Science*. Oxford: Oxford University Press.

Miller, Margaret. 2013. "Clothes and Identity. The Case of the Greeks in Ionia c. 400 BC", in Paul J. Burton (ed.), *Culture, Identity and Politics in the Ancient Mediterranean World. Papers from a Conference in Honour of Erich Gruen*. Antichthon 47, 18–38.

Miller, Nancy K. 1986. "Arachnologies. The Woman, The Text, and the Critic", in Nancy Miller (ed.), *The Poetics of Gender*, 270–295. New York: Columbia University Press.

Mitchel, Fordyce. 1956. "Herodotus' Use of Genealogical Chronology", *Phoenix* 10 no. 2, 48–69.

Möller, Astrid and Wagner-Hasel, Beate. Forthcoming. "Zeitvorstellungen und Weltbilder in der Antike", in: Beate Wagner-Hasel (ed.), *Antike Lebenswelten* (unpublished manuscript).

Momigliano, Arnaldo. 1966. "Time in Ancient Historiography", *History and Theory* 6 Beih. 6, 1–23.

Moraw, Susanne and Kieburg, Anna (eds). 2014. *Mädchen im Altertum/Girls in Antiquity*. Münster/New York: Waxmann.

Mårtensson, Linda, Andersson, Eva, Nosch, Marie-Louise and Batzer, Anne. 2006a. *Technical Report, Experimental Archaeology Part 2:1 Flax*. Danish National Research Foundation's Centre for Textile Research (CTR), University of Copenhagen: Centre for Textile Research, Tools and Textiles – Texts and Contexts Research Programme (https://ctr.hum.ku.dk/research-programmes-and-projects/previous-programmes-and-projects/tools/technical_report_2-1_experimental_archaeology.pdf [last access 15.08.2025]).

Mårtensson, Linda, Andersson, Eva, Nosch, Marie-Louise and Batzer, Anne. 2006b. *Technical Report, Experimental Archaeology Part 2:2 Whorl or Bead?* Danish National Research Foundation's Centre for Textile Research (CTR), University of Copenhagen: Centre for Textile Research, Tools and Textiles – Texts and Contexts Research Programme (https://ctr.hum.ku.dk/research-programmes-and-projects/previous-programmes-and-projects/tools/technical_report_2-2__experimental_arcaheology.pdf [last access 15.08.2025]).

Neils, Jenifer. 1992. "The Panathenaia. An Introduction", in Jenifer Neils (ed.), *Goddess and Polis. The Panathenaic Festival in Ancient Athens*, 13–27. New York: Princeton University Press.

Neri, Camillo. 2016. "Erinna's Loom", in Giovanni Fanfani, Mary Harlow and Marie-Louise Nosch (eds.), *Spinning Fates and the Song of the Loom. The Use of Textiles, Clothing and Cloth Production as Metaphor, Symbol and Narrative Device in Greek and Latin Literature*, Ancient Textiles Series 24, 195–216. Oxford/Havertown: Oxbow.

Nielsen, Mette Dalgaard and Skjold, Else. 2024. "Does Resale Extend the Use Phase of Garments? Exploring Longevity on the Fashion Resale Market", *International Journal of Sustainable Fashion and Textiles* 3 no. 1, 29–48.

Nilsson, Martin Persson. 1920. *Primitive Time-Reckoning. A Study in the Origins and First Development of the Art of Counting Time Among the Primitive and Early Culture Peoples*, Acta Societatis Humanorium Litterarum Lundensis I. Lund: C. W. K. Gleerup.

Nobili, Cecilia. 2018. "Elementi intervisuali nei ditirambi 17 e 18 di Bacchilide", *Acme* 71 no. 2, 21–40.

Nosch, Marie-Louise B. 2012. "The Textile Logograms in the Linear B Tablets. Les idéogrammes archéologiques – des textiles", in Pierre Carlier, Charles De Lamberterie, Markus Egetmeyer, Nicole Guilleux, Françoise Rougemont and Julien Zurbach (eds.), *Études mycéniennes 2010. Actes du XIIIe colloque international sur les textes égéens, Sèvres, Paris, Nanterre, 20–23 septembre 2010*, Biblioteca di "Pasiphae" X, 305–346. Pisa/Rome: Fabrizio Serra Editore.

Nosch, Marie-Louise. 2014a. "Voicing the Loom. Women, Weaving, and Plotting", in Dimitri Nakassis, Joann Gulizio and Sarah A. James (eds.), *KE-RA-ME-JA. Studies Presented to Cynthia W. Shelmerdine*, Prehistory Monographs 46, 91–101. Phildelphia: INSTAP Academic Press.

Nosch, Marie-Louise. 2014b. "Linen Textiles and Flax in Classical Greece. Provenance and Trade", in Kerstin Droß-Krüpe (ed.), *Textile Trade and Distribution in Antiquity/Textilhandel und -distribution in der Antike*, Philippika 73, 17–42. Wiesbaden: Harrassowitz.

Nosch, Marie-Louise. 2014c. "Mycenaean Wool Economies in the Latter Part of the 2nd Millennium BC Aegean", in Catherine Breniquet and Cécile Michel (eds.), *Wool Economy in the Ancient Near East and the Aegean. From the Beginnings of Sheep Husbandry to Institutional Textile Industry*, Ancient Textiles Series 17, 371–400. Oxford/Havertown: Oxbow.

Nosch, Marie-Louise. 2015. "The Wool Age. Textile Traditions and Textile Innovations in Textile Production, Consumption and Administration in the Late Bronze Age Aegean", in Jörg Weilhartner and Florian Ruppenstein (eds.), *Tradition and Innovation in the Mycenaean Palatial Polities. Proceedings of an International Symposium Held at the Austrian Academy of Sciences*, Österreichische Akademie der Wissenschaften. Philosophisch-historische Klasse Denkschriften, 487. Band. Mykenische Studien 34, 167–201. Vienna: Verlag d. ÖAW.

Nosch, Marie-Louise. 2016. "What's in a Name? What's in a Sign? Writing Wool, Scripting Shirts, Lettering Linen, Wording Wool, Phrasing Pants, Typing Tunics", in Susanne Lervad, Peder Flemestad and Lotte Weilgaard Christensen (eds.), *Verbal and Nonverbal Representation in*

Terminology. Proceedings of the TOTh Workshop 2013, Copenhagen – 8 November 2013, Terminologie and Ontologie: Théories et Applications, 93–115. Copenhagen: Institut Porphyre.

Nosch, Marie-Louise. 2019. "Textiles", in Irene S. Lemos and Antonis Kotsonas (eds.), *A Companion to the Archaeology of Early Greece and the Mediterranean*, 589–602. Chichester: Wiley and Sons.

Nosch, Marie-Louise B. 2021. "Textiles, vêtements et parures des royautés en Grèce avant Alexandre", in Ariane Guieu-Coppolani, Marie-Joséphine Werlings and Julien Zurbach (eds.), *Le pouvoir et la parole. Mélanges en mémoire de Pierre Carlier*, Études Anciennes 76, 103–138. Paris: De Boccard.

Nosch, Marie-Louise. 2022. "Klæder skaber Konger: Grækeres syn på kongers dragt i antikken?", in Marianne Pade (ed.), *Monarkier. Et festskrift til Hendes Majestæt Dronning Margrethe II i anledning af hendes 50-års regeringsjubilæum den 14. januar 2022*, 31–42. Copenhagen: Kongelige Danske Videnskabernes Selskab.

Nosch, Marie-Louise. 2023. "I begyndelsen var tøjet", in Sune Haugbølle, Tina Dransfeldt Christensen and Søren Møller Christensen (eds.), *Susanna i badet. Essays om mellemøststudier og den offentlige samtale. Festskrift i anledning af Jakob Skovgaard-Petersens 60 års fødselsdag*, 433–445. Copenhagen: Vandkunsten.

Nosch, Marie-Louise. 2024. "Diachronic Perspectives on the Knossos Textiles (L-Series) in the Room of the Chariot Tablets, the North Entrance Passage and the Main Archival Phase", in John Bennet, Artemis Karnava and Torsten Meißner (eds.), *ko-ro-no-we-sa. Proceedings of the 15th International Colloquium on Mycenaean Studies, September 2021*, Ariadne Supplement Series 5, 325–345. Rethymno: Crete University Press.

Nosch, Marie-Louise. 2025. "Divinely Royal. Garments of Kings and Priests in Ancient Greece with Comparisons from the Ancient Near East and the Levant", in Aleksandra Hallmann (ed.), *Outward Appearance vs. Inward Significance. Addressing Identities through Attire in the Ancient World. The Proceeding of the 14th Annual University of Chicago Oriental Institute Seminar, March 1–2, 2018*, ISACS 15, 279–318. Chicago: Institute for the Study of Ancient Cultures.

Nosch, Marie-Louise B. and Perna, Massimo. 2001. "Cloth in the Cult", in Robert Laffineur and Robin Hägg (eds.), *Potnia. Deities and Religion in the Aegean Bronze Age. 8th International Aegean Conference, University of Göteborg, 12–15 April 2000*, Aegaeum 22, 471–477. Liège/Austin: Université de Liège.

Nosch, Marie-Louise and Sauvage, Caroline. 2023. "Ancient Loom Weights at the J. Paul Getty Museum", *Getty Research Journal* 18, 1–34.

Nosch, Marie-Louise and Ulanowska, Agata. 2021. "The Materiality of the Cretan Hieroglyphic Script. Textile Production-Related Referents to Hieroglyphic Signs on Seals and Sealings from Middle Bronze Age Crete", in Philip Boyes, Philippa M. Steele and Natalia Elvira Astoreca (eds.), *The Social and Cultural Contexts of Historic Writing Practices*, 73–100. Oxford/Havertown: Oxbow.

Oakley, John. 1995. "Nuptial Nuances. Wedding Images in Non-Wedding Scenes of Myth", in Ellen D. Reeder (ed.), *Pandora. Women in Classical Greece*, 63–73. Baltimore/Princeton: Walters Art Gallery/Princeton University Press.

Olofsson, Linda, Andersson Strand, Eva and Nosch, Marie-Louise. 2015. "Experimental Testing of Bronze Age Textile Tools", in Eva Andersson Strand and Marie-Louise Nosch (eds.), *Tools, Textiles and Contexts. Investigating Textile Production in the Aegean and Eastern Mediterranean Bronze Age*, Ancient Textiles Series 21, 75–100. Oxford/Havertown: Oxbow.

Onians, Robert B. 1951. *The Origins of European Thought about the Body, the Mind, the Soul, the World, Time and Fate*. New York: Cambridge University Press.
Panofsky, Erwin. 1967. *Studies in Iconology. Humanistic Themes in the Art of the Renaissance*, 69–93 and plates XXI–XL. New York: Routledge.
Pantelia, Maria C. 1993. "Spinning and Weaving. Ideas of Domestic Order in Homer", *The American Journal of Philology* 114 no. 4, 493–501.
Parke, Herbert William. 1977. *Festivals of the Athenians*, Aspects of Greek and Roman Life. Ithaca: Cornell University Press.
Perlès, Catherine. 1987. *Les industries lithiques taillées de Franchthi (Argolide, Grèce). Tome I: Présentation générale et industries paléolithiques*, Excavations at Franchthi Cave, Greece, 3. Bloomington: Indiana University Press.
Pirenne-Delforge, Vinciane and Pironti, Gabriella. 2011. "Les Moires entre la naissance et la mort. De la représentation au culte", in Martine Hennard Dutheil de la Rochère and Véronique Dasen (eds.), *Des Fata aux fées. Regards croisés de l'Antiquité à nos jours*, Etudes de Lettres 3–4, 93–114.
Pierini, Rachele. 2018. "AB 54+04, Mycenaean *te-pa*, Alphabetic Greek τήβεννα, Latin *toga*. Semantic Remarks and Possible Near East Parallels", *Journal of Latin Linguistics* 17:1, 111–119.
Powell, Barry B. 2017. *The Poems of Hesiod. Theogony, Works and Days, and The Shield of Herakles*. Oakland, California: University of California Press.
Pritchett, W. Kendrick. 1953. "The Attic Stelai. Part I", *Hesperia* 22 no. 4, 225–299.
Pritchett, W. Kendrick and Pippin, Anne. 1956. "The Attic Stelai. Part II", *Hesperia* 25 no. 3, 178–328.
Quercia, Alessandro and Foxhall, Lin. 2012. "Tracing Networks Project. Craft Traditions in the Ancient Mediterranean. I pesi da telaio come indicatori di dinamiche produttive e culturali nelle attività tessili del sud-Italia in età preromana", in Maria Stella Busana, Patrizia Basso and Anna Rosa Tricomi (eds.), *La lana nella Cisalpina Romana. Economia e società. Studi in onore di Stefania Pasavento Mattioli, Atti del convegno (Padova-Verona, 18–20 maggio 2011)*, Antenor Quaderni 27, 367–381. Padova: Padova University Press.
Quillien, Louise. 2019. "Identity through Appearance. Babylonian Priestly Clothing During the 1st Millennium BC", *Journal of Ancient Near Eastern Religions* 19: 1–2, 71–89.
Quillien, Louise. 2022. *Histoire des textiles en Babylonie, 626–484 av. J.-C. Production, circulations et usages*. Culture and History of the Ancient Near East 126. Leiden/Boston: Brill.
Rahmstorf, Lorenz. 2003. "Clay Spools from Tiryns and Elsewhere. An Indication of Foreign Influence in LH III C?", in Nina Kyparissi-Apostolika and Mani Papakonstantinou (eds.), *The Periphery of the Mycenaean World. 2nd International Interdisciplinary Colloquium in Lamia, Greece, 26–30.9.1999*, 397–415. Athen: Ministery of Culture.
Rahmstorf, Lorenz. 2011. "Handmade Pots and Crumbling Loomweights. 'Barbarian' Elements in the Eastern Mediterranean in the Last Quarter of the 2nd Millennium BC", in Vassos Karageorghis and Ourania Kouka (eds.), *On Cooking Pots, Drinking Cups, Loomweights and Ethnicity in Bronze Age Cyprus and Neighbouring Regions. An International Archaeological Symposium held in Nicosia, November 6th–7th 2010*, 315–330. Nicosia: A. G. Leventis Foundation.
Rasmussen, Anders Holm. 2023. "Om attiske offerkalendere i klassisk tid", *Aigis Suppl*. 7.
Raubitschek, Antony E. 1945. "The Priestess of Pandrosos", *American Journal of Archaeology* 49 no. 4, 434–435.

Reeder, Ellen D. 1995. "Women and Men in Classical Greece", in Ellen D. Reeder (ed.), *Pandora. Women in Classical Greece*, 20–31. Baltimore/Princeton: Walters Art Gallery/Princeton University Press.

Reinard, Patrick. 2019. "Used Universe? Zu Kategorisierungsmöglichkeiten ökonomisch motivierter Wiederverwendung anhand archäologischer, epigraphischer und papyrologischer Beispiele", in Patrick Reinard, Christian Rollinger and Christoph Schäfer (eds.), *Wirtschaft und Wiederverwendung. Beiträge zur antiken Ökonomie*. Scripta Mercaturae-Beihefte. Beiträge zur Wirtschafts- und Sozialgeschichte 1, 199–254. Gutenberg: Scripta Mercaturae Verlag.

Reinard, Patrick, Rollinger, Christian and Schäfer, Christoph. eds. 2019. *Wirtschaft und Wiederverwendung. Beiträge zur antiken Ökonomie*. Scripta Mercaturae-Beihefte. Beiträge zur Wirtschafts- und Sozialgeschichte 1. Gutenberg: Scripta Mercaturae Verlag.

Reinecke, Juliane and Ansari, Shahzad. 2017. "Time, Temporality, and Process Studies", in Ann Langley and Hari Tsoukas (eds.), *The SAGE Handbook of Process Organization Studies*, 1–25. Los Angeles: Sage Reference.

Remijsen, Sofie. 2023. "Women on Time. Gendered Temporalities in Greco-Roman Egypt", in Lucinda Dirven, Martijn Icks and Sofie Remijsen (eds.), *The Public Lives of Ancient Women (500 BCE-650 CE)*, Mnemosyne Suppl. 468, 158–172. Leiden/Boston: Brill.

Reuthner, Rosa. 2006. *Wer webte Athenes Gewänder? Die Arbeit von Frauen im antiken Griechenland*. Frankfurt: Campus Verlag.

Reuthner, Rosa. 2019. "Textiles Beutegut und Kleidermärkte in Athen. Überlegungen zum Verbleib der Kleidung aus der Perserbeute", in Beate Wagner-Hasel and Marie-Louise Nosch (eds.), *Gaben, Waren und Tribute. Stoffkreisläufe und antike Textilökonomie. Akten eines Symposiums (9./ 10. Juni 2016 in Hannover)*, 237–250. Stuttgart: Franz Steiner Verlag.

Ricoeur, Paul. 1980. "Narrative Time", *Critical Inquiry* 7 no. 1, 169–190.

Riis, Poul Jørgen. 1993. "Ancient Types of Garments. Prolegomena to the Study of Greek and Roman Clothing", *Acta Archaeologica* 64, 149–182.

Ritter, Hans-Werner. 1965. *Diadem und Königsherrschaft. Untersuchungen zu Zeremonien und Rechtsgrundlagen des Herrschaftsantritts bei den Persern, bei Alexander dem Großen und im Hellenismus*, Vestigia. Beiträge zur alten Geschichte 7. Munich: C. H. Beck.

Rivoli, Pietra. 2014. *The Travels of a T-shirt in the Global Economy. An Economist Examines the Markets, Power, and Politics of World Trade*. Hoboken: Wiley and Sons.

Robertson, Noel. 2004. "The Praxiergidae Decree (*IG* I^3 7) and the Dressing of Athena's Statue with the *Peplos*", *Greek, Roman and Byzantine Studies* 44, 111–161.

Robson, James. 2005. "New Clothes, a New You. Clothing and Character in Aristophanes", in Liza Cleland, Mary Harlow and Lloyd Llewellyn-Jones (eds.), *The Clothed Body in the Ancient World*, 65–74. Oxford/Havertown: Oxbow.

Roebuck, Carl. 1959. *Ionian Trade and Colonization*. New York: Archaeological Institute of America.

Roller, Duane W. 1989. *Tanagran Studies I. Sources and Documents on Tanagra in Boiotia*, McGill University Monographs in Classical Archaeology and History 9. Leiden/Boston: Brill.

Rössler, Detlef. 1974. "Modetendenzen in der griechischen Tracht am Ende des 5. und im 4. Jahrhundert v. u. Z.", in Elisabeth Charlotte Welskopf (ed.), *Hellenische Poleis. Krise – Wandel – Wirkung*, Vol. III, 1539–1569. Berlin: Akademie-Verlag.

Roussel, Pierre. 1941. "Les chlamydes noires des éphèbes athéniens", *Revue des Études Anciennes* 43:3–4, 163–165.

Roux, Georges. 1974. "Commentaires à l'Orestie", *Revue des Études Grecques* 87 no. 414–418, 33–79.

Scheid, John and Svenbro, Jesper. 1994. *Le métier de Zeus. Mythe du tissage et du tissu dans le monde gréco-romain.* Paris: La Découverte.
Scheid, John and Svenbro, Jesper. 2003. *Le métier de Zeus. Mythe du tissage et du tissu dans le monde gréco-romain* (nouvelle édition). Paris: Errance.
Schibli, Hermann Sadun. 1990. *Pherekydes of Syros.* Oxford: Clarendon Press.
Schmitt, Jean-Claude. ed. 2002. *Ève et Pandora. La création de la femme.* Paris: Gallimard.
Schmitt-Pantel, Pauline. 1977. "Athéna Apatouria et la ceinture. Les aspects féminins des Apatouries à Athènes", *Annales. Économies, Sociétés, Civilisations* 32 no. 6, 1059–1073.
Schmitt-Pantel, Pauline. 2016. "Der Gürtel. Körperschmuck, Statussymbol und Geschlechtsmerkmal", in Beate Wagner-Hasel and Marie-Louise Nosch (eds.), *Gaben, Waren und Tribute. Stoffkreisläufe und antike Textilökonomie. Akten eines Symposiums (9./10. Juni 2016 in Hannover)*, 333–355. Stuttgart: Franz Steiner Verlag.
Schneider, Jane and Weiner, Annette B. 1986. "Cloth and the Organization of Human Experience", *Current Anthropology* 27 no. 2, 178–184.
Sellet, Frédéric. 1993. "Chaîne opératoire. The Concept and Its Applications", *Lithic Technology* 18 no. 1–2, 106–112.
Shapiro, H. Alan. 1995. "The Cult of Heroines. Kekrops' Daughters", in Ellen D. Reeder (ed.), *Pandora. Women in Classical Greece*, 39–48. Baltimore/Princeton: Walters Art Gallery/Princeton University Press.
Shaya, Josephine. 2005. "The Greek Temple as Museum. The Case of the Legendary Treasure of Athena from Lindos", *American Journal of Archaeology* 109 no. 3, 423–442.
Singer, Peter N. 2022. *Time for the Ancients. Measurements, Theory, Experience*, Chronoi. Zeit, Zeitempfinden, Zeitordnungen 3. Berlin/Boston: De Gruyter.
Singer, Peter N. 2023. *Galen. Writings on Health. Thrasybulus and Health (De sanitate tuenda).* New York: Cambridge University Press.
Sipiora, Philip. 2002. "Introduction. The Ancient Concept of Kairos", in Phillip Sipiora and James S. Baumlin (eds.), *Rhetoric and Kairos. Essays in History, Theory, and Praxis*, 1–22. Albany: State University of New York Press.
Sipiora, Philip and Baumlin, James S. eds. 2002. *Rhetoric and Kairos. Essays in History, Theory, and Praxis.* Albany: State University of New York Press.
Skals, Irene, Möller-Wiering, Susan and Nosch, Marie-Louise. 2015. "Survey of Archaeological Textile Remains from the Aegean and Eastern Mediterranean Area", in Eva Andersson Strand and Marie-Louise Nosch (eds.), *Tools, Textiles and Contexts. Investigating Textile Production in the Aegean and Eastern Mediterranean Bronze Age*, Ancient Textiles Series 21, 61–74 and appendix A and B. Oxford/Havertown: Oxbow.
Skjold, Else. 2016. "Biographical Wardrobes— A Temporal View on Dress Practice", *Fashion Practice* 8, 135–148.
Snell, Bruno. 1946. *Die Entdeckung des Geistes. Studien zur Entstehung des europäischen Denkens bei den Griechen.* Göttingen: Vandenhoeck and Ruprecht.
Snyder, Jane McIntosh. 1981. "The Web of Song. Weaving Imagery in Homer and the Lyric Poets", *The Classical Journal* 76, 193–196.
Soffer, Olga, Adovasio, James M. and Hyland, David C. 2000. "The 'Venus' Figurines. Textile, Basketry, Gender, and Status in the Upper Palaeolithic", *Current Anthropology* 41 no. 4, 511–537.

Soffer, Olga and Adovasio, James M. 2010. "The Roles of Perishable Technologies in Upper Paleolithic Lives", in Ezra B. W. Zubrow, Françoise Audouze, and James G. Enloe (eds.), *The Magdalenian Household. Unraveling Domesticity*, 235–244. New York: SUNY Press.

Solmsen, Friedrich. 1967. "Electra and Orestes. Three Recognitions in Greek Tragedy", *Mededelingen der Koninklijke Nederlandse Akademie van Wetenschappen. Afdeeling Letterkunde. Nieuwe reeks* 30 no. 2, 31–62.

Sørensen, Tim Flohr. 2024. "Ragpickers. Critiquing the Third Science Revolution with Walter Benjamin", in Anne Drewsen, Ulla Mannering and Marie-Louise Nosch (eds.), *The Common Thread. Collected Essays in Honour of Eva Andersson Strand*, New Approaches in Archaeology 3, 11–23. Turnhout: Brepols.

Sourvinou, Christiane. 1971. "Aristophanes, *Lysistrata*, 641–647", *The Classical Quarterly* 21 no. 2, 339–342.

Sourvinou-Inwood, Christiane. 2011. *Athenian Myths and Festivals. Aglauros, Erechtheus, Plynteria, Panathenaia, Dionysia*. New York: Oxford University Press.

Spantidaki, Stella. 2016. *Textile Production in Classical Athens*. Ancient Textiles Series 27. Oxford/Philadelphia: Oxbow.

Spantidaki, Stella, Flemested, Peder and Nosch, Marie-Louise. 2023. "Interdisciplinary Perspectives on the Sails of the Athenian Trireme", in Martin Bentz and Michael Heinzelmann (eds.), *Archaeology and Economy in the Ancient World. Proceedings of the 19th International Congress of Classical Archaeology, Cologne/Bonn 2018*, Single Contributions, Sessions 6–8, Band 55, 33–35. Heidelberg: Heidelberg University Library (https://doi.org/10.11588/propylaeum.1035.c14045).

Stears, Karen. 1995. "Dead Women's Society. Constructing Female Gender in Classical Athenian Funerary Sculpture", in Nigel Spencer (ed.), *Time, Tradition and Society in Greek Archaeology. Bridging the 'Great Divide'*, 109–131. London/New York: Routledge.

Stears, Karen. 1998. "Death Becomes Her. Gender and Athenian Death Ritual", in Sue Blundell and Margaret Williamson (eds.), *The Sacred and the Feminine in Ancient Greece*, 113–127. London/New York: Routledge.

Studniczka, Franz. 1886. *Beiträge zur Geschichte der altgriechischen Tracht*, Abhandlungen des archäologisch-epigraphischen Seminares der Universität Wien VI, 1. Vienna: Carl Gerold's Sohn.

Swalec, Jennifer. 2016. "Weaving for the People Not a *Peplos*, but a *Chlaina*. Wool-Working, Peace, and Nuptial Sex in Aristophanes' *Lysistrata*", in Giovanni Fanfani, Mary Harlow and Marie-Louise Nosch (eds.), *Spinning Fates and the Song of the Loom. The Use of Textiles, Clothing and Cloth Production as Metaphor, Symbol and Narrative Device in Greek and Latin Literature*, Ancient Textiles Series 24, 161–178. Oxford/Havertown: Oxbow.

Thomsen, Christian Ammitzbøll. 2023. "Vreden og gudinden. Kvinders bønner om retfærdighed i det hellenistiske Knidos", *Aigis Suppl.* 7, 1–15.

Thomsen, Christian Ammitzbøll. 2025. *Stemmer fra Antikken*, AIGIS – Nordisk tidsskrift for klassiske studier 25/1. Frederiksberg: Frydenlund Academic.

Thomsen, Christian Jürgensen. 1836. *Ledetraad til Nordisk Oldkyndighed og Historie*. Copenhagen: S. L. Møllers Buchdruckerei.

Thomsen, Christian Jürgensen. 1837. *Leitfaden zur Nordischen Alterthumskunde*. Copenhagen: Bianco Luno and Schneider.

Thomsen, Christian Jürgensen. 1848. *Guide to Northern Archaeology. Edited for the Use of English Readers by the Earls of Ellesmere*. Copenhagen: Berlin Brothers.

Thomson, George. 1966. *The Oresteia of Aeschylus*, Vol. I–II. Amsterdam/Prague: Hakkert/Academia.

Thomson, George. 1972. *Aeschylus and Athens. A Study in the Social Origins of Drama*. New York: Haskell House Publishers.
Thraede, Klaus. 1962. "Das Lob des Erfinders. Bemerkungen zur Analyse der Heuremata-Kataloge", *Rheinisches Museum für Philologie* 105, 158–186.
Toups, Melissa A., Kitchen, Andrew, Light, Jessica E. and Reed, David L. 2011. "Origin of Clothing Lice Indicates Early Clothing Use by Anatomically Modern Humans in Africa", *Molecular Biology and Evolution* 28 no. 1, 29–32.
Tranberg Hansen, Karen. 2000. *Salaula. The World of Secondhand Clothing and Zambia*. Chicago: University of Chicago Press.
Trédé, Monique. 1992. *Kairos. L'à-propos et l'occasion. Le mot et la notion, d'Homère à la fin du IVe siècle avant J.-C.* (doctoral thesis).
Trédé-Boulmer, Monique. 2015. *Kairos. L'à-propos et l'occasion. Le mot et la notion d'Homère à la fin du IVe siècle avant J.-C.*, Collection d'Études Anciennes, Série Grecque 150. Paris: Les Belles Lettres.
Trier, Jost. 1940. "First. Über die Stellung des Zauns im Denken der Vorzeit", *Nachrichten von der Gesellschaft der Wissenschaften in Göttingen. Philologisch-Historische Klasse IV, Neuere Philologie und Literaturgeschichte, Neue Folge Band* III, 55–137.
Turnbull, Jocelyn, Sparks, Rodher and Prior, Christine. 2000. "Testing the Effectiveness of AMS Radiocarbon Pretreatment and Preparation on Archaeological Textiles", *Nuclear Instruments and Methods in Physics Research* B 172, 469–472.
Ulanowska, Agata. 2020. "The Chaîne Opératoire as a Cognitive Framework for Investigating Prehistoric Textile Production: Production of Clay Textile Tools in Middle Bronze Age Crete as a 'Troublesome' Case Study", in Monique Arntz and Michael Lewis (eds.), *The Chaîne Opératoire. Past, Present and Future*, Archaeological Review from Cambridge 35:1, 212–226. Cambridge: Victoire Press.
Utzschneider, Helmut. 1988. *Das Heiligtum und das Gesetz. Studien zur Bedeutung der sinaitischen Heiligtumstexte (Ex 25–40; Lev 8–9)*, Orbis Biblicus et Orientalis 77. Fribourg/Göttingen: Vandenhoeck and Ruprecht.
Veenhof, Klaas R. 1972. "Aspects of Old Assyrian Trade and Its Terminology", *Studia et Documenta ad Iura Orientis Antiqui Pertinentia* 10. Leiden: Brill.
Vian, Francis. 1948. "Le péplos des Panathénées dans le περὶ θεῶν d'Apollodore", in *Mélanges d'archéologie et d'histoire offerts à Charles Picard à l'occasion de son 65e anniversaire*, Revue Archéologique 31/32, 1060–1064.
Vidal-Naquet, Pierre. 1968. "Le chasseur noir et l'origine de l'éphébie athénienne", *Annales. Histoire, Sciences Sociales* 23 no. 5, 947–964.
Wace, Alan J. B. 1934. "The Veil of Despoina", *American Journal of Archaeology* 38, 107–111.
Wace, Alan J. B. 1948. "Weaving or Embroidery?", *American Journal of Archaeology* 52, 51–55.
Waetzoldt, Hartmut. 1972. *Untersuchungen zur neusumerischen Textilindustrie*, Studi Economici e Tecnologici 1. Rome: Instuti per l'Oriente.
Wagner-Hasel, Beate. 2000. *Der Stoff der Gaben. Kultur und Politik des Schenkens und Tauschens im archaischen Griechenland*. Frankfurt/New York: Campus Verlag.
Wagner-Hasel, Beate. 2001. "Die Reglementierung von Traueraufwand und die Tradierung des Nachruhms der Toten in Griechenland", in Thomas Späth and Beate Wagner-Hasel (eds.), *Frauenwelten in der Antike*. Stuttgart/Weimar: Metzler Verlag, 81–102.
Wagner-Hasel, Beate. 2002. "The Graces and Colour-Weaving", in Lloyd Llewellyn-Jones (ed.), *Women's Dress in the Ancient Greek World*. Swansea: Classical Press of Wales, 17–32.

Wagner-Hasel, Beate. 2006. "*Textus* und *texere*, *hýphos* und *hyphaínein*. Zur metaphorischen Bedeutung des Webens in der griechisch-römischen Antike", in Ludolf Kuchenbuch and Uta Kleine (eds.), ‚*Textus'* im Mittelalter. Komponenten und Situationen des Wortgebrauchs im schriftsemantischen Feld*. Göttingen: Vandenhoek and Ruprecht, 15–42.
Wagner-Hasel, Beate. 2011. *Die Arbeit des Gelehrten. Der Nationalökonom Karl Bücher (1847–1930)*, Frankfurt a.M./New York: Campus Verlag.
Wagner-Hasel, Beate. 2017. *Antike Welten*. Frankfurt/New York: Campus Verlag.
Wagner-Hasel, Beate. 2020. *The Fabrics of Gifts. Culture and Politics of Giving and Exchange in Archaic Greece*. Lincoln: Zea Books.
Wagner-Hasel, Beate. 2022. "Klytaimestra's Weapon and the Shroud for the Dead", *Archimède: archéologie et historie ancienne* 6, 134–145.
Wahnbaeck, Carolin and Groth, Hanno. 2015. *Wegwerfware Kleidung. Repräsentative Greenpeace-Umfrage zu Kaufverhalten, Tragedauer und der Entsorgung von Mode.* (https://www.greenpeace.de/publikationen/20151123_greenpeace_modekonsum_flyer.pdf [last access 04.07.2025]).
Walter, Anke. 2024. "Introduction", in Anke Walter (ed.), *The Temporality of Festivals. Approaches to Festive Time in Ancient Babylon, Greece, Rome and Medieval China*, Chronoi. Zeit, Zeitempfinden, Zeitordnungen 10, 1–10. Berlin/Boston: De Gruyter.
Wees, Hans van. 2005a. "Clothes, Class and Gender in Homer", in Douglas Cairns (ed.), *Body Language in the Greek and Roman Worlds*, 1–36. Swansea: Classical Press of Wales.
Wees, Hans van. 2005b. "Trailing Tunics and Sheepskin Coats: Dress and Status in Early Greece", in Liza Cleland, Mary Harlow and Lloyd Llewellyn-Jones (eds.), *The Clothed Body in the Ancient World*, 44–52. Oxford/Havertown: Oxbow.
Welters, Linda and Lillethun, Abby. 2018. *Fashion History. A Global View.* London: Bloomsbury.
Wersinger-Taylor, Gabrièle. 2018. "L'invention de l'invention. Archéologie ou idéologie?", *Cahiers 'Mondes anciens'* 11, 1–15.
White, Eric Charles. 1987. *Kaironomia. On the Will-to-Invent*. Ithaca: Cornell University Press.
Wilamowitz-Möllendorf, Ulrich von. ed. 1901. *Griechische Tragödien übersetzt von Ulrich von Wilamowitz-Möllendorf, Zweiter Band: Orestie*. Berlin: Weidmännische Buchhandlung.
Wind, Robert. 1972. "Myth and History in Bacchylides Ode 18", *Hermes* 100 no. 4, 511–523.
Witmore, Christopher. 2023. "The Antiquity of Time. Objects Greek", in Graham Harman and Christopher Witmore (eds.), *Objects Untimely. Object-Oriented Philosophy and Archaeology*, 26–60. Cambridge: Polity Press.
Wolkenhauer, Anja. 2011. *Sonne und Mond, Kalender und Uhr. Studien zur Darstellung und poetischen Reflexion der Zeitordnung in der römischen Literatur*, Untersuchungen zur antiken Literatur und Geschichte 103. Berlin/New York: De Gruyter.
Zawadzki, Stefan. 2006. *Garments of the Gods. Studies on the Textile Industry and the Pantheon of Sippar According to the Texts from the Ebabbar Archive*. Orbis Biblicus et Orientalis 218. Fribourg/Götting: Vandenhoeck and Ruprecht.
Zeitlin, Froma. 1995. "The Economics of Hesiod's Pandora", in Ellen D. Reeder (ed.), *Pandora. Women in Classical Greece*, 49–56. Baltimore/Princeton: Walters Art Gallery/Princeton University Press.
Zhmud, Leonid. 2001. "Prõtoi eyretai – Götter, Heroen, Menschen?", in Jochen Althoff, Bernhard Herzhoff and Georg Wöhrle (eds.), *Antike Naturwissenschaft und ihre Rezeption, Band 11*, 9–21. Trier: Wissenschaftlicher Verlag Trier.

Zhmud, Leonid. 2006. "Chapter 1. In Search of the First Discoverers: Greek Heurematography and the Origin of the History of Science", in Leonid Zhmud, *The Origin of the History of Science in Classical Antiquity*, 23–44. Berlin/Boston: De Gruyter.

Index

Achaemenid   67
Adam   9, 10
Aegina   107–109
Aglauros   14, 91, 115
Aischylos   74, 75, 98, 99, 101, 106
Alcman   93
Alexander the Great   68, 77, 79, 80
Ampekhonon   53, 69
Amyklai   93
Anakalypteria   82
Antigonus   86
Apatouria   84
Aphrodite   13, 60, 62, 86
Apollo   15, 93, 104
Apollodorus   86
Appian   68
Arachne   15, 16, 18, 115
Archon   4, 5, 66
Argos   4, 5, 38, 94, 102, 103, 108, 109, 118.
Aristophanes   18, 30, 68, 77, 87, 93, 113
Aristotle   71, 72, 86
Arrhēphoria, arrhēphoroi   14, 72, 85–89, 95, 96
Artaxerxes   67, 79
Artemis   15, 33, 34, 62, 63, 72, 82, 102
Athena   10–14, 16, 72, 84–95, 115
Athenaeus   18, 80
Athens   4, 5, 14, 68, 71, 76, 77, 81, 85–97, 104, 107–109, 117
Atropos   7, 15

Baby   14, 20, 33, 34, 71, 73, 84, 86, 104, 115
Babylonia/Babylon   9, 68, 79
Basket   10, 11, 14, 46, 63, 64, 86, 104, 109
Belt   63, 64, 72, 77–79, 83, 84
Birth   14, 15, 33, 45, 72, 73, 77, 84, 87, 88, 104, 105
Body   8, 9, 19, 20, 33, 42, 52–54, 56, 72, 102, 110, 120
Boeotia   10, 18, 62, 66, 77, 93, 97
Boy   71–73, 78, 84
Brauron   62–65, 72, 73

Calendar   2, 5, 85, 88, 90, 94, 95
Callimachos   15, 94
Carrier Bag Theory   20
Chaîne Opératoire   31, 32, 43, 91, 95
Chalkeia   85, 86, 95–97
Child/children/childhood   16, 42, 62–65, 71–73, 84, 98, 101, 102, 104, 106
Cloak   1, 14, 30, 36, 39, 42, 52, 62, 63, 69, 74, 76–81, 88, 90, 93, 94
Comedy   68, 77, 89, 92
Cotton   23, 50, 60, 120
Creusa   104–105
Cyrus   67

Death   14, 46, 47, 60, 74, 75, 77, 99, 102, 107, 108
Dedication, dedicated   15, 34, 62–67, 69, 72, 84, 93, 108
Delphi   3, 104
Demeter   62, 74
Demetrius Poliorcetes   86
Demosthenes   68, 69
Diodorus   47, 80
Distaff   13, 41, 46, 51, 70
Dorian/Doric   24, 51, 52, 108, 109, 111, 112, 117

Eileithyia   15
Electra   98–106, 115
Embroidery   99, 118
Ephēbeia, ephebe   14, 63, 64, 71, 72, 77–79
Ephor   4, 5
Epigram   4, 84
Ergastinai   13, 86–89, 96
Erichthonios   14, 86, 104, 115
Euripides   74, 75, 98, 99, 102, 104, 106, 115
Experimental archaeology   29, 39–44

Fabric   1, 6, 8, 11, 13, 18, 23, 25, 26, 35, 36, 40, 43, 44, 47, 48, 52, 60, 69, 98, 99, 104, 111, 115, 116, 119, 120
Fashion   107–116, 119–121
Fibres   2, 8, 11, 19–29, 33, 36, 39–41, 43, 50, 94–96, 120

Flax   6, 20, 21, 28, 29, 39–43, 47, 51, 63, 94
Fleece   14, 90–92, 94, 96
Funeral   75, 76

Galen   36, 37
Genealogies   3, 4, 14
Girl   11, 13, 14, 46, 66, 71–73, 81, 82, 84–86, 88, 93, 94, 96, 98, 99, 104–106, 109
Girdle/girded. See belt

Heirloom   69, 70
Hekatombaion   87, 88, 95
Helen   46, 48, 75, 117
Hemp   20, 29
Hephaistos   11, 12
Hera   4, 62, 66, 93, 94, 97, 115
Herakles   16, 48
Hermes   62, 66, 67, 104
Herodotus   3, 4, 6, 24, 73, 74, 107, 109, 117
Hesiod   3, 5, 10, 11, 14, 22, 30
Hesychius   14, 54, 56, 73
Himation   52, 63–65, 69, 72, 75, 88, 90, 91, 109–111, 117
Homer   2, 5, 11, 15, 28, 36, 38, 39, 46–48, 51, 53, 55, 56, 73, 75, 90, 102, 117, 118
Homeric Hymns   13, 74
Household   18, 33, 35, 42, 98, 114
Hyakinthia   93
Hyginus   18
Hyphasma   13, 98, 99, 106

Iliad. See Homer
Indo-European   1, 52
Infant   See baby
Ion   98, 104–106
Ionian/Ionic   18, 24, 51, 52, 107–112, 117, 118
Iphigenia   99, 102–104, 106

Jewish   33, 77, 81
Josephus   81

Kairos   1, 53–59, 67
Kallynteria   88–91, 85
Kalymma   52, 53, 74
Kalypso   48
Kalyptra   53, 72
Katapetasma   53, 67

Kausia   80
Kekrops   14, 91
Kerkis   35, 52, 57, 99
Khitōn, khitōnion, khitōniskos   36, 42, 48, 51, 52, 62, 65, 66, 72, 73, 78, 80, 89–91, 93, 107–111, 115, 117
Khlaina   36, 52, 69
Khlamys, khlamydes, khlamydion   52, 63, 64, 68, 72, 77, 78, 80
Khlanis, khlanides, khlanidion, khlanidiska, khlanidiskion   52, 63–66, 72
Kirke   48
Klothō   15
Korē   62, 71
Krēdemnon   53, 72
Krinō   57
Krisis   57

Lachesis   15
Laconia   93, 97
Laertes   38, 47, 48, 73, 118
Lindos   3
Linear B   29, 50, 51
Linen   4, 6, 18, 24, 28, 28, 39–44, 51, 52, 56, 57, 63, 64, 66, 78, 107, 108, 110–112
Locri   45
Locris   93, 94
Logogram   50
Loom   24, 30, 35, 39, 47, 48, 51, 54, 56–58, 69, 70, 86, 105
Loom-weight   24, 35, 69, 70
Lysias   68

Mantle   12, 39, 54, 73, 77, 90, 93, 95, 99, 113
Marriage/married/unmarried   11, 38, 47, 48, 60–62, 71, 82, 83, 86, 99, 118
Meletius   94
Menopause   72
Mesopotamia   8–10, 21, 68
Metaphor   6, 14, 33, 37, 44, 45, 53, 55, 57, 78, 83
Miletus   62, 63, 78
Minoan   24, 50, 53, 70
Moires   6, 7, 14, 15, 45, 115
Mycenaean   15, 24, 26, 36, 50–52, 117

Nausikaa   46, 90
Nebuchadnezzar   68

Odysseus   36, 38, 48, 118
Odyssey   See Homer
Old Testament   9, 53, 77
Olympia   93, 97, 115
Olympic Games   3, 5
Orestes   98–106, 115

Palaeolithic   19, 20
Panathenaia   87–91, 93, 95–97, 115
Pandora   10–12, 115
Pandrosos   14, 91, 115
Pastoralism/pastoralist   11, 12, 94
Pausanias   13–15, 84, 93
Penelope   38, 39, 47, 48, 57, 58, 73, 117, 118
Peplos   39, 42, 52, 72, 74, 75, 83, 85–91, 93, 95, 96, 104, 107–112, 115, 117
Persian   5, 6, 52, 67, 69, 79, 80, 109, 111, 117
Pharos   12, 39, 42, 73, 90, 91, 93
Pin   24, 107, 108
Pindar   5, 15
Plato   11–13, 53, 57
Pliny the Elder   17, 18, 47
Plutarch   18, 55, 67, 74, 75, 79, 80, 83, 86, 90
Plynteria   14, 87–92, 95, 96
Poikilos   vi, 12, 48
Pollux   16, 74
Praxiergidai   85, 87–90
Pregnancy   2, 33, 84, 86
Priest   5, 66, 67, 81, 92
Priestess   4, 5, 14, 86, 88, 89, 91–93, 102
Prosōpida   53, 63, 64
Purity/impurity   33
Purple   16, 26, 46, 47, 62–66, 74, 75, 79, 80

Radiocarbon/14C   25–27
Rag, ragged   vi, 33, 62, 63, 65–67, 99, 101, 116
Rhakos   See rag
Rhythm   vii, 22, 28, 31, 33–36, 115
Ribbon   59, 63, 64, 83

Sail   2, 35, 43, 44, 48, 68, 88
Samos   62, 63, 66, 84

Sanctuaries   3, 4, 14, 24, 33, 34, 44, 62, 65–69, 78, 85, 89–93, 108, 115, 116
Sappho   62
Sassanian   60
Sculptures   107–109
Seasons   1, 2, 5, 6, 19, 28–32, 36, 94, 115, 119
Semitic   51, 52, 54, 111
Sex   9, 81, 83
Shearing   29, 30, 92, 94
Sheep   8, 9, 28–30, 92, 94
Shepherd   11, 12, 30
Shirt   40, 42, 43
Shroud   1, 38, 73, 116, 118
Silk   23, 25, 26, 63, 64, 118
Sindonites   63, 64
Skirophorion   86, 90, 92, 95, 96
Soldier   69, 107, 116
Solon   5, 75, 76
Sophocles   48
Sparta   4, 5, 46, 77, 83, 93, 103, 112
Spin, spinning, spinner   v, 1, 6, 8, 13–15, 18–20, 25, 28, 30, 38, 40–49, 51, 86, 91, 95, 96, 118, 120
Spindle   7, 13, 15, 18, 41, 46, 51
Spindle-whorl   40, 41, 44
Spools   24
Stamna   26, 27
Stolē   52, 67, 68, 81

Tabby   23, 24, 26, 53, 56
Tanagra   62, 66, 72
Tapestry   vi, 48, 86, 95, 96, 98, 99, 102, 104, 117
Tarantinon   65, 66
Tegidion   53, 66
Temple   3, 62, 63, 67, 68, 85, 87, 89, 104, 108
Temple Inventories   62, 63, 72, 84
Terminology   6, 50, 52, 58, 71, 72, 91, 94, 117
Themis   15
Thread   vi, 1, 6–8, 14, 15, 18, 20–23, 25, 26, 35, 36, 38–45, 53–60, 104, 115
Thucydides   3, 5, 24, 109–111, 117
Trade   17, 23, 68, 112–114, 120
Tragedy   74, 98, 99, 104, 115
Trireme   43, 44
Troy   3, 5, 14, 48, 60, 98, 102, 117
T-Shirt   119, 120

Tunic   36, 42, 43, 48, 51, 60, 61, 80, 108, 110, 116
Twill   23, 24, 44

Unisex   51, 52, 73
Unveil   See veil

Veil   10, 42, 60–64, 67, 72, 74, 77, 81–83, 90, 92, 95
Votive   See dedication

Warp   6, 23–25, 35, 40, 42, 43, 53–60, 86, 95–97, 105
Warp-weighted loom   69–70
Weave, weaving   v, vi, 6–16, 18, 20–26, 28, 30, 31, 34–36, 38–40, 42–44, 47–49, 51, 53, 60, 69, 85–91, 99, 101, 102, 104–106, 110, 115, 118, 120.

Wedding   33, 60–62, 72, 75, 77, 82–84
Weft   6, 23, 24, 26, 35, 36, 42, 54, 55, 57
Wife   10, 11, 42, 46–48, 65, 71, 73, 82, 98, 108
Woman   v, 4, 6, 9–11, 13, 15, 16, 20, 27, 30, 33, 34, 39, 40, 42, 44, 45, 47–49, 52, 56, 62, 65, 68, 69, 71–77, 81–89, 92–94, 96, 103, 104, 107–110, 112, 113, 115–117, 121
Wool   11, 14–16, 18, 21–24, 26, 29, 30, 36, 39–42, 44, 46, 47, 50–52, 59, 63, 64, 69, 73, 78, 91, 92, 94–96, 107, 110, 112

Xenophon   68, 90

Yarn   7, 19, 23, 35, 40–46, 53, 55, 59, 60, 95, 96, 98

Zeus   11–13, 15, 92, 105
Zōnē   53, 72, 83, 84

The following volumes have been published in this series:

Volume 2
Detel, Wolfgang. *Subjektive und objektive Zeit: Aristoteles und die moderne Zeit-Theorie.* Berlin/Boston: De Gruyter, 2021.

Volume 3
Singer, P. N. *Time for the Ancients: Measurement, Theory, Experience.* Berlin/Boston: De Gruyter, 2022.

Volume 4
Gertzen, Thomas L. *Aber die Zeit fürchtet die Pyramiden: Die Wissenschaften vom Alten Orient und die zeitliche Dimension von Kulturgeschichte.* Berlin/Boston: De Gruyter, 2022.

Volume 6
Zachhuber, Johannes. *Time and Soul: From Aristotle to St. Augustine.* Berlin/Boston: De Gruyter, 2022.

Volume 7
Golitsis, Pantelis. *Damascius' Philosophy of Time.* Berlin/Boston: De Gruyter, 2023.

Volume 8
Defaux, Olivier. *La Table des rois: Contribution à l'histoire textuelle des ›Tables faciles‹ de Ptolémée.* Berlin/Boston: De Gruyter, 2023.

Volume 9
Fischer, Julia (ed.). *Zwiegespräche über die Zeit: Dialoge in der Berlin-Brandenburgischen Akademie der Wissenschaften aus Anlass des sechzigsten Geburtstags von Christoph Markschies.* Berlin/Boston: De Gruyter, 2024.

Volume 10
Walter, Anke (ed.). *The Temporality of Festivals: Approaches to Festive Time in Ancient Babylon, Greece, Rome, and Medieval China.* Berlin/Boston: De Gruyter, 2024.

Volume 12
Sieroka, Norman. *Zeit-Hören: Erfahrungen, Taktungen, Musik.* Berlin/Boston: De Gruyter, 2024.

Volume 13
Birk, Ralph/Coulon, Laurent (ed.). *The Thebaid in Times of Crisis: Revolt and Response in Ptolemaic Egypt*. Berlin/Boston: De Gruyter, 2025.

Volume 14
Pallavidini, Marta. *(A)synchronic (Re)actions: Crises and Their Perception in Hittite History*. Berlin/Boston: De Gruyter, 2025.

www.ingramcontent.com/pod-product-compliance
Lightning Source LLC
Chambersburg PA
CBHW051542230426
43669CB00015B/2697